Jack Chri

50 BEST
day trips
from Vancouver

GREYSTONE BOOKS
Douglas & McIntyre Publishing Group
Vancouver/Toronto

For Louise

Greystone Books
A division of Douglas & McIntyre Ltd.
2323 Quebec Street, Suite 201
Vancouver, British Columbia V5T 4S7
www.greystonebooks.com

National Library of Canada Cataloguing in Publication Data

Christie, Jack, 1946–
  50 best day trips from Vancouver

Includes index.
ISBN 1-55054-924-3

  1. Lower Mainland (B.C.)—Tours. 2. Fraser River Valley (B.C.)—Tours.
I. Title. II. Title: Fifty best day trips from Vancouver.
FC3845.L69C495 2002   917.11'3044   C2002-910236-7
F1089.L79C495 2002

Photos by Louise Christie
Maps by Kelly Alm and David Lewis
Editing by Naomi Pauls
Text and cover design by Val Speidel
Cover photograph by Eastcott and Momatiuk/Tony Stone Images
Printed and bound in Canada by Friesens
Greystone Books is committed to reducing the consumption of old-growth forests in the books it publishes. This book is one step toward that goal. It is printed on acid-free paper that is 100% ancient-forest-free, and it has been processed chlorine free.

The publisher gratefully acknowledges the financial support of the Canada Council for the Arts, the British Columbia Ministry of Tourism, Small Business and Culture, and the Government of Canada through the Book Publishing Industry Development Program (BPIDP) for our publishing activities.

CONTENTS

PREFACE

Welcome to the new face of *Day Trips* in the 21st century. When the first editions of *Day Trips from Vancouver* and *One-Day Getaways from Vancouver* appeared more than a decade ago, they helped steer Lower Mainlanders in search of quick access to the neighbouring outdoors. What we've set out to accomplish with *50 Best Day Trips from Vancouver* is to refine the manner in which information is presented. Key data to help with decision-making now appears at the outset of each chapter. This will allow readers to quickly determine which destination best suits the amount of time at their disposal and the activities they most enjoy.

In the past 10 years, the number of both local parks and recreational interests has soared; the amount of leisure time many of us have to enjoy the outdoors has not kept pace. Thus it's more imperative than ever that this time-honoured guide help readers become better organized and informed. With this in mind, distances to destinations appear at the opening of each chapter. These are calculated from the bridges that link Vancouver with the North Shore and Richmond, or from the city's eastern boundary with Burnaby.

Readers will also be able to tell at a glance which activities are best suited to each destination. Since *Day Trips from Vancouver* first appeared, in-line skating, mountain biking, kayaking and snowboarding have grown steadily in popularity, as have the more gentle pastimes of bird watching and nature observation. Our purpose with this new book is to provide readers with the most detailed descriptions of trails and pathways suited to each of these pursuits. For car-free city dwellers, detailed transit information, including telephone numbers and Web sites, is listed. Finally, we have selected a few choice highlights from each chapter to whet your appetite for discovery.

Choosing which destinations to include was a difficult assignment. After all, there are hundreds of trails, lakes and picnic sites alone scattered throughout the Lower Mainland. The number of provincial, regional and municipal parks continues to grow. *50 Best Day Trips from Vancouver* isn't intended to be the most exhaustive guide to our region. It does aim to be the most comprehensive look at 18 provincial parks, 17 regional parks, 31 municipal parks and recreation trails, 5 conservation regions, 2 BC Hydro recreation sites, 2 Parks Canada national historic sites, 3 B.C. Forest Service interpretive forests, plus one outstanding county park in nearby Washington state for good measure. How did we decide? Simple. These are the places we return to time after time, season after season, and which reward us with new approaches and fresh prospects year after year.

ACKNOWLEDGEMENTS

Rob Saunders, publisher of Greystone Books, is chiefly responsible for this new endeavour. He gathered the team to make it happen, principally editor Naomi Pauls and production manager Susan Rana. My companion Louise Christie took and organized the photographs, and David Lewis fine-tuned the maps. Encouragement came from many quarters, including Beverley Sinclair, John Burns, Ian Hanington, Martin Dunphy, Kevin Statham, Dianna Antonsen, Dan McLeod and Yolanda Stepien at the *Georgia Straight*; Mark Forsythe, Elizabeth Hoath and Volkmar Richter at CBC Radio One's *BC Almanac*; and Wanda Chow at BC CTV.

Family and friends who adventure with us and inspire us deserve special thanks. Bob, Jacqueline and Cam Christie, Lillian Thompson, Chris Laustrop, Gord White and Jane McRae, Ian and Sally Wilson, Skyla King, Herb and Erica Muekel, Larry Emrick, Ruth Tubbesing, the Golley-Janz family, Masako Okodaira, Al Grass, Charles Campbell and Lainé Slater, Brigit Goldammer and Bill Sarota, Jurgen and Jackie Rauh, John and Sharon Bidder, the Fragomeni family, Kelly Mortenson, Alexia Russo, Tom Shandel, Kirk and Daniel Tougas, Gwilym Smith and Sharon Masui, the Loadmans, the Collins and the Browns are always there to cheer us on.

Thank you to all those readers, listeners and viewers who have offered constant encouragement and suggestions for new destinations. If you'd care to comment on anything that catches your eye while using this book, write to me care of Douglas & McIntyre, 2323 Quebec Street, Suite 201, Vancouver, B.C. V5T 3A3, or visit our Web site, www.jackchristie.com, where updated information on all our activities is posted.

LIST OF MAPS

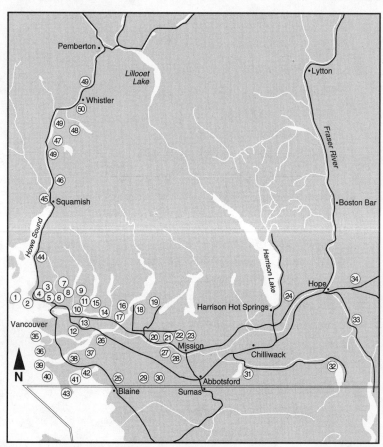

Index map (numbers refer to chapters)

LEGEND

——	Road
----	Trail
——	Railroad
....	Ferry
–··	Park Boundary
===	Canada-U.S. Border
⅄	Picnic Site
▲	Campground with picnic facilities
ⓘ	Information
ⓥ	View
ⓟ	Parking
⑳	Highway
⊶	Gate
⌃	Mountain Peak
⅏	Dike / Dam
⸺	Marsh
✕	Bridge

NORTH SHORE

1 BOWEN ISLAND

DISTANCE: 20 km (12.4 mi.) to Horseshoe Bay, northwest of Vancouver via Highway 1/99

ACTIVITIES: Bird watching, boating, hiking, historic site, nature observation, paddling, picnicking, swimming, viewpoints, walking

HIGHLIGHTS: Ferry ride to beachside picnic grounds; gentle forest trails around a quiet lake

ACCESS: Drive the Upper Levels Highway (Highway 1/99) to Horseshoe Bay. Take BC Ferries' *Queen of Capilano*, which can carry 85 vehicles; the round-trip fee is $16. The round-trip fare for drivers and passengers is $5.50 per person. There is a reduced fare of $2.75 for children aged 5 to 11; children younger than 5 travel free. There is an extra charge of $1.50 for bicycles. Call 1-888-223-3779 for sailing information.

Alternatively, you can travel to Horseshoe Bay by bus along West Vancouver's scenic (and winding) Marine Drive. Call West Vancouver Transit at 604-985-7777 for details.

Islands define British Columbia's coast. It's probably easier to guess the number of molecules of salt in a bucket of seawater than to try to add up how many islands there are along our coastline. Each island adds its own distinct note to the composition that plays out between the Gulfs of Georgia and Alaska. And what an intricate tune it is.

Come the sunny season, almost everyone in Vancouver contemplates an island adventure. If you want to sail over the bounding main on a quick day trip, try Bowen Island. The *Queen of Capilano* has a sheltered outdoor area for foot passengers where you can enjoy the scenery even on a stormy day. The view of the Howe Sound Crest mountains from the ferry's deck is one of the best reasons for making this journey. The Lions stand out in bold relief, oddly rearranged compared to the familiar configuration seen from Vancouver.

Unlike most other islands served by BC Ferries, when you disem-

Bowen Island ferry

bark on Bowen, you're on the doorstep of a park. Crippen Regional Park includes not only green spaces but bakeries, curiosity shops, two pubs and the restored Union Steamship Company store, all clustered around the dock. Head for a large map of the island situated on the store's lawn to orient yourself. The decision you'll face upon your arrival in Crippen Park will be how much of it to explore. For many people, the 1-hour round-trip ferry ride is an adventure in itself.

SNUG COVE The Union Steamship Company was a going concern during the first half of the 20th century, bringing thousands of visitors each summer to its Bowen Island resort at Snug Cove and Deep Bay. Spacious picnic grounds for company outings and games, a lighted waterfront promenade, beaches, a dance hall, a hotel, cottages and the Union Steamship Company store made it as complete a recreation destination as Whistler is today, though on a more modest scale. Stop by the old store—now renovated as an information centre—to learn more.

Just minutes away from the ferry dock on the west side of Snug Cove are a wide beach and the open fields of the picnic grounds. If you follow the signs to this area along Lady Alexandra Promenade, you will pass a few of the diminutive cottages that remain from the Union Steamship days. Should you become enchanted with Bowen,

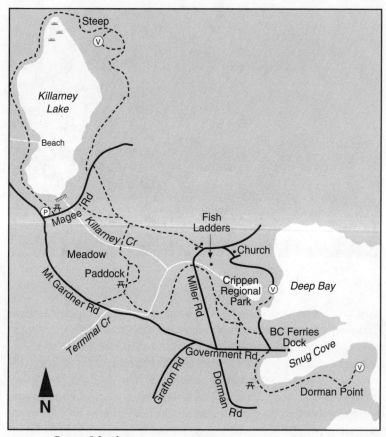

Bowen Island

you can arrange to rent one of them if you wish to spend the night on a subsequent visit. Call 604-947-0707 for rates. A steep trail leads up the hill on the far side of the picnic area to Dorman Point. Look down from here for a vivid illustration of why this is called Snug Cove.

KILLARNEY LAKE TRAIL As you head uphill from the ferry on Government Road past the Union Steamship store, a trail marked with a green GVRD signpost leads off to the right to Killarney Lake. Allow 45 minutes to walk one way. (*Note:* The Killarney Lake Trail is restricted to those on foot; no bikes or horses are allowed.) Secondary growth closes in overhead, but the path is wide and welcoming. Within several minutes the trail passes Terminal Creek, which falls down a sharp embankment and into a lagoon beside Deep Bay.

Snug Cove, Bowen Island

Two generations of fish ladders, the older one of concrete and the other of pressure-treated wood, climb the rocky canyon beside the creek. There is a small hatchery on the west side of Miller Road from which the returning salmon were originally released. Coho and possibly cutthroat trout may be seen running the fish ladders in October and November.

The fish ladders themselves have a pleasingly uniform design, and it's not hard to imagine the salmon jostling for position to leap from step to step. In winter, with snow outlining the ladders and daylight filtering through leafless trees, this is a photographer's playground. A narrow lagoon opens into the ocean at the bottom of the canyon. It can be fun to walk down over the rocks to look out at groups of ducks and geese feeding in this backwater.

The trail continues for a short distance beyond the fish ladders, leading up to Miller Road. A yellow gate marks the entrance to the Killarney Lake Trail, just before the road passes Saint Gerard's Church. Killarney Lake is a 30-minute walk from here. The first third of the trail is on level ground, then it begins to rise gently through second-growth forest. Huge stumps are everywhere.

At the halfway point to Killarney Lake, Meadow Trail leads off to the left and across a small bridge over Terminal Creek. If you take this path you'll discover that a short way along, meadows open up one after another. In one is an exercise paddock for horses. Just beyond the paddock, the trail links up with Mount Gardner Road, which leads back left to the ferry or right to the lake. Island residents often gather around the paddock. A picnic table stands under spreading trees nearby.

The main trail continues from the halfway point towards the lake, linking with Magee Road just before it reaches the shoreline. Bear left at this junction. Walk along Magee as it drops down to the lake and watch for the sign indicating the start of the lake trail. Almost immediately you will see the concrete dam that controls the water level of the lake. There is a small swimming area here and, a short distance beyond, picnic tables in the cool shelter of a fir tree grove.

The going is easy around the north side of the lake, where the ground is level. A 10-minute walk will bring you to a developed gravel beach where a small creek flows into the lake. In summer the waters of Killarney Lake are warm enough for swimming. If you've come to Bowen by car with a canoe or kayak, this is a good place to launch. There is parking beside the picnic area.

Past the beach the trail begins to climb slightly, then joins a boardwalk that crosses the marsh at the far end of the lake. The steepest and roughest parts of the trail are here where the hillside rises, providing several good viewpoints of the lake and Mount Gardner, Bowen Island's highest point (760 m/2,500 ft.). Rustic benches, hewn from some of the old stumps at trailside, line the way until the trail links up once more with Magee Road. Allow an hour to circle the lake.

Bowen's population swells in summer, but in the off-season months, the GVRD's 240-ha (593-acre) Crippen Park is a quiet haven. Although the park is irregularly shaped, all of the trails around Snug Cove, including those leading to and around Killarney Lake, are part of the park. Walk the trails while leaves float gently down and crunch underfoot in autumn. Enjoy the winter wonderland feeling after a snowfall. Catch the first hint of spring as skunk cabbage blooms in a forest where views are not yet obstructed by the foliage of a new season.

Although you don't need to take a car to Bowen, you will have to find a place to park in Horseshoe Bay within walking distance of the ferry. If there are two adults in your party and you have much baggage, such as a stroller, consider dropping off one adult with the youngsters at the BC Ferries foot passenger entrance on Bay Street. Pay parking is usually available near the ferry terminal, except on long weekends, when it may be necessary to find space uphill under the Highway 99 overpass on Marine Drive, across from Gleneagles Golf Course. On long weekends, a local service group rents out spots immediately under the off-ramp to Horseshoe Bay on Marine Drive. Otherwise, there is free parking farther south on Marine in a large cleared area.

Don't walk down the highway entrance to the ferry terminal; use the sidewalk from the top of the overpass. Follow the signs downhill to Bay Street, Horseshoe Bay's main street. If you bring bikes, it's a short swoosh downhill from Keith Road to the foot passenger entrance. (Children should be experienced cyclists to attempt this.) Since Bowen is a hilly island, count on a very challenging bike ride if you want to explore more than Crippen Park.

2 LIGHTHOUSE & WHITECLIFF PARKS

DISTANCE:	20 km (12.4 mi.) northwest of Vancouver, in West Vancouver
ACTIVITIES:	Picnicking, playground, scuba diving, swimming, viewpoints, walking
HIGHLIGHTS:	Beaches and rock outcroppings for sunset viewing, backed by towering old-growth forest rising above the shoreline
ACCESS:	Take the Upper Levels Highway (Highway 1/99) through West Vancouver to Horseshoe Bay. Exiting is tricky—you want to take the Highway 99 exit to Squamish before coming to the BC Ferries toll booth, then make the first left turn onto Marine Drive. (If you find yourself in downtown Horseshoe Bay, simply follow one of the main streets uphill to Marine Drive.)

Lighthouse Park is located just south of Marine Drive a short distance east of Horseshoe Bay. The turnoff is prominently marked by a wooden sign. Turn south on Beacon Lane to reach the parking lot. A wooden bus shelter is also located here. After a short stroll or drive through a residential neighbourhood, you reach the parking lot. There is regular bus service from Park Royal Shopping Centre to Horseshoe Bay and Lighthouse Park; take the #250 Horseshoe Bay.

The way to Whytecliff Marine Park, at the western end of Marine Drive, is well marked at all major intersections.

LIGHTHOUSE PARK Lighthouse Park's towering Douglas fir trees are the sort of treat that somehow you don't expect to find this close to the city. They represent one of the last stands of unlogged forest in the Lower Mainland (aside from the local watersheds). The reason for their protected status is directly related to the lighthouse, strategically

Lighthouse Park

perched atop the rocky outcropping of Point Atkinson at the northern entrance to Burrard Inlet; the forest was preserved as a dark background to contrast with the lighthouse's beacon. This is one of the older lighthouses on the West Coast; the first keeper took up residence here in the late 1880s. All the keepers' names have been recorded on a historic cairn mounted on the rocky hillside above the white-sided, red-capped tower. These days the lighthouse is automated.

At the park's entrance at the south end of Beacon Lane, next to a yellow gate and a bicycle rack, an interpretive sign offers a large map of the park as well as some natural-history notes. A concise map of park trails is also available here for visitors to carry with them. Dogs are permitted in Lighthouse Park provided they are leashed or under voice control.

Walk past the yellow gate and downhill along the paved service road or forest trail to the lighthouse. You'll be there in an easy 10 minutes. Along the way the dimensions of the forest rapidly change. Suddenly, there are trees large enough to build an entire house out of—and occasionally they'll be leaning your way just enough to make you say a prayer of deliverance should you find yourself here

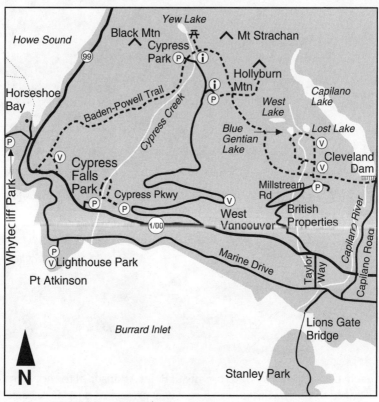

West Vancouver

in a windstorm. If you want to see nature in a state of high arousal, venture through here then, but be wary. Signs of an ancient forest fire blacken the sides of some older trees.

Phyl Munday House and a collection of cabins once used to house conscripts during World War II appear just before the lighthouse. Munday and her husband, Don, were ardent alpinists who explored the unknown wilderness of the Coast Mountains between 1920 and 1949. Among her many accomplishments, Munday was one of the first women to climb 4044-m-high (13,260-ft.-high) Mount Waddington. West Vancouver Girl Guides tend Munday House, which is open on Sundays from 2 P.M. to 4 P.M.

There are good viewpoints over Burrard Inlet on either side of the lighthouse. A well-worn rocky trail winds its way above the shore-line in the trees, leading to East and West Beaches. East Beach is the more sheltered of the two. West Beach is a great place to stretch out on the smooth rock face that slopes gently down to the often-agitated waters off Point Atkinson. There's protected swimming in a narrow bay. The lighthouse rises dramatically on the rocks beside the bay, and you get glimpses of freighters and the outer harbour beyond.

The lighthouse stands in solitary splendour on a rocky promontory, just beyond the dense virgin forest with its thick undergrowth of ferns and berry bushes. The arches of the UBC Museum of Anthropology are visible above the cliffs of Point Grey across the inlet to the south. Scramble out onto the most seaward perch and look back at Burrard Bridge and False Creek, English Bay and Stanley Park. All that civilized expanse was, until relatively recent times, clothed in forest like that here in Lighthouse Park. Next time when you look over from Vancouver at this blinking beacon, imagine yourself back in this wilderness setting.

On calm summer days the waters around the point become more tranquil, making it a quiet place to take in a sunset. A constant parade of boats of all shapes, sizes and speeds streams into Burrard Inlet from Howe Sound and Bowen Island. Walk west towards Jackpine Point, taking care on the rocks that line the undulating trail as it makes its way through the forest. Views of the nearby ocean can be distracting. After a long summer day, the warm rocks or a sturdy arbutus tree trunk make perfect backrests for watching the sun drop behind Bowen, with Lasqueti Island in the far distance. At other seasons this can be a powerfully dramatic theatre for storm watching.

Circle back towards the parking lot from Jackpine Point. Small wooden benches with tables fashioned from old stumps sit beside the trail in places. Some substantial trees grow along here, particularly in one section where the trail climbs through a grove of amabilis fir, past rock walls and boulders covered with moss and licorice ferns. The cool silence of the forest here provides healing for ears strained by harsh city sounds. Plan on taking at least an hour to walk the circuit from the parking lot to the lighthouse, out to Jackpine Point and back to your car or the nearby bus shelter.

Other trails crisscross through the woods. Several of the trails that begin to the left of the yellow gate at the south end of the parking lot quickly lead to the park's high point, a knoll whose open summit offers a bird's-eye view of the majesty of the Douglas fir forest. Bald eagles nest in the craggy tops of some of the park's tallest timber.

WHYTECLIFF MARINE PARK Whytecliff Marine Park is ideal for a quick visit to the rugged ocean shore. With its easy access to the water, you can find an hour or two's exploration when you're in need of a quick getaway under, on or near the water. If you're in no hurry, enjoy the scenic route by taking Marine Drive all the way to the park from the Lions Gate Bridge, rather than taking the Upper Levels Highway. As you make your way along the pebble beach in Whytecliff Marine Park, you may see scuba divers who have come to experience a little weightlessness in the nether world just offshore, where the year-round cold temperatures matter little, provided you dress appropriately.

Although not as large as nearby Lighthouse Park, Whytecliff is surprisingly big and certainly has enough room for visitors to find a secluded spot in which to relax most times of the year. Come summer, the crowds increase noticeably. In 1993, Whytecliff Park was designated as Canada's first Marine Protected Area. This means that nothing in this West Vancouver municipal park may be disturbed: there is to be no harvesting of any marine life beneath the waters of the park. Although B.C. has created dozens of marine parks, you may be surprised to learn that there is very limited protection for the marine life within them. In effect, what has been created at Whytecliff is an underwater sanctuary, which conservationists hope will lead to extended protection in other marine parks.

Most visitors to the park are probably not aware of exactly what lies beneath the waves that beat against this rugged shoreline, but upwards of 200 animal species call these waters home. From above, there is no hint that the speckled sanddab or the sunflower seastar are nestled on the ocean floor nearby, or that the copper rockfish or giant Pacific octopus are feeding below. Few park visitors arrive here in wet suits—for most of us gumboots are a big deal—but Whytecliff Park has become a magnet for local divers over the years.

The setting at the mouth of Howe Sound is dramatic, with the vastness of the Strait of Georgia spread out to the west. Under a low sky, with no sign of Vancouver Island in the distance, the strait seems infinitely wide. Ferry boats are constantly coming and going, serving Nanaimo, Bowen Island and Langdale—chugging in and out of nearby Horseshoe Bay at peak periods. As the wake from the larger boats hits the shoreline, it creates surf, a rather uncommon sight in our sheltered waters. The sound of the waves crunching against the rocks has a scouring, cleansing effect on the ear.

For those who like to experience the extremes exhibited by nature at stormy times of year, Whytecliff provides exposure to the elements in a safe environment. On windy days, pull up your hood and walk down to the narrow cove, where a bench awaits. Stretch your legs along the wide expanse of beach. A rocky bar lies exposed at low tide, leading out to Whyte Islet. Clambering up its steep slopes is harder than it appears from shore. Far easier is to scramble around on the cliffs from which the park takes its name and find a sheltered spot beneath a lone shore pine. There you can find repose without having to constantly check the progress of the tide, which might otherwise cut off your escape route from the island.

Very little of the true nature of the park is revealed when you first arrive. It all looks rather sedate and well ordered: rolling lawns beneath spreading limbs of cedar and oak, a children's playground and a covered picnic area just inside the park entrance. You begin to notice a difference here when you see the list of rules of conduct, prominently displayed in the parking lot. These regulations are directed primarily at the divers, who are encouraged to change in the washrooms and to keep their language clean. (It looks more like an admonition to a group of bikers than one to divers!) *Note:* Dogs are not allowed in Whytecliff.

Follow one of the rough but well-trodden trails that run along the top of the cliffs. Small sets of rock stairways lead here and there. In various places signs have been installed, explaining the variety of marine life to be found beneath the waves. Although you have to take most of it on faith, occasional life forms do bob to the surface, such as the head of a curious seal or sea lion.

3 CYPRESS PROVINCIAL PARK

DISTANCE: 17 km (10.5 mi.) from the Lions Gate Bridge, in West Vancouver

ACTIVITIES: Cross-country skiing, driving, hiking, mountain biking, nature observation, picnicking, skiing, tobogganing, viewpoints, walking

HIGHLIGHTS: Panoramic views, ancient forests, inviting trails

ACCESS: Take Cypress Bowl Road (Cypress Parkway) from the Upper Levels Highway (Highway 1/99) at Exit 8, via an 8-km (5-mi.) paved highway. See West Vancouver map, page 10. Cypress Mountain runs a shuttle bus from Park Royal Shopping Centre. Call 604-926-5612 for details.

With over a million visitors a year, Cypress Park in West Vancouver is the most popular provincial park in B.C. Stop on the drive to or from the 2996-ha (7400-acre) park to admire the views of the Lower Mainland and Washington state from both the Cypress Park Viewpoint and the nearby picnic grounds. These views, along with the park's proximity to the city and its easily accessible trails, account for Cypress's prominence with the public.

Although most visitors ride up on four wheels, others make do with two, sometimes with a pair of skis strapped to the bicycle frame. On the way to the top there are four major switchbacks. You'll usually see cars parked near each one. From the gate at the first switchback, the old Cypress Creek logging road leads west towards Cypress Falls Park (see next chapter), climbing from there to the parking lot at Cypress Bowl (also called Cypress Mountain, a major misnomer as there is no peak by that name within the park), a distance of 7.6 km (4.7 mi).

The Cypress Park Viewpoint is at the second of the switchbacks. There is ample parking here and an interpretive sign that identifies the geographical landmarks laid out before your eyes.

Just above the third switchback are two rough entrances to trails on the lower slopes of Hollyburn Mountain. The well-marked turnoff to the Hollyburn cross-country and toboggan centre and its parking lot is located farther uphill. Cypress Bowl is just a short

Cypress Park Viewpoint

drive past the Hollyburn turnoff. In springtime, the snowbanks lining this last stretch of road become "Cypress Beach," as sun worshippers unfold their lawn chairs atop the towering mounds of snow pushed up by ploughs during the winter months and soak up rays as part of an annual ritual welcoming the return of warm weather to the coast.

Since 1985, winter operations in the park have been run by a private company, Cypress Bowl Recreation Limited. Currently owned by Boyne USA, CBRL leases a fifth of the park's 3000 ha (7410 acres), which includes the downhill runs on Black Mountain and Mount Strachan, plus the cross-country and toboggan trails on Hollyburn.

Long before chairlifts came to Cypress Bowl, alpine skiers, ski jumpers and cross-country skiers enjoyed the terrain on adjacent Hollyburn Mountain. In the 1920s and 1930s, as many skiers trekked out around West Lake as do today. Hollyburn is the only one of the three mountains within Cypress Park that has not been extensively logged. Hence one of Hollyburn's unique features is that it has the last accessible stand of old-growth western hemlock in the Lower Mainland between Garibaldi Park and Chilliwack. Add to this the fact that upper reaches of the mountains have not been touched by forest fires in the past one to four millennia, and you have an ecological area that many people passionately wish to preserve. Rings on a stump atop Mount Strachan indicated it was nearly 1200 years old when cut in 1988 as part of a previous expansion.

HOLLYBURN SUMMIT Hollyburn Mountain is best known for its popular cross-country ski trails; however, Nordic activities take up at most only half the calendar. The rest of the year, hiking boots make their mark on the trails that crisscross the slopes below the mountain's 1326-m (4350-ft.) peak. Hollyburn's companions, Mount Strachan to the north and Black Mountain to the west, stand at 1454 m (4770 ft.) and 1224 m (4016 ft.), respectively. Hollyburn's unlogged summit allows unimpeded views of the mountain ranges to the north, for the most part not visible from Vancouver. You can hike to the summit in less than 2 hours.

From the cross-country parking lot, head uphill underneath the hydro lines. A service road doubles as a trail for the stretch from the parking lot to the warming hut beside Third Lake. (The hut is for winter use only, as are several of the privies, which stand head and shoulders above the landscape without the benefit of snow to provide easy access.) A kiosk at the trailhead on the east side of the parking lot features a detailed diagram of trails on Hollyburn. It also lays out a sensible approach to exploring all wilderness settings: dress warmly, always let someone know where you're going and when you can reasonably be expected back, and never hike the mountains alone. *Note:* At almost any time of the year, you'll find water running in the rocky creekbeds that double as trails on the mountain. Waterproof footwear is advisable but not absolutely necessary.

The skiers' warming hut lies 15 minutes uphill from the parking lot. As the trails pass beside hydro lines you can see the open ski runs through the forest, with their names—Burfield, Sitzmark, Telemark, Wells Gray—posted high in the trees. A trail marker beside the warming hut, announcing the approach to Hollyburn Mountain, bears a map of the area and a summary of distances and times. The warming hut is at 1093 m (3586 ft.), which means you have a 233-m (764-ft.) ascent before you reach the summit.

Once you set out, you'll find that the trail divides after about 15 minutes, with the Hollyburn Trail heading straight ahead and the Baden-Powell Trail branching off to the left towards the parking lot at Cypress Bowl, a 40-minute journey. The hike to the top of Hollyburn from this divide takes another 50 minutes.

As the trail climbs from the warming hut, it passes a series of six small lakes, four of which can be glimpsed from the trail. The trail leads along the shoreline of Fourth Lake several minutes past the warming hut, then begins to snake through the woods, traversing the forested slopes and coming out into the open on an old ski-trail cut. On the east side of the trail, weathered signs warn against trespassing in the restricted Capilano watershed, whose boundary is nearby.

The forest shields almost everything else from view, which allows you to concentrate on your footing. As on many of the trails on Hollyburn, much of the route is over exposed roots around the base of the sturdy firs. (On the way down, you'll be treated to views galore out over the Fraser estuary as far south as Boundary Bay.) Along the trail, you'll frequently catch sight of Hollyburn's beckoning summit, surmounted by a dense crown of old growth. Late in the summer berry bushes line the way; snow flattens them in winter, creating a challenging descent on skis for those who've made the trek to this elevation.

Just before the final ascent, where the going does get tricky in several places owing to rocks made slippery by running water or ice, a charming viewpoint appears, with a rustic bench. It's well situated for catching your breath—*and* the geographical display. The sides of Hollyburn drop away into the Capilano Valley, hidden below. Rising vertically to the north and east are the walls of Grouse Mountain and its companions; in the distance are the peaks and ridges of Coliseum and Seymour mountains. Although the view from the top is more panoramic, it somehow can't match this setting. Must be the bench.

The actual peak of Hollyburn is open and rocky, an encouragement in the last 10 minutes of the hike when you can see the sky beginning to appear above you, no longer masked by trees. A dangling rope offers assistance to ascend the last steep rock section before the top, which is only several footsteps beyond. If you've really pushed to get here, maybe with an incoming squall dogging your heels, you can at last catch your breath before hurrying back down. It feels as good to have accomplished this climb as it would if you'd mastered any other significant peak, a reminder that everyone has their own Everest within. From the summit you can look west to Mount Strachan, past Black Mountain to the waters of Howe Sound and over to Gibsons on the Sunshine Coast in the distance.

A rough, steep trail leads from the summit of Hollyburn to Mount Strachan. Rather than attempt this traverse, I recommend that you retrace your steps to the warming hut; if you've still got strength in your legs, walk down the Wells Gray Trail to First Lake or follow the

Mobraaten Trail to its intersection with the Grand National Trail, and around on Grand National to West Lake. Both Wells Gray and Mobraaten start from the warming hut, and both intersect with Grand National. Part of an old chairlift can still be seen at the north end of West Lake.

To experience the flavour of the original development on Hollyburn begun in the 1920s, be sure to return to the parking lot on the Burfield Trail, which passes beside a nest of old cabins and the Hollyburn Ski Lodge, built in 1926.

OTHER DESTINATIONS Cypress Bowl presents an opportunity for visitors to make easy, moderate or extensive explorations of the park. A short, 1.5-km (0.9-mi.) interpretive trail leads from the parking lot to nearby Yew Lake. (Cypress Creek originates in the marshy wetland surrounding this lake.) This trail has been upgraded to provide wheelchair access and is also designed with visually impaired visitors in mind. Yellow cypress trees, from which the park takes its name, ring the little lake.

Those with more time and energy to burn can hike trails that ascend Black Mountain to its summit, a 30-minute climb, or head north along the Howe Sound Crest Trail towards the Lions and the provincial park at Porteau Cove (see chapter 44), a one- or two-day trek. Even if you don't intend to go all the way to the Lions on this trail, several hours' hiking will bring you past good viewpoints leading up to St. Marks Summit, 5.5 km (3.4 mi.) from Cypress Bowl. Along the way you'll be treated to a view of the Lions from Strachan Meadows (2.6 km/1.6 miles) and then of Howe Sound at St. Marks Summit. Snow may cover parts of this trail, especially at higher elevations, well into July. North of St. Marks the trail deteriorates as it approaches aptly named Unnecessary Mountain.

This may well be as far as you wish to come. North of Unnecessary Mountain, the Howe Sound Crest Trail skirts the base of the Lions, then crosses the ridges of Mounts Harvey and Brunswick before descending past Deeks Lake to a trailhead on Highway 99 near Porteau Cove. This hike is only for those who are experienced and well equipped. A cleared area suitable for camping is located at the outlet of Deeks Lake, otherwise there are only emergency huts at Magnesia Meadows and Brunswick Lake. *Note:* Campfires are forbidden.

The best time to attempt the Howe Sound Crest Trail is between mid-July and October. Some hikers prefer to use the Howe Sound Crest Trail as a route to the Lions, then descend along the Lions Trail to Lions Bay. From Cypress Park to Lions Bay is a strenuous 18 km (11.2 miles). Allow 9 hours to complete this hike one way. Allow two full days to complete the entire Howe Sound Crest Trail, a 15-hour trek one way. *Note:* Trail markers on open sections of Unnecessary Mountain and other exposed sections are often difficult to follow even in good weather. Do not attempt this route unless you are confident in your pathfinding abilities. Consult topographic map 92G/6 (North Vancouver), available from the Geological Survey of Canada, Suite 101, 605 Robson Street, Vancouver, B.C. v6b 5J3, phone 604-666-0271. More detailed information on the Howe Sound Crest Trail is available on a special map designed for trail users by BC Parks. For more information and to request a map of Cypress Provincial Park, including a detailed description of the Howe Sound Crest Trail, contact BC Parks at Mount Seymour Park, 604-929-4818, or the district office, 604-924-2200. Maps are also available on-line at wlapwww.gov.bc.ca/bcparks.

Other trails to pursue in Cypress Park include the Black Mountain Loop trail, a moderately difficult, 2.5-km (1.6-mile), 2-hour tour of the mountain's subalpine meadows and pocket lakes with a terrific viewpoint on top. The loop trail ties in with the Yew Lake Trail, both of which begin at the base of the Black Mountain chairlift.

Cypress Park has only one official mountain bike trail, named BLT ("Boulders, Logs and Trees"), which begins just north of the entrance to the old logging road at the first switchback on the Cypress Parkway. Another entrance is from the maintenance yard above the fourth switchback. BLT may be the only one, but at least it's got length (16 km/10 mi., return) in its favour. There are a number of trails just outside the park, ranging from the idyllic Fern Trail to the psychotic Sex Boy, both of which link with BLT. Fern Trail begins where BLT meets the road's third switchback. Entrances to upper and lower Sex Boy occur along BLT north of a BC Hydro substation and the third switchback. Mountain biking elsewhere in the park is illegal and rigorously enforced. Expect fines or bike confiscation if caught. Another series of trails is found at the second switchback of the Parkway. These trails, including Skyline, Panorama, No Stairs Allowed and My Friend the Stupid Grouse, run through the forested British Properties neighbourhood.

4   CYPRESS FALLS PARK

DISTANCE:
15 km (9.3 mi.) from the Lions Gate Bridge via the Upper Levels Highway (Highway 1/99), in West Vancouver

ACTIVITIES:
Hiking, nature observation, viewpoints, walking

HIGHLIGHTS:
A soothing waterfall in a sheltering forest

ACCESS:
There are two approaches to Cypress Falls Park (see West Vancouver map, page 10). Take the Cypress Park exit (#5) from the Upper Levels Highway (Highway 1/99) and drive to the first major switchback. Park on the west side of the road beside a yellow-and-black striped gate. A road runs west, well used by walkers and cyclists. After an easy 15-minute walk to the site of a hydro substation, look for a narrow single-track pathway that leads into the forest just downhill from the substation. The path descends over an old creekbed and through gradually taller trees to a bridge just above the lower falls on Cypress Creek.

Alternatively, take the Caulfeild-Woodgreen exit (#4) from the Upper Levels Highway. Once on Woodgreen, follow it to the third street on the right, Woodgreen Place. The park lies at the end of this street. The trail to the falls begins here.

You can travel to Cypress Falls Park on West Vancouver Transit. Take the Caulfeild bus (#253), which leaves from Park Royal Shopping Centre at 20 minutes past each hour. For more information, call 604-985-7777.

Even in the depths of winter there are times when a day trip is in order—if only to get you out of the house and away from the threat of cabin fever. Of all the ingredients that make for a good winter outing, proximity is paramount. Since the sun supplies us with only eight hours of daylight in December and January, choose a place that's close at hand so getting there doesn't

Cypress Falls Park

waste precious time. Wind chill is another factor in the equation: the place you visit should be sheltered. Thirdly, your destination should catch Nature displaying herself at her seasonal best.

One of the wintry manifestations I like most is the sight of frozen spray, layer upon layer of ice coating trees, rocks and earth like ceramic glaze. Cypress Creek in West Vancouver spills down the slopes of Black Mountain, creating just such an effect in two places where the water really falls. A small park surrounds one of the most dramatic sections of the creek. Viewpoints of the upper and lower falls are easily reached from the parking lot even when snow is deep and crisp.

Anyone who has travelled west along the Upper Levels Highway will have crossed Cypress Creek near the falls. A road sign marks the location of the creek, but the falls are hidden in a gorge, surrounded by the forest. Unless you know where to search them out, they remain a local secret.

Ancient trails crisscross the banks around Cypress Falls. Although they're not as well marked as the Brothers Creek (see next chapter) or Capilano-Pacific Trails, finding your way is not difficult. There has been a minimum of logging on this part of the mountain, and trails stand out against the dense forest background as if Nature herself were inviting visitors.

In places there are stands of original growth that sprouted around Shakespeare's time. At some point in the past 400 years a fire swept across the lower face of Black Mountain (hence its name). You can still discern dark scars on the trunks of the older Douglas firs and western hemlocks. Some of these trees tower nearly 70 m (230 ft.) above the forest floor. Their almost 3-m (10-ft.) girth means that you *really* have to stretch your arms to give them a full hug.

From Woodgreen Place, walk down a staircase to the playing field, bearing left for a short distance towards some bleachers. From here the trail enters the woods in two directions. To reach the falls, head uphill on the left-hand trail. (The right-hand trail, suitable for jogging, is a soft bark-chip ring trail that circles the field.) The sound of the creek will almost immediately impress itself on your ears. (Watch for a rough trail that leads downhill on the right and connects with an old roadway. If you have time, explore this short diversion, which leads uphill to a good viewpoint of the canyon at the foot of the lower falls.)

The gentle nature of the main trail makes it suitable for walkers of all ages, even in slippery wintery conditions. Parts of the trail can be mucky, so bring high-top footwear for this walk. Leave your cotton socks behind in winter, because when wet they will leach warmth out of your body much faster than it can be replaced. Instead, wear wool, silk or polypropylene.

You'll come to a viewpoint of the lower falls within 5 minutes. The spray here coats the walls of the gorge as this part of the cataract drops away to a pool 17 m (56 ft.) below. A small fence here prevents anyone from venturing too close. Otherwise, this is a very non-threatening version of the Capilano Canyon (see chapter 6). No need to worry about slipping. A bridge links trails on both sides of the creek. Roots from a stand of old-growth forest hold the mountainside together. This is the steepest part of the park. Stay on the west bank, travelling in a clockwise direction to the upper falls.

Keep close to the creek as the trail rises gradually on the west bank. Smaller trails occasionally cut off up to the left, allowing neighbourhood access to the creek. The main trail is demarcated by wooden railings in places. No matter where you might turn, as long as you can hear the creek clearly you can't go wrong. You may have to backtrack, but you should have no trouble finding the right path. In an easy 10 minutes you will have reached the upper falls viewpoint.

There are two magnificent old Douglas fir trees next to this viewpoint. On the forest floor below them a network of roots stands out, gleaming black as if lacquered. Up above, the broad spreading limbs catch much of the snow (or rain), keeping it from reaching the trail. Where snow does appear on the ground, it stands out in contrast to the reddish-brown bark and leaf mulch. Even when the outer boughs are coated with white, the interior limbs of many trees are sparkling green. Ferns persist where all else has perished from the frost. The odd holly tree with its spiky leaves puts the finishing touch on this seasonal scene.

The trail climbs again for a short distance beyond the upper falls viewpoint. A stand of young hemlocks lines the trail on either side. You may have to move sideways between them in order to keep snow from dislodging and finding its way down your collar. If you want pictures you will have to use a low-speed film, a tripod and a flash to capture an impression.

Turn right onto the wide roadbed of an old logging road that climbs to the McCrady Bridge; from the bridge you can look down into the gorge carved by Cypress Creek's relentless flow. The road runs downhill past a hydro substation. Pick up the trail back to the lower falls on your right, just after you pass the humming wires. (If you stay on the logging road, it will take you east to the Cypress Bowl Road, 1.1 km/0.7 mi. away.) Pick your way carefully down through this section and you will be at the lower falls bridge in 15 minutes. The round trip takes an easy 2 hours, by which time you should be ready for a hot toddy if you didn't think to bring along a thermos of cocoa to enjoy along the trail.

One good reason for paying a visit to Cypress Falls now is the increasing evidence that municipal and private development near the falls may well disturb the wilderness feeling of this park. British Pacific Properties owns much of the land surrounding the park—including the upper falls area—and the company plans to begin residential construction here over the next five to 20 years. However, only a new municipal waterline road near the upper falls and a new municipal works yard next to the BC Hydro substation currently intrude on a visit to Cypress Falls Park.

5 BROTHERS CREEK TRAIL

DISTANCE: 3 km (1.9 mi.) north of the Lions Gate Bridge, in West Vancouver

ACTIVITIES: Hiking, picnicking, swimming, viewpoints, walking

HIGHLIGHTS: Big, bigger and biggest trees parade beside one of the North Shore's most historic drainages

ACCESS: From the Lions Gate Bridge via Marine Drive, go to the north end of Taylor Way, then west (left) on Southborough Road to Eyremount Drive in the British Properties neighbourhood. Follow Eyremount to Millstream Road, then turn east (right). The trailhead lies on the north (left) side of Millstream and is prominently marked by a large wooden signpost (see West Vancouver map, page 10). There is room in front of the yellow gate for several cars to park. Nearby is a bus stop. The #254 British Properties bus leaves Park Royal Shopping Centre at 20 minutes before the hour. Check with West Vancouver Transit (604-985-7777) for more details.

Sometimes it seems there can't be much of the North Shore that hasn't been walked through at least once. At the turn of the century there was no such certainty: when the little settlement of Ambleside was hardly more than a few cabins in size, residents had to guess at the origins of several creeks that flowed into the Capilano River from on high.

So it was that by the 1920s at least four creeks in the region came to be known as Sisters Creek. Speculation had it that each could trace its headwaters to the runoff from the Two Sisters, the twin peaks that today are referred to by the non-Native community as the Lions. Finally, a provincial-park survey team went to work. They determined that Sisters Creek ought to be the small, rather insignificant stream that flows into the north end of Capilano Lake (now off-limits to the public as it is in the restricted Greater Vancouver Water Supply Area). The remaining streams were rechristened. One of the larger ones became Brothers Creek.

Brothers Creek Trail

An exciting network of trails follow Brothers Creek on the mountainside above the British Properties. As a reward for overheated hikers there are two small lakes near the creek's origins.

Depending on your time and hiking companions, a visit to Brothers Creek can last anywhere from an hour to half a day. With the network of trails around the creek, it's possible to tailor a visit here to fit any circumstance and any age group.

A rocky old fire road serves as the beginning of the Brothers Creek Trail, no matter which circuit you attempt. Take a good look at the scenery below as you set out on this trail—in a matter of minutes the tall trees will close in around you, shutting out all signs of the city until your return. Soon only an occasional sound—perhaps the *whoof* of a diesel locomotive in the BC Rail yards—will float up from the world you've left behind. Almost immediately the past will rise to greet you. Thick wooden planks used in the construction of skid roads are still evident in places. They are studded with heavy spikes and act as reminders, along with some enormous cedar stumps sprinkled throughout the forest, of the logging activity here 70 years ago.

Within minutes of starting the trail you are presented with a choice of routes. Three bridges cross Brothers Creek, approximately 20 minutes' walk apart. You might follow soft and mostly level Baden-Powell Trail west to the first of these if your time is limited.

Lost Lake, West Vancouver

The trail parallels a power line and crosses several small board-walks. Watch for a tall snag that stands out above the forest just as the trail begins its descent to quaint First Bridge. The round trip to this point is 1 hour.

From First Bridge, Brothers Creek Trail climbs beside the creek, with staircases built into the slope to assist you. A number of shel-tering western red cedars stand on the west side of the creek. They'll amaze you with their girth. Who would have thought big trees such as these could exist so close to the city? As it happens, some of the largest trees on the West Coast grow in the nearby Capilano and Seymour watersheds, restricted areas since the 1920s.

If you circle back over Second Bridge, rejoining the fire road, you will have had a brief but stimulating 2-hour introduction to the area. Along the way between Second Bridge and the fire road is a stand of old-growth fir trees. These escaped the saw blade because they were too tall for early loggers to handle. Though not as dramatic as the fir and cedar higher up the slope near Third Bridge, they are still mighty impressive.

If you have another hour or two at your disposal, there's a most rewarding adventure in store. After climbing up the fire road or the trail beside Brothers Creek to Third Bridge, follow the trail markers to Blue Gentian Lake. This small lake lies on the west side of the creek, a half-hour above Third Bridge. Lily pads dot its surface and, in truth, it more closely resembles a pond than a lake. Small Stoney Creek can be heard nearby.

To complete a circle trip, follow an older trail that cuts east across both Stoney and Brothers Creeks to Lost Lake. Somewhat larger and more inviting, it takes 20 minutes of up-and-downing to reach. If it's a warm day, have a swim in the fresh water under the open sky. A shorter approach to Lost Lake runs from Third Bridge: simply follow the trail on the east side of Brothers Creek. This takes only 15 minutes, but then you will have to retrace your footsteps. One of the rewards of using the circle route to both lakes is the view of the upper falls on Brothers Creek that appears only between the two.

Across the fire road below Third Bridge are the tallest stands of trees on the entire journey. Some of the firs and cedars measure 2.4 m (8 ft.) in diameter. Many have had their tops snapped off, but green life persists in the remaining branches.

Each time I visit Brothers Creek I end up exploring farther. It's a perfect spot to escape the heat of the day or the falling rain, so well does its canopy of trees shelter visitors. The forest swallows you up, and it's not until you return to the trailhead that the city intrudes on your consciousness once more.

The West Vancouver Historical Society, in cooperation with the District of West Vancouver and the West Vancouver Museum and Archives, publishes a detailed map and forestry heritage walking guide to Brothers Creek entitled "Shakes, Shinglebolts and Steam-pots." For a free copy, contact Parks and Community Services, 604-925-7200.

6 CAPILANO RIVER TRAILS

DISTANCE: 1 to 7.5 km (0.6 to 5 mi.) from the Lions Gate Bridge, depending on starting point, in West and North Vancouver

ACTIVITIES: Hiking, nature observation, picnicking, viewpoints, walking

HIGHLIGHTS: A walker's paradise; sandbars in the depths of Capilano Canyon

ACCESS: Almost all of the Capilano River's west bank and forest perimeter is included in a regional park, a length of over 7 km (4.3 mi.). The river's steep-walled west side is best approached from several park trailheads in West Vancouver. Good places to begin are at the mouth of the Capilano River at the south end of Taylor Way, on Clyde Road by the Park Royal Hotel, or on Keith Road. Walk east to the river and the Town Trail, a municipal route that connects with the river's major route—the Capilano-Pacific Trail—as well as Park Royal Shopping Centre and Ambleside Park.

The upper section of the Capilano-Pacific Trail begins north of the Upper Levels Highway (Highway 1/99). To find it, follow Keith Road east off Taylor Way and park on either side of the underpass beneath the Upper Levels Highway.

To reach Capilano River Regional Park by bus from downtown Vancouver, catch a West Vancouver Transit bus to Park Royal Shopping Centre and begin exploring on the Town Trail nearby. A Pemberton Heights/Grouse Mountain (#236) bus from North Vancouver's Lonsdale Quay will drop you at the parking lot and picnic area beside the Cleveland Dam. Call TransLink, 604-953-3333, for bus numbers and schedules or visit their Web site: www.translink.bc.ca.

Capilano-Pacific Trail

Hugging the Capilano River's banks are numerous well-marked trails. Much of this 26-km (16-mi.) network is concentrated on both sides of the river below the Cleveland Dam. That's a lot of ground to cover, so you should be selective when planning a visit. Choose an easy outing to begin; then, once you become more familiar with the park, explore it more deeply.

TOWN TRAIL On sunny weekends, visitors pack the Town Trail near where the Capilano River flows into Burrard Inlet. With the Lions Gate Bridge soaring above, this is a magnetic setting. A modest beach rewards those who stay with the trail to its oceanside terminus.

North of the Marine Drive bridge, the trail passes beside the Park Royal Hotel, crosses Brothers Creek (see previous chapter), winds its way around a retirement home and links with the Capilano-Pacific Trail. The Greater Vancouver Regional District has signs posted in several places beside the river, detailing the way north into the canyon.

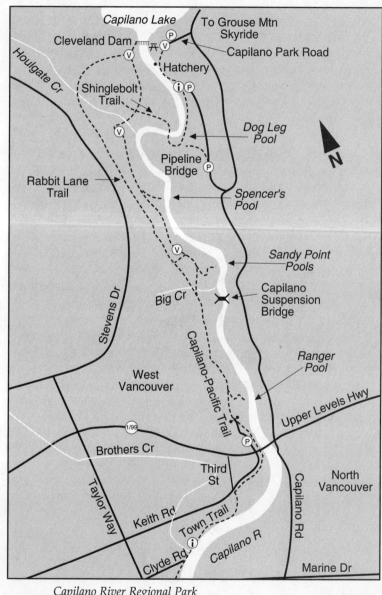

Capilano River Regional Park

CAPILANO-PACIFIC TRAIL The Capilano-Pacific Trail is Capilano River Regional Park's most popular route and runs 7.5 km (4.7 mi.) between the Cleveland Dam and the ocean at Ambleside Park. The trail is mostly level and takes about 3 hours to complete one way.

This is a good place to explore the forest and some of the pools where the Capilano River narrows dramatically as it flows through a steep-sided canyon.

At its south end, the Capilano River is shallow and wide, with only slight banks on either side. The riverbed is a field of melon-sized stones. At low-water times, scramble down to walk on the smooth boulders exposed above the stream. From here the trail leads away from the bank up to Keith Road as it nears the Upper Levels Highway bridge. Keith Road runs north to its terminus at the bridge, where a GVRD signpost indicates the start of the next section of the Capilano-Pacific Trail. At this point the trail is a charming old lane. Occasionally you'll see signs of fainter branch trails. This is one of the oldest parks in the Vancouver region. Opened in 1926, the 160-ha (395-acre) park today has more than a million visitors year round.

The first trail that descends into the canyon off the main Capilano-Pacific Trail leads down to a section known as the Ranger Pool. Although the trail is moderately steep in places, it's worth the effort for the view of the canyon from the riverbed. A short distance beyond the Ranger Pool trail, the Capilano-Pacific Trail passes a wire fence surrounding the private property of the Capilano Suspension Bridge. The entrance to the bridge is on Capilano Road in North Vancouver, on the river's east side.

Just past the fenced area the trail divides at a trail marker, with Rabbit Lane continuing in the open while the Capilano-Pacific heads into the forest. The overstorey of tall evergreens perfumes the air with one great green essence throughout the year. One of the joys of visiting here is the quiet that permeates the atmosphere. Even when it's raining, the branches of the forest are so sheltering that much of the precipitation never reaches the trail.

The Capilano-Pacific Trail begins to lead gently through a silent forest, above and slightly removed from the river sounds below. This is a good trail for people who enjoy exchanging hellos. There is almost always a pleasant stream of visitors, many accompanied by their dogs, to be met along the way. From one magnificent viewpoint the canyon can be seen dropping away sharply to the river below. A bench beside some towering Douglas firs welcomes hikers here. Just before this viewpoint a trail leads off the Capilano-Pacific to the Sandy Point Pools below.

From Houlgate Creek, the second of two major creeks north of the viewpoint, a branch of the main trail leads to a viewpoint called Shinglebolt, close to the park's North Vancouver entrance. (A shinglebolt is a section of a cedar log from which shakes and shingles are cut.) The Shinglebolt Trail is best explored on clear days when the path isn't too muddy. This is the route used by the Capilano Timber Company railway from 1917 to 1933, which accounts for its gentle grade. A maze of trails runs through the woods here, past some beautiful old trees along the west bank. The easygoing Rabbit Lane Trail feeds into the Capilano-Pacific Trail at several places around the Shinglebolt Viewpoint below Cleveland Dam.

NORTH VANCOUVER TRAILS There are several fine viewpoints of Capilano Canyon and the North Shore mountains—particularly the Lions—as well as picnic locations around the Cleveland Dam. At many times of the year, kayakers challenge the river in the region just below the dam, one of the best places in Vancouver to spot them in action.

An aquarium-like salmon hatchery sits at the north end of the river, below the Cleveland Dam. Palisades Trail connects the hatchery with a picnic area beside the dam at the corner of Capilano and Prospect Roads. Explore farther south along the river on the Coho Loop Trail, which begins at the parking lot at the north end of well-marked Capilano Park Road, off Capilano Road below the Cleveland Dam. There's even more variety here, including two bridge crossings of the canyon and a descent to riverside at the Dog Leg Pool. Allow at least an hour to complete the loop, especially if you spend time beside the river, where your thoughts are likely to be caught up in the current as all else comes to a momentary standstill.

7 LYNN HEADWATERS REGIONAL PARK

DISTANCE: 10 km (6.2 mi.) north of Highway 1/99, in North Vancouver

ACTIVITIES: Cross-country skiing, hiking, nature observation, picnicking, swimming, viewpoints, walking

HIGHLIGHTS: Sheltered valley with gentle creekside trails

ACCESS: To reach the park entrance, follow Mountain Highway or Lynn Valley Road north off the Upper Levels Highway (Highway 1/99). Signs pointing to the park begin at the turnoff to popular Lynn Canyon Park (see next chapter). Stay on Lynn Canyon Road until it ends, then follow Intake Road for about 1 km (0.6 mi.) to the parking lot where the trail begins. (For busy months there are two overflow parking lots on Intake Road close to the trailhead.) If you're travelling on foot, catch the #228 Lynn Valley bus from the SeaBus terminal at Lonsdale Quay. It drops you where Intake Road begins, the last stop on its route.

Tucked in behind Grouse Mountain and leading north for 15 km (9.3 mi.), Lynn Headwaters Regional Park has been welcoming visitors since it opened to the public in 1985, after being off-limits for decades as part of the extensive North Shore watershed system. Stone, water and wood characterize much of the park's nature. Silence is another component. Turn the corner at the top of North Vancouver's Lynn Valley Road and suddenly you leave behind the sounds of the city and enter another world. Even if the parking area is full, Lynn Headwaters is so large that it absorbs people quickly. You often feel as if you have the place to yourself.

Lynn Headwaters Park is a welcoming place where first-time visitors may be content to picnic just inside the entrance beside the old flood-control bridge. Several tables, toilets and a public telephone are located here. Getting to the creek is easiest via a gentle approach just upstream on the east side of the bridge, where a visitor registration

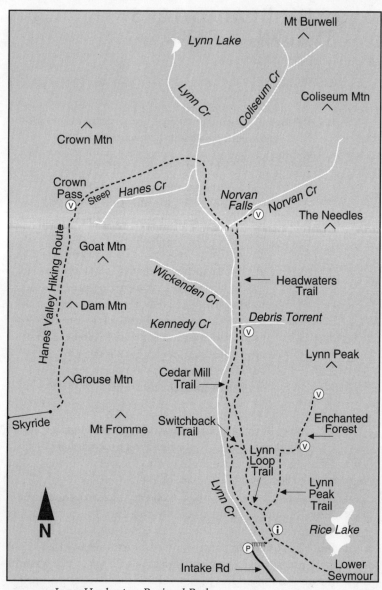

Lynn Headwaters Regional Park

kiosk displays all you need to know about the park. Fires are not permitted; neither are bicycles, except on a connector road between Lynn Headwaters and the Lower Seymour Conservation Reserve (formerly the Seymour Demonstration Forest). *Note:* Although dogs

Lynn Creek

are welcome in Lynn Headwaters, you are not permitted to take Fido into the Lower Seymour Conservation Reserve.

Roughly half the trails in Lynn Headwaters are fairly level and thus suitable for all. One arm of the Lynn Loop leads north to easy-going Cedar Mill, a creekside trail that runs through the folds of the valley for 3.8 km (2.4 mi.). Finding more challenging terrain is easy in this narrow-sided valley. Get to know it one bight at a time.

If you want to test yourself, try the Switchback Trail. Although the Switchback is only 0.7 km (0.4 mi.) in length, its ups and downs will get your heart rate up quickly. If you're here for the first time, try it from top to bottom. Ascend Lynn Loop Trail in a counter-clockwise direction from the kiosk, then go down Switchback to meet the creekside trail in the valley. (Before making the descent, walk a short distance farther north on Headwaters Trail to see the old snag and viewpoint of the valley below.) The trail's switchbacks, staircases and serpentine layout provide a good way to gauge your fitness level. And don't let winter deter you: this part of the park is one of the most pleasantly sheltered environments in which to view a snowfall. The broad branches of hemlock trees catch much of the load, leaving the trail bare below.

LYNN CREEK Lynn Creek cuts through the valley over a wide bed of boulders. The mountains on either side rise so steeply that it is difficult to get a good perspective of them from Headwaters Trail. Only Mount Fromme is really prominent in the west. As you explore northwards along Lynn Creek beyond the debris torrent where Cedar Mill Loop Trail and Headwaters Trail link, a spiny ridge of peaks known as the Needles comes into view to the east. Walking the trail is quicker and easier than boulder-hopping in the rough creekbed. During spring months the water in the creek rises and rushes through the valley. As the unrepaired dam at the Headwaters trailhead suggests, North Vancouver gave up trying to control this as a watershed in the early 1980s.

For those who wish to really stretch their legs without much elevation gain, the 7-km (4.3-mi.) Headwaters Trail to Norvan Falls and the Cedar Mill Loop Trail are both ideal. (Consult the GVRD trail guide, available at the park's visitor registration kiosk, for estimated round-trip times for a variety of destinations within the park.) Plan on a 2-hour journey to reach the debris torrent across from Kennedy Creek on the valley's west side. Headwaters Trail rises above the valley while Cedar Mill Loop Trail travels along the creek bank. People of all ages use these easy trails, and in winter they're popular with cross-country skiers. In places along both trails, particularly at the "4.5 km" sign on Headwaters Trail, there are logging-camp debris—kettles, boot soles, logging equipment, bottle shards, saw blades—placed atop nurse logs or hung from branches.

The water in Lynn Creek is much colder than in the neighbouring Seymour River, and swimming spots are hard to come by. Some of the best pools lie between the debris chute, where the Cedar Mill and Headwaters Trails converge, and Norvan Creek, 30 minutes farther north. The water is very soft. A cool breeze normally blows through the valley, keeping bugs down.

ENCHANTED FOREST If you are prepared to hike several kilometres up the steep Lynn Peak Trail, it is possible to find a small grove of original trees that for some reason were left standing. This spot is appropriately named the Enchanted Forest. The trail to reach it is identified as the route to Lynn Peak on the large map at the trailhead. The forest is not marked as such but is located between two viewpoints near the summit. To find the turnoff from the main trail, follow Lynn Loop Trail to the right of the registration kiosk for 15 minutes. Near two lightning-blasted snags, one on each side of the trail, and three large stumps is a trail sign indicating the continuation of Lynn Loop Trail. A secondary trail that is signed as the Lynn Peak route branches off at right angles.

The sound of Lynn Creek begins to diminish as the trail climbs to the peak. A smaller stream becomes evident, one that often dries up for months once the spring runoff finishes. The trail follows the stream in places and there may be some wet climbing over small rocks. Pack along something to drink, because the steep hiking trail increases in difficulty from this point.

Moving at a moderate pace you will get to the first viewpoint about 35 minutes after leaving Lynn Loop Trail. From here you look directly east to the Mount Seymour ski area and down into the Lower Seymour Conservation Reserve in the valley below.

The forest floor begins to dry out as you climb up the spine of Lynn Peak. The sound of wind high in the trees accompanies you. The trail is narrow but begins to open up for a short distance beyond a large blowdown over which you will have to clamber. You will sense your arrival in the Enchanted Forest by the hush that falls around you. The underbrush becomes much less dense. The sound of Lynn Creek rises and harmonizes with the wind. In the centre of the grove are fir trees that begin to put out branches at the 30-metre (100-foot) level and continue upwards from there. It takes four adults stretched fingertip to fingertip to encircle one of the smaller trees. Some are so old that their lower trunks have begun to crumble.

Upward from here the trail narrows and becomes rougher again as it climbs to its finish at the site of what was once a blimp tethering station, 10 minutes farther along. No effort was spared in logging Lynn Peak; 20 years ago, the blimp was used to lift logs off the mountain.

HANES VALLEY HIKING ROUTE The GVRD makes a distinction between hiking *trails* and hiking *routes* in Lynn Headwaters. The trails are well marked, and though you are guaranteed an energetic workout, they are also well maintained. In contrast, hiking routes in the park are much more of a challenge, particularly in adverse weather conditions. The terrain is rockier, the paths much less distinct in places and the difficulties much more pronounced. Still, if you've explored other aspects of the park and are hungry for further adventure, prepare yourself for the long trek through the Hanes Valley. Total distance on this route is more than 15 km (9.3 mi.) one way, a 7-to-8-hour trek from the park entrance to Grouse Mountain.

Getting to Grouse Mountain requires you to first cover the 7-km

(4.3-mi.) Headwaters Trail to Norvan Falls. From the bridge over Norvan Creek follow the trail west to Lynn Creek, then up a treacherous scree slope beside Hanes Creek. Don't hesitate to turn back should the weather close in—this section is difficult even with good visibility. Snow patches may persist well into the summer in places shaded from the sun. One of the most satisfying stages of this route is at the top of Crown Pass, where you leave the scree behind and once more enter the forest. From this point on the trail gently rises and falls as it makes its way towards the Grouse Mountain alpine area. Ride the Skyride down to the parking lot at the foot of the gondola. (Hardier souls could hike down the Grouse Grind.) If you haven't arranged to be picked up here, you can catch the #236 bus back to Vancouver.

VARLEY TRAIL As the palette of colours in local forests shifts with the seasons, bright pockets almost always persist. Such highlights lend an added poignancy for day trippers who walk the Varley Trail, which links Lynn Headwaters Regional Park with the Lower Seymour Conservation Reserve (see LSCR map, page 45). The trail commemorates Frederick Varley, considered the bohemian of the Canadian painters the Group of Seven. Between 1934 and 1937, Varley lived in a house that still stands on what is now Rice Lake Road. The gifted colourist who painted on the west bank of Lynn Creek included many scenes from the immediate surroundings in his work. Lynn Peak (which he dubbed "the Dumpling"), Mount Seymour and Grouse Mountain were all subjects in both his drawings and watercolours. And what an ideal location he had from which to view these landmarks.

Today, as one walks the trails that link an astounding amount—10,535 ha (26,033 acres)—of protected area on both the east and west banks of Lynn Creek, one encounters the same sounds, sights and smells that Varley did. It's easy to see the influences that inform his work. In autumn, one of the most dazzling times of year, shafts of sunlight light up foregrounds of pumpkin-yellow alder groves against a backdrop of forest green. Lynn Creek rushes by at a faster clip than it has in months, as if celebrating its release from the summer drought. Its motion produces a constant melody that permeates the atmosphere. As the wind rises and falls, so too do the notes from the creek, like music from a concert hall orchestra. A heady, resinous odour emanates from millions of newly shed needles that carpet the forest floor.

This is the kind of trail that welcomes a variety of users, from walkers to equestrians, many of whom already make use of the many other trails on both sides of Lynn Creek. In fact, portions of the Varley Trail cover sections of other trails to form a loop that leads through the GVRD's Lower Seymour Conservation Reserve and Lynn Headwaters Regional Park, as well as Lynn Canyon Municipal Park. One stretch of Varley Trail runs for about 1 km (0.6 mi.) from the old Varley home at the north end of Rice Lake and Marion Roads to the entrance of Lynn Headwaters Park.

Along much of the way, the trail parallels Lynn Creek's winding course. Boardwalks convey adventurers above some of the muddier parts. Signs warn that heavy rains may make the trail immediately adjacent to Lynn Creek "challenging" to pass. Be particularly careful if exploring the unstable riverbanks during periods of high water. Never underestimate the strength of the current, which flows faster at the shoreline than anywhere else in the creek's boulder-strewn channel.

For much of its length, Lynn Creek is easier to detect with ears than eyes. Its unseen cataract often carves through steep-sided granite gorges as it drops towards Burrard Inlet. Sounds of the creek are amplified by the canyon walls and the towering forest. However, as you walk the Varley Trail along the west side of Lynn Creek, flashes of its white water signal through the forest. It's easy to imagine that this relentless clamour must have provided Varley with a transcendent environment in which to create.

The Varley Trail is best approached from either of two locations: the Lower Seymour Conservation Reserve parking lot located at the north end of Lillooet Road (see chapter 9) or the entrance to Lynn Headwaters Regional Park at the north end of Lynn Valley Road. If you're travelling on foot from Vancouver, catch the #228 Lynn Valley bus from the SeaBus terminal at Lonsdale Quay to Intake Road. Walk a short distance north on Intake Road to Rice Lake Road. All the trails are well signed, including the rustic Baden-Powell Trail, which provides additional walking south of the Varley Trail through Lynn Canyon Park.

8 LYNN CANYON PARK

DISTANCE: 7 km (4.3 mi.) north of Highway 1/99, in North Vancouver

ACTIVITIES: Mountain biking, nature observation, viewpoints, walking

HIGHLIGHTS: A suspension bridge links with easygoing trails on both sides of Lynn Creek's narrow canyon

ACCESS: Take either Mountain Highway (Exit 21) or Lynn Valley Road (Exit 19) north from the Upper Levels Highway (Highway 1/99) in North Vancouver near the Ironworkers Memorial (Second Narrows) Bridge. Both roads intersect near the park (see North Vancouver map, page 54). From there, follow Lynn Valley Road north to Peters Road. Turn right (east) where a sign indicates Lynn Canyon Park. The suspension bridge, an interpretive centre and a concession stand are next to the parking lot at the end of Peters Road. If you're travelling on foot, catch the #228 Lynn Valley bus from the SeaBus terminal at Lonsdale Quay, which stops at Peters Road, several blocks west of the park entrance.

In these days when home life is so comfortable, it's important to occasionally expose yourself to the powerful forces of nature. North Vancouver's Lynn Canyon Park is a good place to do this. Younger children may find the canyon trail too steep for their little legs, but they will thrill at the sight of Lynn Creek as it carves its way through a narrow, granite-walled canyon. To heighten the excitement, there's a suspension bridge from which the hypnotic motion of the water can be observed. Although not as long as the Capilano Canyon suspension bridge, the one spanning Lynn Canyon will make just as big an impression, with the added advantage of being free of charge and just steps away from the parking lot.

Stop at the Lynn Canyon Ecology Centre to pick up a map of the park. Plan on spending some time in the centre as part of your visit. Younger children will especially enjoy the kids' "exploratorium cor-

Lynn Canyon Park suspension bridge

ner," which features a puppet theatre. There's also a film room where you can choose from a catalogue of nature-related National Film Board shorts that are projected on request. The Ecology Centre's hours are 10 A.M. to 5 P.M. on weekdays, noon to 4 P.M. on weekends and holidays. Call 604-990-3830 for information on special seasonal programs.

Lynn Canyon Park is one of the oldest parks on the North Shore, having opened in 1912. Relatively modest in area, it's adjoined by two immense tracts of neighbouring wilderness, the Lower Seymour Conservation Reserve and Lynn Headwaters Regional Park. It's taken a while for them to become knitted together, but these days the three—totalling about 10,535 ha (26,033 acres)—are linked by a network of trails, bridges and old logging roads. You can spend an hour or a full day adventuring on foot or, where permitted, on bicycle or horseback without ever coming in sight of civilization.

Visiting Lynn Canyon Park is like attending a banquet where dessert is the first course served. Within a minute's walk of the parking lot, you reach the suspension bridge. Sturdy steel cables support the narrow walkway that is slung across the canyon. Enjoy the experience of standing high above a series of waterfalls cascading into Lynn Creek, 50 m (164 ft.) below. The walkway is ribbed like a gangplank for secure footing; its sides are encased in wire mesh for further safety. Below, white water comes to rest in placid emerald-green pools, then becomes white again in a flash; the pools reflect the thick conifer forest growing out of the canyon walls. On a quiet day you can be mesmerized by the motion in the creek. At other times, when you share the bridge with other walkers and cyclists, there is just enough room for everyone to squeeze by when travelling in opposite directions.

A number of well-marked trails proceed from each end of the bridge. Tall fencing keeps visitors away from the most dangerous sections of the canyon. One of the fascinating aspects of this park is how quickly the landscape transforms the creek from a wide, meandering swath into a narrow funnel of surging energy. Within a 10-minute walk north of the bridge, you can be relaxing beside a gravel bar where the creek widens at a place named 30 Foot Pool. Water spills out of a narrow canyon into the pool. Nearby a staircase leads up to the eastern rim of the canyon. On clear days, sunlight lances through the towering forest to brighten landings at several places on the staircase. In autumn, golden maple leaves spin and slice through the air. The sound of needles being shed by fir trees is like a shower of raindrops as they fall on the understorey of ferns.

From the top of the staircase, it's a short walk farther north to a wooden footbridge that leads west across Lynn Creek and connects with the Varley Trail, which in turn connects with Lynn Headwaters Park (see previous chapter and map page 45). An alternative route runs east from the footbridge and connects in minutes with the nearby Lower Seymour Conservation Reserve (see next chapter). Once you've experienced the proximity of one park to the other, you can understand their popularity with cyclists, who flit through the woods along the wide trails.

If you'd rather not retrace your steps, return to the suspension bridge using an alternative route, a section of the North Shore's extensive Baden-Powell Trail. This level pathway meanders along an old logging road on its way to the suspension bridge. You can do the round trip from the suspension bridge to the footbridge in an easy hour, breaks included.

If you have time, take a 20-minute walk south of the suspension bridge on either side of the canyon to reach the Twin Falls bridge. The route offers a stunning view as water plummets over a tall waterfall into the canyon below. Once on the bridge, you stand much closer to the wildness of the creek than when on the suspension bridge: you're enveloped in mist and in one of nature's most profound sounds. The canyon walls are quite steep here, and towering Douglas firs cut the amount of sunlight reaching the forest floor.

9 LOWER SEYMOUR CONSERVATION RESERVE

DISTANCE: 7 km (4.3 km) north of the Ironworkers Memorial (Second Narrows) Bridge, in North Vancouver

ACTIVITIES: Cross-country skiing, cycling, fishing, hiking, in-line skating, nature observation, picnicking,˙ swimming, viewpoints, walking

HIGHLIGHTS: A paved recreation trail, ancient forest and warm-weather swimming holes

ACCESS: The entrance to the LSCR is at the north end of Lillooet Road, reached by taking the Mount Seymour Parkway exit off Highway 1/99 in North Vancouver near the Ironworkers Memorial Bridge. A large green GVRD sign at the intersection of the Parkway and Lillooet Road points straight ahead on Lillooet to the LSCR. Follow Lillooet past Capilano College, where it narrows. Beyond an entry gate, the road becomes gravel for 4 km (2.5 mi.), to the main gate. The entry gate is locked towards dusk. There is a small parking area just before this gate for those who wish to explore the reserve without fear of being locked in for the night. The main road to the dam is paved and always open to those on foot; bikes and in-line skates are permitted after 5 P.M. on weekdays and all day on weekends and holidays. *Note:* Dogs are not permitted in the LSCR.

If you are travelling on foot from Vancouver, catch the #228 Lynn Valley bus from the SeaBus terminal at Lonsdale Quay to Intake Road. Walk a short distance north on Intake Road to Rice Lake Road, where the Varley Trail (see chapter 7) provides a link between the LSCR, Lynn Headwaters Regional Park and Lynn Canyon Park. Lynn Headwaters and the LSCR are also linked by a kilometre-long stretch of old logging road.

Seymour River

For the better part of the 20th century the Seymour Valley watershed was designated off-limits to the public and held in reserve for future water supply. Stretching below the peaks of Mount Seymour, the watershed was a "look, but don't touch" jewel in our treasure trove of local wilderness areas. In 1987, the Greater Vancouver Regional District decided to open the lower valley south of the Seymour reservoir after a study determined that the site would not be required until well into the 21st century, if at all. Gone are the warning signs forbidding entrance, and no longer do guards chase locals from the old trails used by homesteaders at the turn of the century. Known as the Seymour Demonstration Forest for the first 12 years, the recreation area operated by the GVRD's watershed management department had its name changed in 1999. It is now called the Lower Seymour Conservation Reserve, or LSCR.

A paved road runs about 12 km (7.5 mi.) north through the valley from the LSCR's main gate to the Seymour Falls Dam. Due to construction on the dam that is expected to last until at least 2012, in 1999 work began on a recreation trail to parallel the main road beyond Rice Lake. A wide trail that begins just north of the LSCR's visitors' centre leads to Rice Lake and beyond to the entrance to Lynn Headwaters Regional Park.

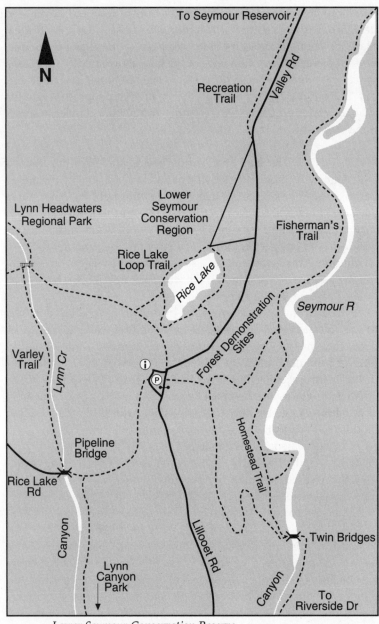

Lower Seymour Conservation Reserve

RICE LAKE Only a short walk from the LSCR's entrance, Rice Lake is a small freshwater destination. Trails and broad boardwalks ring the lakeshore for easy access. All of the amenities here have been designed with wheelchairs in mind. Rice Lake's dock is an ideal place for young and old fry alike to try out their casting technique. Several picnic tables with views of the lake are located nearby. Look for salamanders in the small creek. If there are none in sight, check out the natural-history interpretive trail that loops through the shaded woods on the lake's west side. You're bound to learn something interesting.

RIVER TRAILS The trail that winds beside the Seymour River's west side will interest those who want to walk longer distances. Because the Seymour cuts a deep channel through the valley, there are only a few approaches to the river. From the main gate a dirt road winds down to the forest's southern end, where a trail begins beside an old bridge. On foot this journey takes 30 minutes, by bike 20 minutes. This is the quickest route to the river. There are several rough spots for cyclists, and on the way back uphill bikes have to be pushed around these patches.

A third of the way down to the bridge an alternative pathway to the river appears. Inaccessible by bike, this walking trail leads down into the river valley and joins the Homestead Trail 30 minutes upriver from the bridge. If you're headed upriver, this is a shortcut.

Just before reaching the bridge, the Homestead Trail splits off to the north and follows the river past the site of an old logging settlement and 15 km (9.3 mi.) beyond to the reservoir. After 5 minutes' walking on this trail, watch for an old narrow-gauge rail tunnel on your left, partially concealed. Approximately 3 m (10 ft.) in diameter and 25 m (82 ft.) in length, it is one of the many remnants of the logging operations that cleared the valley of its original forest. Walking through its darkened interior is one of the highlights of a visit to the LSCR.

Two well-used paths branch off to the right of the Homestead Trail a short distance apart. The paths link up to form a semicircle at riverside. Bricks from an old chimney litter the ground at one point. The bank is steep heading down to the river, so watch for the several easy approaches. On the opposite shore are many good locations for sunning and swimming where the afternoon light remains long after it leaves the western riverbank in the shade. Wading across is easy when the river is low during the summer.

Another entrance to the river is located at midvalley just east of Valley Road where a gravel logging road descends to a bridge. From the bridge the elusive peaks of Mount Seymour are visible.

From here, the signed Fisherman's Trail south can easily be picked up as it runs along the river's western bank.

From the LSCR's main gate the 5-km (3.1-mi.) walk to midvalley along Valley Road takes an easy 90 minutes. Walking at riverside, this same distance can take twice as long. However, numerous swimming holes along the way provide bathers with a good reason for choosing the longer route. The 20-km-long (12-mi.-long) reservoir behind the Seymour dam soaks up the sun's rays, and a steady volume of water is released downstream in order to sustain fish habitat. Summer temperature in the Seymour is a soothing 21°C (70°F), just several degrees lower than the air. By comparison, nearby Lynn Creek is a brisk 16°C (61°F). Not only does the Seymour register just right for refreshment, an almost constant breeze blowing through the valley wicks away moisture without the need for a towel.

There are plunge pools galore, including one that's just the right size for you. Remember to wear an old pair of running shoes or sandals to negotiate the boulders, some of which are slippery with algae. You might find that you are sharing the river with the occasional group of anglers; however, the Seymour is of generous enough proportions that there is plenty of room for all.

VALLEY ROAD TO SEYMOUR FALLS DAM On a hot summer day it's a pleasant surprise to discover a soft breeze blowing through the Seymour Valley when there's hardly a whisper in the city. On the road or recreational trail to the Seymour Falls Dam you'll find not only fresh air but comforting stretches of shade. Cool green fragrances waft from the forest's interior. All this makes for a delightfully easy ride to the dam, and groups of cyclists and in-line skaters of all ages and abilities pass in each direction. In winter, this open roadway becomes a cross-country ski trail.

When you finally arrive at the dam you can peer through the high chainlink fence surrounding Seymour Lake, much longer than it is wide. Its blue surface stretches out of sight, running 20 km (12.4 mi.) to the Seymour River's headwaters. Rising above to the west is the full face of Coliseum Mountain, barely visible from Vancouver. In times of plenty, water spills over the top of the dam in thundering white torrents. In drier years, its voice is practically mute. A wooden viewing platform commands a good view of the dam's spillway and the river.

The Hurry Creek salmon hatchery sits just south of the dam, a short distance downhill from the main road. Outdoor ponds are stocked with fingerling coho and steelhead, fattening up for their release in spring. Walk past the fence that surrounds the hatchery to find the Old Growth Trail, which leads south from here.

OLD GROWTH TRAIL During the 1990s, public attention was drawn to the significant stands of old growth that remain in local watersheds, particularly along the river valleys, where western red cedar, amabilis fir and Sitka spruce thrive in a moist environment ideally suited to promoting their growth. To allow public access to some of these giants, a gravel-surfaced loop trail has been constructed on the east side of Valley Road about 1 km (0.6 mi.) south of the Seymour dam. The Old Growth Trail's northern terminus is beside the Hurry Creek fish hatchery. It leads for almost 2 km (1.2 mi.) through the forest here. Much of the distance is over boardwalk above the rain forest floor, with its tangle of devil's club and huckleberry and salmonberry bushes, as well as downed tree trunks coated with thick moss. To bushwhack through here would be no contest: this bush would whack the daylights out of you in short order.

Several strategically located viewing platforms along the Old Growth Trail allow visitors to observe this habitat. One special stop has been constructed beside the largest of the smooth-barked Sitka spruce on the trail. The tree rises like a pillar, casting a spell enhanced by the soothing, melodious gurgle of the river, passing unseen nearby.

Branches of the Seymour River channel through backwaters in which skunk cabbage thrive. Their leafy abundance, along with the imposing upper canopy of branches, lends this environment the air of a steamy Louisiana bayou. Although the gators won't git you, the skeeters might, so bring your bug spray.

After the close quarters of the forest, you might long for the release of the open sky above the river. Unfortunately, there's little more than a glimpse of the river at the end of a short side path that leads from the main trail to an eroding riverbank. Take care where you stand to view the water. The Old Growth Trail gives the river's main course a wide berth, and with good reason: it would be a shame to see the trail washed away by the flooding river. Over the centuries, the Seymour has dug itself a deep channel in the valley floor. There are far safer places downstream to approach the water as you make your way back to the park's entrance. Meanwhile, just keep breathing in the rich forest air.

During the summer, the GVRD operates a shuttle bus from the main gate to the Old Growth Trail. For more information, call 604-987-1273.

10 MAPLEWOOD FLATS CONSERVATION AREA

DISTANCE: 2 km (1.2 mi.) east of the Ironworkers Memorial (Second Narrows) Bridge, in North Vancouver

ACTIVITIES: Bird watching, nature observation, picnicking, walking

HIGHLIGHTS: More than 200 species of birds flock to this haven on Burrard Inlet

ACCESS: Follow the Dollarton Highway exit (#23) east of the Ironworkers Memorial Bridge towards Deep Cove (see North Vancouver map, page 54). Opposite the landmark Crab Shack seafood store stands the Pacific Environmental Science Centre. Next to it, at 2645 Dollarton Highway, is the Maplewood Flats Conservation Area. A road sign displaying the BC Wildlife Watch logo of a pair of binoculars indicates where to pull in. Bus service on Dollarton Highway (#212 Deep Cove) originates from the Phibbs Exchange at the north end of the Ironworkers Memorial Bridge. Call TransLink for schedule information, 604-521-0400, or visit their Web site: www.translink.bc.ca.

For a glimpse of the natural world around the mud flats of Burrard Inlet, head along the Dollarton Highway in North Vancouver, an easy 20-minute drive from Vancouver. The Maplewood Flats Conservation Area officially opened in 1999 and is run by the Wild Bird Trust of B.C. Upon arrival, stop by the sanctuary office, where helpful information on the trust is available. Open daily, the office provides visitors with pamphlets for self-guided viewing of as many as 210 species of birds. Members of the public are invited to join guided bird surveys on the first Saturday of each month (8 A.M. to 12:30 P.M.) and nature walks on the second Saturday of each month (start time 10 A.M.). The nature walks are led by wildlife educator Al Grass, who has gained a reputation as a leader among provincial naturalists during the past three decades.

Maplewood Flats

Grass shares his wide-ranging knowledge of the natural world on a 90-minute ramble along an extensive network of wheelchair-accessible trails.

Sweet birdsongs greet visitors even on overcast winter days here beneath forested Mount Seymour. It's as if the birds sense that this is their new drop-in centre. After leaving the sanctuary office, where recent bird sightings are posted, make your way past the adjoining plant nursery and head for the ocean. Almost immediately you must choose to either follow the loop trails to the west via a stately wooden footbridge or head east beside the mud flats. Although helpful, rubber boots aren't essential to exploring the shoreline. Binoculars, on the other hand, are mandatory. Within minutes in either direction, you'll find yourself at a viewpoint overlooking Burrard Inlet.

Begin your visit by searching for signs of an osprey nest. Ospreys were once a fairly common sight around Burrard Inlet. As the waterfront was developed during the past 50 years, the keen-eyed raptors were crowded out. So aggressive has infilling of the mud flats been that this 126-ha (311-acre) sanctuary is almost all that remains of what was once a 2600-ha (6425-acre) habitat.

For the past several years, a pair of ospreys has returned here to rear two chicks each year, the first such occurrence in living memory. Typically, ospreys build a spacious home atop a sturdy piling or "dolphin." Such nests are easily spotted in the Fraser Valley in places such as the Pitt River. Bundles of twigs indicate that a family of ospreys are in residence. However, in winter you'll have a harder time sighting the birds, as their nests are vacant: ospreys spend the season in California. (Many bird watchers would agree that such behaviour betrays their Canadian roots.)

Ospreys are "snowbirds" as much in appearance as in their migratory habits. When viewed from the underside, these bald eagle–sized raptors display a brilliant white plumage that contrasts markedly with their blackish top feathers. Unlike eagles, which fly low over the waves and reach out their talons to snatch prey from the surface, ospreys hover above the water before plunging in feet first for their catch. Also called fish hawks, ospreys only eat fresh fish.

With binoculars, scan a line of evenly spaced pilings that march south into deep water. Atop the farthest one is the pile of twigs that constitutes the ospreys' nest. Lucky visitors are rewarded with a close-up look at the adult birds, who often swoop low overhead as they scout the inlet for fish. During berry season, a less likely encounter will be with one of the black bears that frequent the reserve in autumn. Signs are posted when a bear is known to be in the area.

A sturdy footbridge allows visitors access to both sides of an old barge channel that cuts through the middle of the sanctuary. An immature stand of alder is starting to add forest cover to the marshland above the mud flats. Sanctuary staff have begun to augment the existing groundcover with plantings from their native-plant nursery. Carefully examine the broadleaf maple and red alder trees that border the hard-packed trail. Tiny Pacific tree frogs may be sitting motionless at the centre of the larger leaves. The trick is spotting the green or iridescent-coloured amphibians in the first place. Once you know what to look for, they're everywhere.

For more information on Maplewood Flats and the Wild Bird Trust of B.C., call 604-924-2581.

11 MOUNT SEYMOUR PROVINCIAL PARK

DISTANCE: 8 km (5 mi.) northeast of the Ironworkers Memorial (Second Narrows) Bridge, in North Vancouver

ACTIVITIES: Hiking, mountain biking, picnicking, skiing, snowboarding, snowshoeing, tobogganing, viewpoints, walking

HIGHLIGHTS: Big views and technical trails in the spiritual home of Vancouver's mountain biking and snowboarding scene

ACCESS: Take Exit 22 from the Upper Levels Highway (Highway 1/99) just north of the Ironworkers Memorial Bridge and follow Mount Seymour Parkway east to Mount Seymour Road. Turn left and drive a short distance north to the park's entrance. The #211 Seymour bus stops at the intersection of Mount Seymour Parkway and Mount Seymour Road, south of the provincial park's entrance. In winter, a private shuttle bus transports skiers and snowboarders from this intersection to the winter sport facilities.

Vancouver's North Shore is blessed with three provincial parks: Cypress, Mount Seymour and freshly minted Indian Arm. Even before bridges spanned Burrard Inlet, day trippers made their way to West and North Vancouver to explore the mysteries of Hollyburn Mountain (in what is now Cypress Park) and Mount Seymour (which achieved provincial-park status in 1936). Not surprisingly, most of the trails in these parks have felt the impact of countless bootprints. Winter recreation was just as much a draw then as now and became increasingly so as rope tows and chairlifts were installed in the 1960s and '70s.

Although modernization may have occurred elsewhere, the facilities at Seymour Ski Country, as its known, retain an "old school" feel. An overwhelming majority of Lower Mainlanders take their

Seymour Ski Country

first lessons here. The groomed runs are wide and gentle; those in search of more challenging terrain hike to a series of small peaks beyond the range of the chairlifts, particularly to First Pump and Second Pump. A friendly family feeling pervades Seymour Ski Country, which is why it retains a loyal following among even the most accomplished local snowboarders and "new school" skiers. Recently, snowshoeing the gentle trails that lead from the base of the Mystery Peak chairlift towards Dinkey Peak and Goldie, Flower and First Lakes has begun to rival the popularity of hiking these same routes in summer.

Part of the enjoyment of visiting Mount Seymour Park is the drive. Mount Seymour Road ascends 12 km (7 mi.) from sea level to a large parking lot beside Seymour Ski Country's facilities at 1034 m (3392 ft.). Along the way are several picnic areas adjacent to spectacular viewpoints. It is difficult to overstate how sweeping the prospects are from the Vancouver Lookout at the second switchback and the Deep Cove Lookout at the fifth switchback.

If you enjoy hiking to viewpoints, Mount Seymour Park offers a wealth of moderate trails. Use extreme caution when exploring the park's open summits, especially in the region around Mount Bishop, at 1508 m (4947 ft.) the tallest peak in the park. Weather conditions change quickly during storm season and the route between peaks quickly becomes obscured. Each year this mountain confounds an unwary hiker or two.

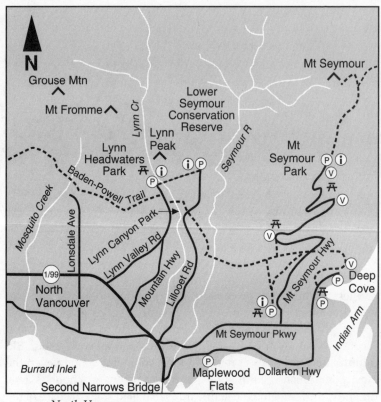

North Vancouver

In summer, once the snow has melted, short hiking trails lead from the parking lot at the top of Mount Seymour Road to Dinkey Peak and Goldie, Mystery and Flower Lakes. Distances to these spots are short, the elevation gain is minimal, and hikers are rewarded with views of Greater Vancouver that are among the best in the Lower Mainland.

For a more extended hike, try the First Lake Trail to Dog Mountain from the parking lot at the top of Mount Seymour Road. Plan on taking 2 hours to complete the 5-km (3.1-mi.) round-trip journey. Wear waterproof boots as this trail is often soggy. If you set your sights on reaching Mount Seymour's summit, try the moderately difficult 4-km (2.5-mi.) hike to Mount Seymour's First and Second Pump peaks. The trail traverses Brockton Point on its way to the peaks. Owing to the panoramic view from here, this is a very popular trail. Other hiking routes on Mount Seymour include the 10-hour, 14-km (8.7-mi.) round-trip trek to Elsay Lake. The initial section of the trail covers the same route as that used to reach First Pump Peak. From there the trail to Elsay Lake passes Gopher Lake, then narrows as it crosses the most exposed section of the mountain. Trail markers are often difficult to locate in bad weather along this rugged portion of the trail, and hikers should not hesitate to turn back if the weather deteriorates. Only experienced, well-equipped hikers should attempt this difficult trail. An emergency shelter is located at Elsay Lake.

BADEN-POWELL TRAIL A 5-km (3.1-mi.) portion of the 48-km (29.8-mi.) Baden-Powell Trail that runs between Horseshoe Bay and Deep Cove passes through Mount Seymour Park. Although there are no major creeks or rivers to cross, plenty of small brooks and streams carry moisture down off the slopes of Mount Seymour. Many are bridged, but you can expect to do a little rock-hopping across others.

Begin from the parking area and picnic grounds at the Baden-Powell Trail's well-marked junction with Mount Seymour Road. From here it's a 15-minute walk to the junction of the Baden-Powell and Mushroom Trails. (A metal trail marker indicates that this is 42 km/26 mi. east of Horseshoe Bay.)

The historic Mushroom parking lot is marked by a sign that explains the important role once played by this site, where travellers to cabins on Mount Seymour left their vehicles before proceeding on foot. Almost overgrown by moss, ferns and alder now, an aging picket fence surrounds the cedar stump to which a mushroom-shaped notice board was once affixed. A short distance beyond the Mushroom parking lot are the Vancouver Lookout picnic grounds, a great place to take a break after making the effort to get this far.

To rejoin the Baden-Powell Trail, simply retrace your steps, or take the Buck Access Trail—a joy of a trail, overflowing with green essences—east from the Vancouver Lookout parking lot to where it joins Old Buck Trail, a 25-minute journey. Old Buck Trail has been upgraded to accommodate mountain bikes as it descends to meet Mount Seymour Road. Cross the road to rejoin Old Buck Trail, restored here to its original width. Although gated against vehicular traffic, this is part of the bicycle trail system in Mount Seymour Park, where many of the pathways are open for riding. Descend to the intersection with the Baden-Powell Trail, 15 minutes from the Buck Access Trail junction. Mount Seymour Road is 10 minutes east of here. If you want to connect with a bus you can follow Old Buck Trail 2.2 km (1.4 mi.) downhill to the park headquarters. Buses stop on nearby Mount Seymour Parkway.

East of the parking lot on Mount Seymour Road, the Baden-Powell Trail enters a much rougher section than the smoother trail that leads west towards the Lower Seymour Conservation Reserve (see chapter 9). In the short distance between Mount Seymour and Indian River Road there are boardwalks, bridges, stairs and a ladder to negotiate. Go left at Indian River Road for a short way to where the trail picks up again beneath the hydro lines. From here east is one of the prettiest sections as views of Indian Arm open up. There is one particularly rewarding location atop an open cliff, worth the scramble up beneath the hydro lines for its views of both Indian Arm and Burrard Inlet.

Having gone as far east as possible, the Baden-Powell Trail cuts south towards Deep Cove. In an hour you'll be out at its terminus on Panorama Drive, a short distance north of Gallant Avenue. This is as good a place as any to begin or end a visit to the trail, with a park, a pub and coffee shops nearby. At busy times there's still ample parking in the lot just south of the beach.

Deep Cove has changed considerably in the years since the Baden-Powell Trail was built. As well as being a jumping-off point for explorers heading up Indian Arm, it has a spruced-up main street and a renowned bicycle shop, handy if you're in need of advice or repairs.

CYCLE TRAILS Begin at the base of Mount Seymour just inside the provincial-park gates with an ascent of the Old Buck Trail. After a grunt up Old Buck, follow a route that touches on the BC Hydro power line service road, the Baden-Powell Trail, Dale's Trail, the Bridle Path and the notoriously steep Severed Dick Trail. In response to the growing number of cyclists who use the park, over the past several years BC Parks has reinforced several trails such as Old Buck to withstand the impact of mountain bike tires. This not only assists riders but also provides a smooth surface for those pushing strollers. Parts of this loop, particularly the technical drops where riders must call on all of their skills to pull off a clean run without having to dismount, are quite challenging. On foot, allow 90 minutes to hike the entire loop and keep your eyes on the trail markers. On more than one occasion even experienced riders have lost their way.

For more information and to request a map of Mount Seymour Provincial Park, contact BC Parks at Mount Seymour Park, 604-929-4818, or the district office, 604-924-2200. Maps and trail information are also available on-line at wlapwww.gov.bc.ca/bcparks.

NORTH OF THE FRASER

12 FRASER RIVER TRAILS

DISTANCE: 3 km (1.9 mi.) east of Boundary Road

ACTIVITIES: Bird watching, cycling, in-line skating, paddling, picnicking, playground, viewpoints, walking

HIGHLIGHTS: Work and play on the Fraser River's North Arm as seen from recreational trails and waterfront piers

ACCESS: For Fraser River Park, head east on Southeast Marine Drive to Burnaby, turning south (right) on Byrne Road, which leads several blocks to the park. To access the west end of the Burnaby River Trail, drive south to the foot of Boundary Road. Vancouver's Riverfront Park (see map page 172) has entrances at the south end of both Victoria Drive and Kerr Street. For bus information, phone TransLink at 604-953-3333 or check out their Web site: www.translink.bc.ca.

Lower Mainlanders are beginning to take more interest in the health of the Fraser River. It's easy to see why. In the past decade, strategic blocks of industrial land along the banks of the North Arm near the boundary of Vancouver and Burnaby have been rezoned as residential. When the Fraser flows past your front window, you want it to look—and smell—pretty. With this in mind, planners have greatly enlarged some small street-end parks that once served as little more than picnic areas for workers on their lunch breaks. Pathways have been created for walkers, joggers, families pushing strollers, cyclists and in-line skaters. Eventually a trail will run the length of the Fraser River's North Arm, from Pacific Spirit Park near the University of British Columbia east to New Westminster.

BURNABY RIVER TRAIL One good stretch with a forested feeling is the Burnaby River Trail. This hard-packed dirt pathway, more than 5 km (3 mi.) long, runs east beside the river from the south foot of Boundary Road towards New Westminster. In the distance the spires and guy wires of two bridges, the Queensboro and the Patullo, frame distant Mount Baker's snow cone. In the foreground is the

Vancouver Riverfront Park

wide, muddy Fraser River. When the earth begins to warm in March, dozens of skunk cabbage bloom in marshy sections of the trail. Their yellow blossoms and unmistakable odour announce spring's arrival on the West Coast.

Weyerhaeuser (formerly MacMillan Bloedel) has a large particleboard and specialty wood operations yard beside the Boundary Road trailhead. A long line of booms moored just offshore corral western red cedar logs. The air is ripe with their woody aroma, and their deep auburn colour flames in the light of the late afternoon sun. Appropriately, much of the trail is lined with fledgling cedars.

Walk down to the river beside the trail at the foot of Boundary Road. You never know what you'll see on the river—something always seems to be going on. In early summer, a riverboat festival has become an annual tradition. Watch for a colourfully-decked-out flotilla of vessels to sail up the Fraser past the trail when visiting on the second full weekend in July.

No matter when you time your visit, there are bound to be tugboats with imaginative names like *Sea Imp* emblazoned on their stubby prows pulling barges and booms. Bring along a pair of binoculars so that you can read them. Shorebirds such as sandpipers, kingfishers and herons also warrant close inspection. It's not all work on the river; speedboats tow water-skiers on weekends, while kayakers and canoeists paddle close to shore to avoid their wake. Sunday mornings are always the quietest times to explore here.

Walking along the river is a popular pastime, especially on weekends. The path is wide enough for everyone to share. Looking south across the river, you can see runners and cyclists on the dike road encircling Lulu Island silhouetted against the open sky. Along the trail, the forest of alder and cottonwood is rapidly approaching its climax. Cedars will eventually replace these deciduous trees and help reinforce the riverbanks against the erosion from the wakes of tugs and barges on the Fraser. The log booms, to their credit, help with this task, too.

The trail passes through Fraser River Park, where log booms give way to a stretch of open beach. For small children this beach is a worthwhile destination and a welcome place to take a break and enjoy a snack on an extended outing. If you're looking for a place to begin a paddle on the Fraser River, this park is a good site to launch a small hand-carried boat.

On the east side of the park, Commonwealth Construction allows public access through the company's dockyard. Rather than having to detour around its considerable property, you can follow the Fraser River trail upstream continuously for several more kilometres. Along the way you'll pass the CNR swing bridge that links Burnaby to Lulu Island. East of the bridge, a long, broad straightaway leads to a sandy beach, perfect for picnicking. Beyond the beach the trail quickly degenerates into a skunk cabbage wetland, but if you don't mind getting mucky, explore on. The broad leaves of this plant become progressively taller during the summer months until they assume tremendous proportions.

If you don't want to retrace your steps, circle back along the side roads north of Fraser River Park through the rich delta, where a wide variety of vegetables are grown year round. Since the route is quite level, you can complete this riverside adventure in a morning or an afternoon.

VANCOUVER RIVERFRONT PARK Quick access to Vancouver Riverfront Park, with its broad pier, twin multi-use trails, a beach and a children's play area, has no doubt saved more than one relationship. When you need to get out of the house in a hurry, head for this stretch of waterfront, bookended by a set of piers strategically positioned for optimum river viewing. The path between the two piers is easygoing, and equally enjoyable for those on foot, bikes, scooters, in-line skates or young (and lucky) enough to be pushed in strollers. This is the sort of place that, once discovered, you can return to at a moment's notice.

13 BURNABY PARKS

DISTANCE: 15 km (9.3 mi.) east of Boundary Road

ACTIVITIES: Bird watching, cycling, paddling, picnicking, viewpoints, walking

HIGHLIGHTS: Exotic totems and tree-lined pathways with dozens of species of birds for company

ACCESS: The most convenient way to reach Burnaby Mountain Park from Vancouver is to take Parker and then Curtis Streets east off Boundary Road, turning north (left) on Centennial Way as Curtis begins to climb Mount Burnaby towards Simon Fraser University. The park is at the end of Centennial Way and is well marked.

The main entrance to Deer Lake Park is located just south of the Trans-Canada Highway (Highway 1) in Burnaby. Take the Canada Way exit (#33). Turn left on Canada Way and immediately right on Sperling to Deer Lake Park. An alternative approach leads east from a parking area on Royal Oak Avenue between Kingsway and Canada Way. For bus information, phone TransLink at 604-953-3333 or check out their Web site: www.translink.bc.ca.

BURNABY MOUNTAIN PARK Here's one of the most exotic parks in the Lower Mainland. Burnaby Mountain Park's proximity makes it perfect for a quick morning or afternoon getaway. No matter what your age, you'll feel as if you've entered another world here. The location is stunning, with the city spread to the west below Mount Burnaby's long incline. Spacious fields offer plenty of romping room. Japanese ceremonial, or totem, poles lend a truly fantastic appearance to the setting. The place where the poles are installed seems custom-made for works of such simple grandeur. A wide-open, grassy field descends the mountain's western slope in a series of gently rolling steps to meet the surrounding poplar forest. The

Deer Lake

poles were raised on the top third of the slope. Populating one of the steps is a group of perhaps 50 poles gathered as a community—some in pairs, some alone.

Although similar to the outdoor area beside the University of British Columbia's Museum of Anthropology, where several large ceremonial poles from a number of West Coast First Nations soar skyward, Burnaby Mountain Park's installation is different. The poles were carved by a Japanese artist, Nubuo Toko, and his son, who are among the Ainu people, Japan's first inhabitants. The totem poles were erected to commemorate the friendship between the sister cities of Kushiro and Burnaby.

The spectacular setting in the park inspired Toko to imagine it as Kamui Mintara, or Playground of the Gods. Set out in an orderly, eye-pleasing fashion, the poles represent the story of the gods who descended to Earth to give birth to the Ainu. Familiar animal spirits such as the whale, bear and owl adorn the tops of the slender, bleached logs. Incised into the sides of some poles are suggestions of human forms, while other poles are simply ringed and notched like the pieces of an ultramodern chess set. Particularly pleasing are four poles set in a square and linked by diagonal cross-beams, with a killer whale riding atop. Nearby, the lone pole in the collection to be installed at right angles to the others supports a whale accompanied by the brooding figure of a raven gazing towards the west. All of the poles rise from gravelled pads, which gives the area a formal look. Harmony, balance and order reign here. Perhaps this is why a visit to Burnaby Mountain Park provides such a pleasant change for most people.

Not only is the vista to the west enchanting, but so, too, are the cliffside views down to Burrard Inlet, the sight of several bends in Indian Arm and the view north to the sprawling slopes and glacial expanses of Mamquam Mountain near Squamish. A fence keeps visitors back from the edge, providing a sense of security while still imparting a thrill.

The poles and views are not the sole attractions. Burnaby Mountain Park is ringed by a network of pathways that crisscross the perimeter of the SFU campus, including the Trans Canada Trail. When spring temperatures heat the earth, the smell of the resin-rich buds of poplar trees fills the air, along with birdsongs. This park is the ideal place to celebrate the annual seasonal renewal in the Playground of the Gods. Its formal rose garden is also a big draw for wedding parties who wish to be photographed among the blossoms. Horizons Restaurant is located next to the garden. Walking and cycling trails run through the forest uphill towards Simon Fraser University and in the woods below the totems.

DEER LAKE PARK Deer Lake lies just south of the Trans-Canada Highway. A wall of deciduous trees, interspersed with the occasional hemlock, shields it from view. Even passers-by on Canada Way are deprived of a glimpse of the demure lake, as shy as its name suggests. Which is perhaps what makes the lake so special. Only those who make an effort to get out of their cars and approach on foot are rewarded with a full view of its surface.

Open slopes preside over Deer Lake's western shoreline just east of Royal Oak Avenue. This meadow is particularly significant to wildlife, particularly birds. It is classified as "old field," a former cow pasture that years ago was left to go wild, and Burnaby Parks now manages the hillside as a nature reserve. In the late 1980s, when Burnaby assumed control of the Oakalla prison lands, they built a unique biofiltration pond here, complemented by a wildlife viewing platform. Aquatic vegetation planted in the pond, such as cattails, removes oily particles and other contaminants from storm sewers that drain the slope. This prevents sedimentation and phosphates from entering Deer Lake farther downhill.

During annual spring and fall bird migrations, it pays to scan the horizon from the viewing platform. You'll see not only raptors such as hawks, merlins and peregrine falcons making their way, but also turkey vultures winging between the Interior and their winter homes in the Fraser Delta. Silken-voiced meadowlarks and barn owls have begun to frequent the former pasture as well. Along the shore, Virginia rail and cinnamon teal share space in the shallows with the occasional angler. Each fall, the provincial Ministry of Water, Land and Air Protection stocks Deer Lake with rainbow trout to encourage city dwellers to toss in a line. Just remember to have a freshwater fishing licence if you do.

Over the past several years, wildlife educator Al Grass (see chapter 10) has been keeping a detailed record of birds seen around Deer Lake for BC Wildlife Watch. Such scrutiny is long overdue and is part of an extensive inventory of wildlife being carried out by the municipality. What makes this park so fascinating even for those who have difficulty pinning names on all but the most common birds is the sheer number of feathered creatures liable to be encountered. On a casual walk visitors can easily spot upwards of 40 species. On a good day Grass routinely sees between 50 and 70 species. It helps to know which spruce tree in which to spot owls, one of the more elusive residents. (Watch for them at the west end of the lake beside the boardwalk.) Creeks and gullies indent the hillside directly above the lake's south shore. Dense foliage here provides the perfect shelter for the diminutive western screech-owls.

Although not as large as nearby Burnaby Lake, Deer Lake is just as admirably suited for a canoe or kayak paddle. There's a beach on the lake's east side with a boat launch (non-motorized vessels only). In summer, you'll find canoes for rent here. On special evenings you can enjoy sunsets that just won't quit. The sky lights up with vivid colours that would rival a Navajo blanket. A stately heron shares a log with a rakish-looking mallard and his more modestly festooned mate. A mat of lily pads spreads out before them, dotted with white blossoms as fat as dahlias.

For a map and further information on both parks, call the Burnaby Parks and Recreation office, 604-294-7450, or visit their Web site: www.burnabyparksrec.org.

14 BURRARD INLET & PORT MOODY ARM

DISTANCE:	As much as 15 km (9.3 mi.) east of Boundary Road
ACTIVITIES:	Bird watching, cycling, fishing, in-line skating, kite-flying, nature observation, paddling, picnicking, playgrounds, swimming, viewpoints
HIGHLIGHTS:	Harbour views, beaches and recreational pathways
ACCESS:	New Brighton Park sits on the north side of McGill Street across from the PNE site. Turn north off McGill onto Commissioner Street and follow the signs.

To find Barnet Marine Park, drive east from Vancouver on Hastings Street towards Port Moody. This route leads to the Barnet Highway (Highway 7A). In 2.5 km (1.6 mi.) you'll see the signed entrance to the park on your left.

Rocky Point Park is located in Port Moody, an easy 30-minute drive on weekends from downtown Vancouver via the Barnet Highway (see map page 72). Drive along St. Johns Street, Port Moody's main street. Watch for signs that point to Rocky Point Park. Turn north on Moody Street and follow it to an overpass over the railway tracks that leads to the park. For schedule information on the #160 bus to Port Moody from Vancouver, call TransLink, 604-953-3333, or visit their Web site: www.translink.bc.ca.

Vancouver's harbour is a fascinating whirl of marine activity. Huge freighters come and go, slipping in and out of port with the help of tugboats, those little dynamos that ride herd on their foreign-flagged charges. Watching them in action in Burrard Inlet and Port Moody Arm is a gentle way to spend a few afternoon hours. On sunny weekends the harbour is also filled with pleasure craft that range in size from slim racing canoes to fat cruise ships.

Some of the best vantage points for viewing the action are a series of waterfront parks located on the shores of Burrard Inlet. Getting to any of them involves a quick drive from Vancouver—New Brighton Park, for example, is inside the city limits near Burnaby. All of them share an abundance of attractions. It's not just the sight of boats from the shoreline that you'll enjoy, but also the wildlife that work the shore in search of food.

NEW BRIGHTON PARK Although you may often have driven down McGill Street past the Hastings racetrack on the way to the Iron-workers Memorial (Second Narrows) Bridge, you may not have stopped to explore New Brighton Park. After all, traffic moves through this area at a good speed, and making the turn into the park requires some foresight. Not that you'll find it difficult; you simply have to slow down to make the turnoff into the park. The entrance is well signed, but that doesn't make the park any easier to spot, hid den as it is by a railway overpass. In summer there are plenty of other cars in the parking lot. New Brighton boasts a heated outdoor pool that attracts many families here on the east side of town.

In the off-season the pool is fenced in and off-limits unless you fly in. On spring and fall days, ducks have it to themselves; floating on the calm waters of the pool, they look like ideal bathtub duckies. The nearby grain elevators cast their reflection on the pool's surface. The rich smell of this year's grain crop being loaded onto a waiting freighter is so thick you'd think you could make bread from the air itself.

It's a short walk from the pool to the small pier for a look across Burrard Inlet at the Lions, which are perfectly twinned when seen from here. This is one of the best vantage points in the city from which to see these peaks. Perhaps this is why in 1863 the first build-ings put up by Europeans in what is now Vancouver were situated here, at the Hastings townsite. A heritage plaque gives details of how the Douglas Road linked this spot with New Westminster and for years carried visitors to a resort that flourished in the days before the wheat pool arrived.

Judging from the currents that suck and eddy around the pier's pilings, ocean swimming never has been much of an option, but there are a couple of sheltered beaches on which to roam out of the cool breeze. Not much point in getting the bike out here, though, as the riding at New Brighton is limited unless you're going on a long jaunt west along Commissioner Street for more views of the inner harbour. However, the open playing fields around the shoreline lend themselves to tossing a Frisbee, flying a kite or romping with a

Rocky Point Park

dog. If you're looking to stretch your legs even more, there is a short stretch of paved pedestrian and cycling trail that runs east from the park entrance to the grain elevators.

BARNET MARINE PARK When you want to get more of a feel for the inland reaches of the Pacific Ocean where it meets Vancouver's shores, head to Barnet Marine Park. As its name implies, this park provides visitors with access to the waters of Burrard Inlet's Port Moody Arm. You don't need a canoe or kayak to enjoy yourself here; there is much to experience on land. Preschoolers will find the spacious sandbox very entertaining, and larger expanses of sand form a wide beach that will appeal to kids of all ages.

Thick foliage hides any view of the park from the road, and railway tracks obscure the shoreline. From the parking lot, walk across the tracks to reach the green spaces. If you've got strollers and toddlers with you, you may wish to drop them off with an adult at the end of the road and then return uphill to park. Parking for people with physical disabilities is available closer to the water, near a viewing pier. True to the park's marine nature, there is a boat launch for canoes, kayaks or sailboats. Belcarra Regional Park (see next chapter) lies directly north across the narrow inlet. The waters close to shore are serene because no motorized boats can be launched from here. (*Note:* Dogs are not allowed in the park.)

Burnaby has improved the grounds of Barnet Marine Park tremendously over the past few years, and it now has one of the prettiest beaches in the entire Burrard Inlet area. A large boomed-off swimming section fronts the hard-packed sandy beach. Picnic tables with barbecue stands are shaded by tall poplars. Swings, slides and toy ponies are enclosed in a large sandbox beneath their boughs.

The park is located on the site of Barnet, a small town that flourished with the help of a lumber mill from 1889 until its demise in 1949. All that remains today are several large concrete towers and a squat scrap burner hunkered on the beach. In spring, piles of fresh sand awaiting spreading are mounded up beside a pier perched on tall pilings and provide a challenge for young hill-climbing explorers. The wide curves of Barnet's shoreline lead off to the west and east. Watch for the occasional pelagic cormorant, its long neck iridescent in the sun, as it paddles around, working the shoreline with its long thin bill. It's just one of many species of waterfowl you might see here. Other wildlife that inhabit the park include coyotes; signs warn visitors not to feed them.

A service road runs west through Barnet Park and a good distance beyond towards an oil refinery. Follow it on foot or by bike for a look up Indian Arm, across to Deep Cove and Cates Park, and at much maritime activity. Large freighters lie at anchor, with the green slopes of Mount Seymour rising behind. The setting is so sheltered that it is easy to imagine how welcoming Vancouver's inner harbour has always been to sailors. That same sense of peace extends to all those in need of a refreshing outdoor experience. The gracious lines of the Ironworkers Memorial (Second Narrows) Bridge stand half-revealed in the distance. Burnaby intends to extend this trail west in the future, perhaps even linking it with New Brighton someday. One recent transportation link between Vancouver and Mission transects the park: In early mornings and late afternoons, watch for the distinctive blue cars of the West Coast Express commuter train. The engineer has a heavy hand on the whistle as the train passes beside Burrard Inlet. Seeing it roll by adds a special thrill to a visit here.

ROCKY POINT PARK Travellers have been coming to Port Moody for centuries. Native people had summer homes here long before Canadian Pacific's transcontinental rail line first reached the West Coast in November 1885. Port Moody was chosen as its terminus.

Only in subsequent years was a branch line run into the upstart town of Vancouver.

If you ever owned a toy train set, you may enjoy visiting the real thing. The Port Moody Museum is housed in a restored 1904 train station on Murray Street near the foot of Moody Street, next to the park. Tours of the museum may be arranged by calling 604-939-1648. If you're just passing by, there's plenty to be seen just by looking in the windows. On a siding next to the museum is an old CPR passenger car, "Venosta," named for one of the many stops along the vast cross-country rail line.

Rocky Point Park has a lengthy pier running out into the shallow waters of Port Moody Arm's eastern end. There's swimming here, both in the ocean and in a freshwater pool. A children's playground features slides, swings and climbing apparatus housed in a miniature train setting.

These days, some of the more prized destinations for families with older children are those where everyone can in-line skate together. Although that's not the only attraction at Rocky Point Park, it's high on the list of favourite activities here. A scenic, paved bicycle and in-line skate trail runs east from Rocky Point Park to Old Orchard Park, about a 5-km (3.1-mi.) round trip. Paralleling it is a pedestrian-only walkway through the park. Both trails run beside the inlet to a marshy area around Rocky Point, a good place to observe waterfowl.

Several ancient cement foundations anchor the point. Kids will enjoy perching and playing on a parapet here, looking over at a squat, truncated step pyramid about 5 m (16 ft.) high. A larger-than-life, industrial-size rubber tire sits mired up to its rim in sludge. The old tire, the pillars and pyramids all seem perfectly positioned, like a piece of found art. Salmonberry bushes hem the trail. In wet seasons, the little streams and creeks that pass underneath gurgle like newborns. Here, at the very east end of the inlet, the wind often blows so strongly in your ears that you can't hear any sounds—industrial or wildlife—just the cleansing strains of Nature calling.

15 BELCARRA & BUNTZEN LAKE

DISTANCE: 30 km (18 mi.) east of Boundary Road, in the villages of Belcarra and Anmore

ACTIVITIES: Fishing, group functions, hiking, mountain biking, paddling, picnicking, swimming, viewpoints, walking

HIGHLIGHTS: Oceanside walks, mountain biking and hiking trails, warm-water swimming, fresh and saltwater paddling

ACCESS: Belcarra Regional Park and Buntzen Lake Recreation Area lie on the north side of Port Moody Arm across from Burnaby. From Vancouver, head to Port Moody on Hastings Street and the Barnet Highway (Highway 7A). Turn east onto St. Johns Street and north six stoplights later onto well-marked Ioco Road. Ioco Road soon turns left at an intersection marked by a green GVRD sign pointing the way to the park. (If you're headed to the village of Anmore and Buntzen Lake, continue straight ahead onto Heritage Mountain Boulevard.) Turn right at the Ioco School and follow First Avenue towards the village of Belcarra. (An alternative route to Anmore and Buntzen Lake via Sunnyside Road appears on the right just after you've passed through Ioco.) Just before Sasamat Lake, signs direct traffic left towards Belcarra Park. *Note:* There is no vehicle access to the park from the community of Belcarra, where parking is restricted to residents only.

For schedule information on the #148 Ioco bus to Belcarra and Anmore via the #160 bus to Port Moody from Vancouver, call TransLink, 604-953-3333, or visit their Web site: www.translink.bc.ca.

Buntzen Lake

Since 1996, major changes have occurred in the parkland that surrounds the communities of Belcarra and Anmore. Three separate stakeholders—the Greater Vancouver Regional District, BC Hydro and BC Parks—oversee recreational land here; the GVRD's Belcarra Regional Park, BC Hydro's Buntzen Lake Recreation Area and Indian Arm Provincial Park border one another. Thanks to the efforts of a local citizens' group, the Buntzen Ridge Wilderness Recreation and Parks Association, trails connecting the three parks

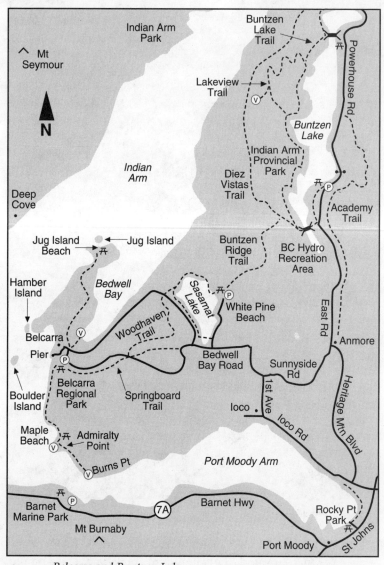

Belcarra and Buntzen Lake

that once served only hikers and horseback riders have been upgraded to accommodate a mixed group of outdoor enthusiasts, including mountain bikers. Strategically placed "Shared Trail" interpretive signs have helped to minimize conflict between users.

This is one of the most varied destinations for day trippers in the Lower Mainland. There's far more ground to explore here than can be covered in a week, let alone a day. Walk oceanfront trails in Belcarra Park, hike lakeside trails on Buntzen Ridge, swim in freshwater Sasamat or Buntzen Lakes, mountain bike through the forest of Indian Arm Park that surrounds Anmore and Belcarra, picnic on Buntzen's grassy lawns, launch a kayak into Indian Arm or paddle a canoe in Buntzen Lake. Decide how big a piece you want to bite off, pack a lunch and away you go.

BELCARRA REGIONAL PARK Belcarra welcomes about 850,000 visitors a year. Granted, the park bulges with swimmers, paddlers, picnickers and mountain bikers in summer months. In the off-season, though, it reverts to the quiet little hideaway it was when GVRD Parks first began acquiring land here in the early 1970s.

Belcarra is an Irish name meaning "fair land on which the sun shines." Approximately 4000 years before the arrival of Judge William Norman Bole, the Irishman who christened this corner of Indian Arm and Burrard Inlet, ancestors of the local Stó:lō First Nations, a people known as the Sleil-waututlh, called it *Tum-ta-mahy-tun*, meaning "land" or "biggest place for people" or just plain "home." Three significant archaeological sites have been unearthed in this area since 1971 that highlight its importance over the millennia. One large midden, a mound of shells and shards, rises above the beach. From it you have an unobstructed view west across the waters of Indian Arm and Burrard Inlet, which sustained the Native population. Small wonder that First Nations peoples treasured this land as their winter home.

In 1923, the Harbour Navigation Company developed resort facilities here. Vancouverites rode the ferry to visit the dance pavilion, wharf and cabins. All but the cement stairway to the beach is now gone, but tour boats from Vancouver still come here in the summer with groups who picnic and play on the large open lawns. Anglers and crabbers use the dock. The Belcarra picnic area has reservable picnic shelters and even a reservable wharf. Call 604-432-6352 for more information.

As you near Belcarra Park, you will see several small parking lots beside the road. These are for the benefit of cyclists and hikers who wish to explore the forested 4-km (2.5-mi.) Springboard Trail without having to drive all the way to the main parking lot. The trail links Sasamat Lake with Belcarra's waterfront on Indian Arm beside the picnic area, concession stand and open park grounds.

At the picnic grounds there is a choice of activities. Head for the beach, stroll out on the dock or stretch your legs along some of the scenic oceanfront trails. Admiralty Point Trail begins at the main parking lot and heads south through second-growth forest to several good viewpoints. New boardwalks have improved footing on a steep-sided section that overlooks Burrard Inlet. A 30-minute walk will have you at Admiralty Point and the Maple Beach picnic area. It won't take long before your eyes begin to pick out things on the forest floor that rarely appear in Vancouver neighbourhoods. Chocolate-brown mushrooms the size of freshly baked muffins glisten at the foot of fire-charred snags covered by velvety, emerald-green moss. Sword ferns colonize the sides of soaring alders, giving the trunks a bristly outline. The graceful skirts of western red cedar branches shelter low-lying salal bushes that line the trail. At places like Cod Rock and Periwinkle Notch, paths lead out to panoramic viewpoints of Burrard Inlet. Kayakers and canoeists paddle by, enjoying a tranquillity on the water similar to that on land.

Hours of afternoon sunlight warm the shores of Belcarra on clear days. On cloudy days an air of quiet reflection hangs over the trail. Besides Burrard Inlet and Mount Burnaby to the south, you can also see Deep Cove to the west and Mount Seymour rising above the entrance to Indian Arm, a fiord that stretches 18 km (11.2 mi.) north.

The most beautiful beach in Belcarra presents itself at Whiteshell Bank, just minutes beyond Admiralty Point, as the trail bends south-east and leads beside Port Moody's outer harbour. The pathway to the beach was obviously fashioned long before this became a park. Indeed, in the early 1980s, squatters were finally ousted after having enjoyed this location since the 1950s. Thanks to their efforts over the years, rocks on a portion of the little beach were cleared away. Over time, pulverized shells streaked the sandy surface a powdery white. Drifts of delicate green periwinkle carpet the foreshore, suggesting human occupation. Confirmation of this is provided by a companion hydrangea bush whose greenish-blue blossoms add yet another splash of colour to the surroundings. Here is a quintessential West Coast setting: a quiet cove outlined in cedar where small streams splash out of the forest and down into the ocean. Gulls wheel above as a harbour seal bobs up to check you out.

JUG ISLAND BEACH TRAIL One of the lengthier walks in Belcarra leads to Jug Island Beach, which overlooks Jug Island. Depending on your pace, it will take between 30 and 45 minutes to reach it from the Belcarra picnic grounds. Jug Island Beach Trail begins in the woods beside the covered picnic shelter. Much of the route is either up or downhill, with a series of wooden staircases for assistance in the steepest sections. Although there are few views along the way, one branch of the trail leads out to an opening beside Bedwell Bay. From here you look east to the slopes of Eagle Ridge and the broad flank of Coquitlam Mountain rising above unseen Buntzen Lake. Farther along, a new branch of the trail leads through a fragrant pine forest to another lookout on Bedwell Bay

The beach trail leads through a forest of second-growth hemlock and alder as well as broadleaf maple. In summer the dense leaf and needle canopy is an omnipresent green. Come autumn the leaves turn shades of gold, and once they fall, their shades range from deep purple to rich terra cotta. So dense is the layer of leaves covering the trail that little, if any, of the bare earth can be seen.

Jug Island lies offshore at the north end of a narrow peninsula and can be viewed from a small beach at the end of the trail. The island has steep, rocky sides with no visible landing sites. Looking north from the little beach, you can make out the concrete walls of the hydro station whose turbines are driven by water from Buntzen Lake. Visible beyond Jug Island are several small islands that comprise Indian Islets Provincial Marine Park. A number of wilderness campsites on the islands make them a desirable destination for kayakers who set off from Belcarra's shore. The broad, glaciated slopes of Mamquam Mountain dominate the skyline to the north. Mount Garibaldi's peak juts up to the left of Mamquam.

SASAMAT LAKE In the hills above Belcarra are two freshwater lakes, Sasamat and Buntzen. The sandy White Pine Beach on Sasamat Lake is among the most popular in the Lower Mainland, perhaps because the water here is so warm. As well, a pleasant walking trail circles the lake (about half as big as nearby Buntzen Lake) beneath the shelter of graceful western red cedars. A 200-m (656-ft.) floating bridge spans the south end of Sasamat Lake and provides welcome relief from the close quarters of the forested trail.

One of the region's best-built hiking and cycling trails links Belcarra with Indian Arm Provincial Park. The Buntzen Ridge Trail begins from the south end of parking lot "F" above White Pine Beach at Sasamat Lake. It switchbacks 2 km (1.2 mi.) to link with the Saddle Ridge Trail (see next section) on Buntzen Ridge, to the west of Buntzen Lake.

BUNTZEN LAKE RECREATION AREA Buntzen Lake draws its water from a tunnel connected to the Coquitlam reservoir and is much chillier than Sasamat. A wealth of riding, hiking and cycling trails lead north from here beside the long lake and onto the ridges above. Those who enjoy exploring by water can rent a canoe year round at the nearby Anmore Grocery (604-469-9928). As Buntzen is closed to powerboats, you'll enjoy the quiet as you paddle past loons and Canada geese. In 1970 BC Hydro, which draws water down from the lake to run two hydro generating plants on Indian Arm, developed Buntzen for recreation, pouring a wide, gently sloping sand beach.

Millennia earlier, the Coquitlam tribe of the Coast Salish journeyed here. Legend has it that as the seas began to rise they built a big boat, put the children in it with plenty of provisions and anchored it to an enormous boulder in Buntzen (which they called "Lake Beautiful") to ride out the Great Flood. After the waters receded, a giant reptile known as Scnoki, with a head at either end of its body, straddled the entrance to Indian Arm. No one dared go near, so Lake Beautiful was used as an alternative route from Burrard Inlet to the rich fishing grounds of Indian Arm.

Buntzen Lake's South Beach picnic area is laid out in a tidy fashion. Large, well-spaced picnic tables sit under a forest of Douglas fir, and broad lawns run down to the beach. You can drive to the dock to unload boats. It's possible to swim from the beach or dock to a small treed island just offshore with a rocky point for diving. Another such island lies a short boat ride north of the dock. The lake is stocked with kokanee, cutthroat trout and Dolly Varden char, among other species. It will take you half an hour to paddle the length of the lake, if you're in a hurry. Otherwise, Buntzen is the kind of place where, once you've arrived, there's no need to rush anything.

Avoid the park during peak weekend hours in July and August; it's just too busy. Otherwise, plan your trip for as early in the day as possible to avoid traffic and long walks from the overflow parking lots. *Note:* Dogs are not permitted on Buntzen's beaches between May and October. An aerial photo of the lake at the head of the trail gives prospective boaters a detailed look at the shoreline and helps determine where to head on this 6-km-long (3.7-mi.-long), narrow, steep-sided lake. The photo is also of great assistance to cyclists, walkers and hikers interested in circling the lake via a series of roads and trails. For much of the distance these mostly level routes hug the lake. In addition, there is a network of more challenging trails that climb to viewpoints above the lake's east and west sides. Printed maps with detailed route descriptions are available at the afore-mentioned sign during summer months. Contact BC Hydro to obtain a copy, 604-469-9679, or visit their Web site: www.bchydro.bc.ca/recreation.

Cyclists and those pushing strollers will particularly enjoy the well-maintained gravel road that runs for 3 km (1.9 mi.) along the lake's eastern shore from the South Beach parking lot to the power-house near North Beach. Those who'd prefer a lakeside walk should try the 8-km (5-mi.) Buntzen Lake Trail, which circles the lake. Allow 4 to 5 hours to walk the trail.

The well-marked Academy Trail provides a more challenging route. This pleasant 4-km (2.5-mi.) hard-packed pathway is a shared equestrian-hiker-cyclist trail. A good place to begin exploring Academy Trail on foot or by bike is from the first parking lot on the right as you enter the recreation area. Academy Trail links up with Powerhouse Road halfway to North Beach. Although views of the lake are scarce along this trail, views of Mount Seymour on the western horizon more than compensate.

Watch for the well-marked entrance to the Halvor Lunden Trail just north of South Beach on Powerhouse Road (see below). Named for a renowned local trail builder, the trail comprises three loop routes: the Lindsay Lake Loop (15 km/9.3 mi.), the Swan Falls Loop (20 km/12.4 mi.) and the Dilly Dally Loop (25 km/15.5 mi.). Only experienced and fit hikers and mountain bikers should attempt these longer trails. The loops traverse the steep hillside above Buntzen Lake's east side in Indian Arm Provincial Park. Viewpoints on Eagle Ridge and a nest of 10 lakes make the effort worthwhile. Depending on your route, allow between 6 and 12 hours to complete the individual loops.

As both Powerhouse Road and the Buntzen Lake Trail approach North Beach, they pass the tunnel for water entering Buntzen from Coquitlam Lake. You'll hear the sound of the water flowing from the tunnel beneath Eagle Ridge well before it comes into view near North Beach. You can walk down from the road to view the tunnel on a staircase that also leads to the North Beach picnic area. If you con-tinue a short distance farther along the road as it descends downhill, you'll arrive at an entrance to North Beach. An interpretive map is located where the lake narrows, next to an open playing field. This is also a good destination should you be exploring by boat. A warning sign advises boaters to keep well away from the tunnel. Paddling north from South Beach will give your arms a good workout. Because of Buntzen's sheltered setting, its surface is most often calm, and you'll find that the water in the lake is extremely clear.

Look for Swan Falls cascading down the eastern slopes above the lake, just as the road descends towards the pumphouse. The road continues in hard-packed condition as it rounds the north end of the lake past the large intake pipe that feeds water to the generators. For many visitors, especially those with children, this will be as far as you wish to go before retracing your route. Don't pass up a chance to cross the suspension bridge over the lake's north end before you turn back.

If you're up for more adventuring, you can choose to return along the west side of the lake on the Buntzen Lake Trail, a round-trip distance of 8 km (5 mi.). Alternatively, the Lakeview Trail (6 km/3.7 mi.), which leads uphill from Buntzen, provides a much stiffer challenge to those on foot or bike. Novices should not attempt this route. It involves a long series of ups and downs along a series of bumpy switchbacks. In contrast, the Buntzen Lake Trail, which skirts the shoreline, is far easier to handle.

If you choose to explore Buntzen Lake in a clockwise direction from South Beach, cross to the lake's west side on the boardwalk that leads over the lake's south end. Pumphouse Road leads 1.5 km (0.9 mi.) along the lake's west side as far as the Burrard Pumphouse. A 4-km (2.5-mi.) portion of the Buntzen Lake Trail leads north from the pumphouse along the west side of the lake. Allow 2 to 3 hours to walk the trail one way to North Beach.

As you climb above the lake's western shoreline you enter Indian Arm Provincial Park. Four multi-use trails originate here, including a series of steep loop trails called Bear Claw, Saddle Ridge and Horseshoe. Thigh- and quad-burning 7-km (4.3-mi.) Diez Vistas Trail is the longest and most demanding route. Ten viewpoints (hence *diez vistas*) are sprinkled along the trail, which overlooks Burrard Inlet, Indian Arm, Eagle Ridge and Buntzen Lake. Near the junction of Diez Vistas and Saddle Ridge Trails is the 2-km (1.2-mi.) Buntzen Ridge Trail, which leads to Sasamat Lake in Belcarra Regional Park.

16 MINNEKHADA REGIONAL PARK

DISTANCE: 17 km (10.5 mi.) east of Vancouver, in Coquitlam

ACTIVITIES: Bird watching, group functions, hiking, nature observation, picnicking, skating, viewpoints, walking

HIGHLIGHTS: Challenging knoll trails reward with sweeping views

ACCESS: From Vancouver, take either the Lougheed Highway (Highway 7) or Highway 1 to Exit 44 (United Boulevard North/Mary Hill Bypass) to Port Coquitlam. As Highway 7 passes through Port Coquitlam's town centre, watch for the green GVRD sign indicating the turnoff to Minnekhada at Coast Meridian Road. Turn north at the lights at this interchange and follow Coast Meridian for several blocks. You'll see another GVRD sign at Apel Drive. From here the park is an easy 10-minute drive along Victoria Drive, Cedar Drive and Oliver Road.

When ducks are flying south and wild mushrooms dot the logs on forest floors, think of visiting Minnekhada Regional Park. This unusual area is tucked into a narrow zone between Mount Burke and the Pitt River. Following the most recent ice age, and long before an elegant hunting lodge that overlooks the Pitt River was built here, knobby knolls were thrust up from the floor of the Fraser Valley. These features are unique in the region. From the tops of these modest but steep hills, visitors enjoy a panoramic lookout over a network of marshes ringed with leafy softwood trees.

Minnekhada is particularly attractive when the leaves start to change colour. While trees in the city may be slow to turn, a touch of frost at the higher elevations around the park can bring out red and golden tones much sooner. Fog settles in the folds of the mountain but burns off with the warmth of the sun, revealing silver birches in changing hues. Spiral staircases of fungi cling to some of the older trunks. Walking is easy on the soft forest floor, cushioned by generations of fallen leaves.

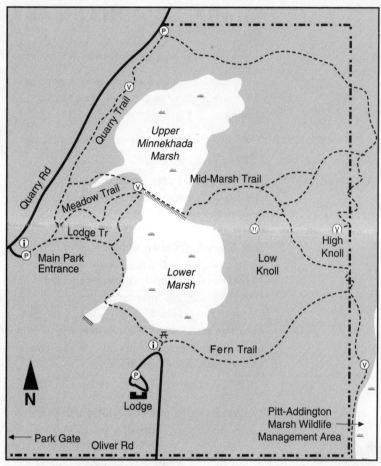

Minnekhada Regional Park

Two large ponds ringed by marshes sit squarely in the middle of the 225-ha (556-acre) park. A figure-eight trail skirts the water's edge. The distances you cover while circling the park fit neatly into the shortened daylight hours of spring or fall. Even in midwinter I like to walk sections of the park, ignoring the drizzle, looking for the first signs of bud-push on the salmonberry bushes. When a winter cold spell hits and the ponds freeze over, this is a fine place to bring your blades.

The GVRD took over management of Minnekhada from the provincial government in 1983. The property was once home to Lieutenant Governor Eric Hamber, who built a Scottish-style hunting lodge on

Minnekhada Regional Park

the hillside above one pond. Several subsequent governors also used the lodge as a retreat. It is now available for meetings, small conferences and weddings, its vice-regal style mellowed by the pastoral surroundings. Each Sunday afternoon from early April to the end of October, the lodge is open to the public for viewing. The first of three entrances to the park leads along Oliver Road past Minnekhada Farm's heritage buildings to the lodge at the park's southern end. (A short distance farther east on Oliver Road is another approach to the park on the PoCo and Coquitlam Dike Trails beside the Pitt River. See next chapter for details.)

There is an information kiosk next to the lodge, as well as parking and several picnic tables beside one of the outbuildings. From Minnekhada Lodge you can quickly walk to the Lower Marsh pond on Lodge Trail or follow Fern Trail east towards Minnekhada's boundary with the Pitt-Addington Marsh Wildlife Management Area. This rolling trail leads to a lookout over the marsh that requires only a moderate climb. Plan on taking 30 minutes to reach it.

The main entrance to the park is from the parking lot off Quarry Road. An information board at the trailhead often carries news of bird sightings. One bulletin listed more than 60 species seen around the marsh during a recent migration season. From here you have a choice of approaches to the ponds and marsh area, as well as to the lodge. Soon after you enter the main trail, it divides. Lodge Trail leads off to the right. Meadow Trail to the left soon divides again. Quarry Trail meanders around some pretty areas where moss and forest intermingle. Bridges span the wetter parts, finally bringing visitors to the shores of the north or upper pond. Meadow Trail leads to a lookout over the ponds before descending to cross an earthen dam that divides the two ponds. Log Walk leads to the dam along more level ground. The banks of the ponds are thick with bulrushes, and there are several open spots where you can sit with binoculars and search for birdlife.

If you're feeling energetic, you might wish to climb to the top of High Knoll to take in the view of Golden Ears to the east, the nearby Fraser and Pitt Rivers, and the Cascade Mountains south across the Fraser Valley. The park's distinctive knolls are largely free of underbrush, and the walking is easy amid the groves. The steepness of the High Knoll does make climbing it a challenge. However, the trail is well constructed, and you can reach the top within an hour from the parking lot. If your time is limited or you're not inclined to climb, a shorter section of trail leads through a lovely stand of cedars and western hemlocks to the lookout at Low Knoll. From here you can look back down on the ponds and west to Mount Burke.

Minnekhada Park is just one part of a large wilderness area on the west side of the Pitt River. As you become more familiar with the region, you can extend your visit to include the PoCo and Coquitlam Dike Trails and the Pitt-Addington Marsh Wildlife Management Area (see next two chapters).

17 POCO & COQUITLAM DIKE TRAILS

DISTANCE: 25 km (15.5 mi.) east of Vancouver, in Port
Coquitlam and Coquitlam

ACTIVITIES: Bird watching, boating, cycling, fishing, viewpoints,
walking

HIGHLIGHTS: Views of the Golden Ears reflecting in the Pitt
River as dozens of species of birds swoop above

ACCESS: From Highway 1, take Exit 44 and follow signs to
Highway 7B/United Boulevard North, which leads
to Port Coquitlam via the Mary Hill Bypass. Be
prepared to turn left (west) onto Highway 7 at
its intersection with the Mary Hill Bypass. From
Highway 7, turn north onto Coast Meridian Road
and east on Prairie Avenue. Follow it to its terminus, next to the Pitt River dike, on top of
which runs the PoCo trail. Alternatively, once
you're on Coast Meridian, follow the green GVRD
signs towards Minnekhada Regional Park (see
previous chapter).

Despite the fact that in the Halkomelem language the
word *coquitlam* means "stinking of fish slime," a visit to
the outlying suburb of this name can be nothing but a breath of fresh
air. In fact, there is often such an enchanting stillness on a section of
the PoCo (short for Port Coquitlam) and Coquitlam Dike Trails that
it feels as if you're sealed inside a capsule and set apart from the
nearby world. So calm is the surface of the Pitt River that it exactly
mirrors the surrounding mountains in all their glory. On a winter's
day your vision, under a clear, pale-blue sky, is of a world so white
that it will erase all of the smudges and fingerprints left on your
mind by the cares and concerns of everyday life.

There is a trend in some of the local municipalities to preserve or
create "town trails." Coquitlam and Port Coquitlam have done this.
Part of their circuit winds along the banks of the Pitt River, one of
the more active rivers to flow into the Fraser. The Pitt's motion is
affected by the tidal action on the Fraser, and depending on the time

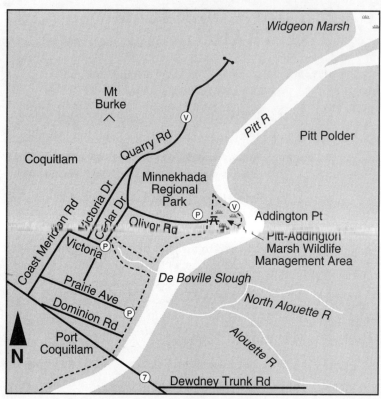

PoCo and Coquitlam Dike Trails

of day its waters can be moving either north or south. The banks of the Pitt have been built up to prevent flooding on the adjacent lowlands.

Families with carloads of bikes and the occasional stroller make these dike trails their year-round destination when a quick outing is called for. It gets everyone out of the house; the kids can ride on ahead at their own rate while those on foot fan out at a more sedate pace. The trail leads north beside the river for more than 10 km (6.2 mi.), far enough to let cyclists really know they've spent some time in the saddle when they finally dismount, particularly after a round trip.

PRAIRIE AVENUE ENTRANCE When you leave your vehicle behind and climb up onto the dike, your eyes must adjust to the wide views east across the river to Pitt Meadows' open prairie. Log booms march north towards Pitt Lake along both banks, and there is plenty of open

PoCo Trail along Pitt River

water in the river's channel to accommodate flocks of waterfowl. You may have to duck as squadron upon squadron of geese rise honking from the river, cresting the dike at low altitude before making their descent to feed in the open green fields to the west. Lunchtime! The birds have been resident on the Pitt for such a long time that they even have a section of marshland—Goose Bar—named for them.

Although during warmer months this region is a swath of mixed greens, by late fall and early winter this exposed piece of wetland looks washed of colour. Flaxen hues predominate along the dike and on the slopes of Mount Burke to the northwest. This makes the thick evergreen forest covering much of Minnekhada's High Knoll at the far northern end of the dike trail stand out in exaggerated relief.

DE BOVILLE SLOUGH No matter from which direction you explore the dike, you'll have to spend some time away from the river where the PoCo Dike Trail cuts inland to circumvent De Boville Slough, whose snaking course provides shelter for ducks and spawning salmon. All the land north of the slough, including Mount Burke and the dike trail to Minnekhada, lies within Coquitlam. (If you are planning to adventure by canoe, kayak or small hand-carried boat, there is a launch at the Pitt River Boat Club. To find it, go north on Coast Meridian, turn right on Prairie Avenue, left on Devon Road and right on Lincoln Avenue. The boat club is at the end of Lincoln.)

Stay with the Coquitlam Dike Trail that hugs De Boville Slough's north side. It will bring you back out to the banks of the Pitt River in a matter of 5 minutes. Blackberries grow along this section of the trail in great numbers; despite the best efforts of the well-organized pickers with their gloves, hooking poles and loppers, there will still be lots left if you visit here in September.

ADDINGTON POINT Back beside the river, the country alongside the trail becomes even more rural, with tilled fields running right up to Mount Burke's steep sides. In another 10 minutes you'll reach the caretaker's heritage home beside Addington Marsh. Visible on the slope of the knoll ahead is a sheltered lookout over the marsh, a good place to stop and picnic, for this is where the dike trail ends.

Just north of the caretaker's house another long trail curves out over the marsh, with two-storey observation towers poised above the wetland in several places, hardly visible from here. You can add another half-hour of cycling to your journey if you roll out here. Or, if you're hankering for a little vertical relief after all the level riding or walking you've just experienced, consider climbing the trail behind the shelter to the top of Minnekhada's High Knoll.

The GVRD maintains a trail that runs north of the lookout shelter to several additional viewpoints overlooking the marsh. This trail leads out onto the marsh, linking with the trail you passed earlier on your way past the caretaker's home. The lodge at Minnekhada is only minutes away. You can see it in the distance, nestled in the forest, as you approach Addington Point. A narrow paved road leads off to it from the left side of the dike as you near the shelter. (For more information on the lodge, see previous chapter.)

Fields of bright foliage colour the eastern shore in an area called Pitt Polder (see next chapter). Mount Burke with its dark forest closes in on the west side of the trail beside Addington Marsh. You've come a long way to reach this point. Catch your breath before turning back, and remind yourself that the view on the return journey will be refreshingly different than it was on the way here.

18 PITT RIVER & PITT POLDER

DISTANCE: 50 km (31 mi.) east of Vancouver, in Pitt Meadows

ACTIVITIES: Bird watching, boating, camping, cycling, fishing, hiking, nature observation, paddling, picnicking, walking

HIGHLIGHTS: Dramatic location for walking or cycling dike trails or paddling tranquil backwaters

ACCESS: To reach Grant Narrows Regional Park, drive east of the Pitt River Bridge on the Lougheed Highway (Highway 7). Turn north on Harris Road at the traffic lights where a large sign points to Pitt Lake. Turn right on McNeil Road, then left on 132nd Avenue and left again at Neaves Road, following it north past the Swaneset Bay golf course, with its imposing clubhouse. Neaves crosses both the south and north arms of the Alouette River, along whose 17 km (10.6 km) of dike trails you might see people walking, jogging, cycling or horseback riding. Beyond the narrow bridge that spans the North Alouette, the road becomes rougher as its name changes from Neaves to Rannie. The park lies 10 km (6.2 mi.) north of here at the end of Rannie Road.

L ooking for a place to head on a moment's notice that will give you a sampling of our local wilderness: mountains, trees, water, wildlife—the works? One of the best and most accessible such spots is in Pitt Meadows at Grant Narrows Regional Park, where Widgeon Creek and the Pitt River meet. And with the trails through Pitt-Addington Marsh Wildlife Management Area leading right up beside it at the foot of thickly forested Alouette Mountain (site of the UBC Malcolm Knapp Research Forest), this part of Pitt Meadows offers a complete outdoor experience.

PITT POLDER After the settled character of Pitt Meadows' cultivated farmland, there is a sudden shift to one of remoteness as you head beyond the bridge over the North Alouette River into Pitt Polder.

Houses appear infrequently, fields with no fencing predominate, and only an occasional horse, cow, emu or even camel (!) can be seen. Vancouver seems a world away. Deep ditches line both sides of the road. The mountains close in on either side. You are now travelling beside the broad Pitt River towards Pitt Lake, with the entrance to Widgeon Valley across the way shielded behind rocky knolls to the west.

Polders are low-lying sections of land near rivers and oceans, dried out using a technique perfected in the Netherlands, a country famous for its ability to pry land from the sea. It takes a polder—the word is Dutch in origin—about 20 years to become productive agricultural land. The northern half of Pitt Polder is part of the 2882-ha (7119-acre) Pitt-Addington Marsh Wildlife Management Area. A colony of endangered greater sandhill cranes nest in a part of the polder that is closed to visitors from April 1 to June 30 to ensure the nesting birds are not disturbed.

GRANT NARROWS REGIONAL PARK Grant Narrows Regional Park serves as a gateway for several different user groups headed in a variety of directions. By land, visitors can begin walking or cycling around the Pitt-Addington Marsh wildlife area, with its extensive series of dike trails and imposing observation towers. Boaters can venture onto the waterways of Pitt River and Pitt Lake or paddle southwestern B.C.'s largest freshwater marsh on nearby Widgeon Creek.

In the mid-1990s, the Greater Vancouver Regional District took control of a large area of Widgeon Marsh, now a regional park in its own right, at the mouth of the creek where it flows into the Pitt River. Together with the public lands at Grant Narrows and Pitt-Addington, this constitutes a sizable package of protected habitat.

PITT RIVER AND WIDGEON CREEK One of the pleasant aspects of visiting Grant Narrows is that you don't need to own a boat or canoe to explore the waterways here. Daily rentals are available on site from March through October. The current rate is $40 for the day. At present this service is provided by Ayla Canoe Rentals, 604-941-2822.

The advantages of exploration by canoe or kayak are numerous: fewer people (though on a busy day Ayla may rent as many as 100 canoes), more scenic vistas and the chance to approach wildlife in a quiet, less-threatening manner. The current allows boaters to drift beside creek and riverbanks in silence, sometimes viewing birds and other animals at a much closer range than on foot. *Note:* The weather

Widgeon Falls

in this area can turn quite windy with little warning. As a result, canoeists should not venture out onto Pitt Lake. Be content to explore Pitt River's shoreline or the quieter backwaters in the marsh or Widgeon Creek.

The waters of Pitt River originate in the wild, remote heart of Garibaldi Park. Mount Pitt (unseen from here), with its twin blades, is one of the grander, rarely glimpsed spectacles in Garibaldi. The Pitt River flows south from its slopes, fed by rain, snow and glacial streams. The river widens dramatically as it moves southwards between high granite bluffs, eventually forming Pitt Lake. Narrowing again at its south end, the Pitt returns to being a waterway, this

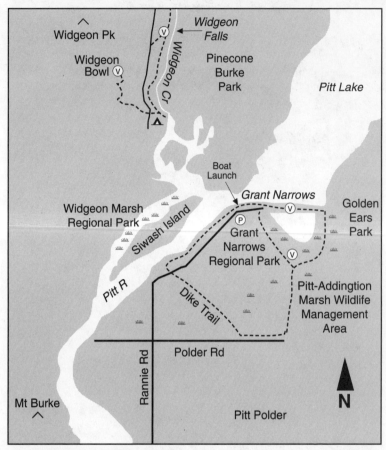

Pitt River and Pitt Polder

time a broad tidal estuary influenced by the rise and fall of the Fraser River. Silt built up at the south end of the lake presents an obstacle for boaters, who cannot make their way directly up the lake from the river but must cross beside a diked roadway almost to the east side of the lake before heading north. Open water and a wide marsh extend south on the opposite side of the dike from the lake.

On the Pitt River itself, large log booms are tethered to mooring posts at regular intervals, especially along the eastern shore. These booms help cut the wake of passing motorboats. Once you've left the boat launch, paddle south between the shoreline and the booms. In these quiet waters you'll have the best chance of observing ospreys nesting on the tops of the mooring posts.

Paddle downstream to where cottages appear on the opposite shore and cross over to explore the backwaters along the river's western side. From the east, large Siwash Island conceals the river's bank at the foot of Mount Burke. The channel between the bank and the island is shallow, with marsh marigolds blooming in summer. A very wild scent fills the air. This is the GVRD's Widgeon Marsh Regional Park, a wildlife sanctuary with numerous signs prohibiting hunting—especially of widgeons!

Crossing Pitt River from Grant Narrows Park to reach Widgeon Creek takes only 10 minutes. However, as mentioned, this is the most exposed section of the journey, where canoeists are liable to encounter winds blowing south off Pitt Lake late in the day. *Note:* Basic canoe instruction for novice paddlers is included in the rental price from Ayla Canoe Rentals.

Once you're in Widgeon Creek's main channel, a sense of tranquillity prevails. You're bound to find at least one great blue heron stalking along Siwash Island's marshy shore on your left as you head upstream. Signs posted along the way will help you follow the creek, which divides into two long arms. The branch to the left leads upstream to a campground and hiking trails in Pinecone Burke Provincial Park and to Widgeon Falls; the right arm ambles into a series of secluded backwaters perfectly suited for wildlife observation and fishing.

By late in the summer, water levels are at their low point for the year in Widgeon Creek. Chances are that if there are more than two of you in the canoe, you'll have to hop out to float it across a sandbar or two. A pair of river shoes will come in handy.

The campground is located on the banks of Widgeon Creek an hour's paddle northwest of Grant Narrows. Along the way are many fine sandy areas well suited for sunning and picnicking. Tall cottonwood and hemlock trees line the shore in many places. Sitka spruce stand apart from the rest, easily identified by their solitary splendour. The creek lazily winds its way into the folds of the nearby mountains, whose slopes rise sharply towards unseen peaks. Silence envelops the valley. Rocky knolls, characteristic geologic formations in the Pitt River flood plain, thrust up in advance of the mountains.

The sight of other canoes pulled up on a broad bank of the creek will alert you to the fact that you've arrived at the campground. Above the pullout is a broad grassy field from which both an old road and a trail begin. The trail to Widgeon Falls is a winding affair, with several sets of steep staircases, and takes an hour to cover; the road leads gently uphill and will bring you close to the falls within 40 minutes. Watch for signs beside the road pointing to the trail at several stages along the way. One of the advantages of taking the trail is that it follows Widgeon Creek for the last half of the journey, a much more scenic approach than the road, which is lined on both sides by poplars and maples. Visitors with young children in tow might prefer the road over the trail; others might well enjoy taking the trail in and the road out.

Widgeon Falls drops through a series of smooth granite boulders. Much of the year the force of the water rushing through here will keep visitors at their distance. During hotter, drier times of the year when water levels drop, it's possible to walk out on the rock shelf beside the creek for a better look. On a sunny day the water in the creek is a beautiful blend of green shades. At any time of year the sound of water dropping over the falls dominates all else, enclosing visitors in a capsule of white noise.

PITT-ADDINGTON MARSH WILDLIFE MANAGEMENT AREA A gated dike trail runs east from Grant Narrows Regional Park in a long arc along the south end of Pitt Lake, right to the slopes of Alouette Mountain. Along the way is an observation tower for momentary relief from the flatness of the dike. The nearby mountain slopes also do their best to counter the landscape's flatness. Still, out here on the dike, the broad, level surface of Pitt Lake that lies stretched out in front of you holds sway.

The dike roadway is wide and smooth until it reaches the mountain slopes. It turns south here, with the UBC Malcolm Knapp Research Forest on one side and the marsh on the other. The dike narrows, and its crushed granite surface becomes harder to walk or cycle. Follow it to another observation tower, visible in the distance, where a trail back to Grant Narrows leads off to the right. This rough, rolling trail is often strewn with trees brought down by beavers. Some of the larger trees still standing are netted with wire in an attempt to protect them from the castor's chisel-like chompers. Cyclists beware the low-hanging branches, which will give an unsuspecting rider a hefty swat. Bird-houses are affixed to many of the tree trunks.

If you'd like to take the long way back to Grant Narrows, follow the dike road south of the observation tower rather than taking the trail. It eventually meets a side road on your right that will take you back out to Rannie Road. Plan on taking 2 to 3 hours to complete this circle route.

19 GOLDEN EARS PROVINCIAL PARK

DISTANCE: 11 km (6.8 mi.) north of Highway 7 in Maple Ridge, about 50 km (31 mi.) east of Vancouver

ACTIVITIES: Boating, camping, climbing, hiking, horseback riding, mountain biking, picnicking, swimming, viewpoints, walking

HIGHLIGHTS: From the beach to the peaks, more ways to veg or explore than you can shake a stick at

ACCESS: Take either the Lougheed Highway (Highway 7) or Highway 1 from Vancouver. (Travelling east on Highway 1, take Exit 44, just west of the Port Mann Bridge. Follow signs to Highway 7B/United Boulevard North, which leads to Maple Ridge via the Mary Hill Bypass.) As Highway 7 enters Maple Ridge from the west, it intersects with the Dewdney Trunk Road. Turn left at the lights here and follow Dewdney east to 232nd Street, where you make another left turn. Provincial-park signs direct you to Golden Ears. (There are also signed approaches on Highway 7 in downtown Maple Ridge.) Follow 232nd as it crosses the Alouette River, then turn right on Fern Crescent as it passes through the municipal Maple Ridge Park. (This park is an excellent destination for groups looking for camping facilities, a treed setting and a playing field. Call 604-463-5221 for information.)

Within the boundaries of 56,000-ha (138,320-acre) Golden Ears Park it is possible to swim, boat and camp at Alouette and Pitt Lakes; to walk or ride horseback along trails to the two waterfalls pouring off Gold Creek into Alouette Lake; or to hike to the Golden Ears themselves or several other peaks that rise high above the lake. The park is large enough to accommodate all these activities within its borders and still have plenty of wilderness left over into which few visitors venture.

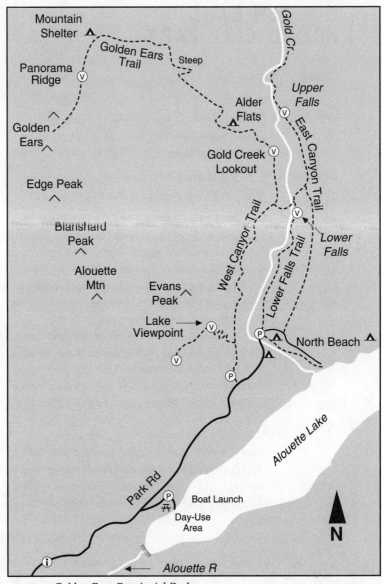

Golden Ears Provincial Park

Horses and riders will begin to appear even before you reach the park. Unless privately owned, the horses are most likely to have come from the Golden Ears Riding Stable at 232nd Street and 136th Avenue, north of Fern Crescent, 604-463-8761. Open daily from

Golden Ears Provincial Park

9 A.M. to 6 P.M., the stables are quite busy on weekends. During summer months, horses are also stabled in the park beside the Gold Creek parking lot. Gold Creek Stables and Tours offers a range of equestrian possibilities, from one lap around the pony track to overnight excursions, both escorted and self-directed. Call 604-202-5190 for information on rates and hours.

As you enter the provincial park you will be met by a strikingly large carving of a white mountain goat, symbolic of the fascinating wildlife found at higher points in the Coast Mountains around Golden Ears. Close at hand, horse trails forming a network parallel the road and lead off into the surrounding forest.

ALOUETTE LAKE Beyond the park gates you have a leisurely drive for 7 km (4.4 mi.) until the first of several parking lots appears. Along the way is an information kiosk, where maps of the park are on display. Farther along is the road leading off to park headquarters and diminutive Mike Lake, and shortly thereafter is the turnoff to the Alouette Lake day-use area at the lake's south end. As this road nears the day-use area, parking for the Spirea Universal Access Interpretive Trail appears on the right. This trail, the first of its kind in a B.C. park, affords those with disabilities a natural-history experience. Unique interpretive signs in a variety of languages appear along the trail, much of which is covered by boardwalk. These signs also feature solar-powered audio systems for hearing-impaired trail users and brass re-creations of some of the park's natural features for the visually impaired.

A beautiful wide beach lies at the south end of Alouette Lake, next to an unobtrusive BC Hydro dam. There are a large boat launch and a dock at the north end of the beach, and during the summer months you can rent canoes. Rentals are on a first-come, first-served basis. If you arrive before noon there is usually a good chance of getting one.

NORTH BEACH Near the end of the 12-km (7.5-mi.) road that runs through Golden Ears is the entrance to the Gold Creek and Alouette campgrounds, with an astounding 343 campsites between them. (For reservations, call 604-689-9025.) For many, camping here is their first introduction to overnighting in the outdoors. Long weekends in May and October are particularly popular with school, Girl Guide and Boy Scout groups. Adjacent to the Gold Creek campground is a parking lot for the West Canyon Trail, which leads to the Golden Ears themselves (see below).

Beyond the West Canyon Trail parking lot the road crosses a one-lane bridge over Gold Creek. The North Beach campground at the north end of the road has an additional 55 campsites. If you're just here for the day, leave your vehicle in the day-use-only Gold Creek parking lot. A gentle walking trail leads from this parking lot along the north bank of the creek to a broad, sandy gravel bar where the creek meets the lake at North Beach. The short (2-km / 1.2-mi.) walk is one of my favourites. Decades of duff deposited on the forest floor give the trail a welcoming sponginess that will put a spring in your step. The clear blue-green water in boulder-filled Gold Creek delights the eye. Mostly level, the trail climbs slightly as it nears the lake. At this point the creek widens and deepens, and you get some of the prettiest views of its colour. Out on the gravel bar at North Beach, look west to Evans Peak, which dominates the horizon.

If you explore the lake by boat, numerous submerged snags soon make you aware that this was once a forested valley. The east side of the lake is particularly heavy with snags, and the shoreline there drops straight down to the water with few landing sites. The northwest side of the lake features both wilderness camping and make-shift picnic sites, accessible only by water. Many visitors rent canoes and journey to these sites from the south end of Alouette Lake. It's an hour or more's steady paddling from there to North Beach, and the shoreline between the two is not particularly inviting. Better to launch from the parking lot beside the new outdoor learning centre at North Beach. Its post-and-beam construction is typical of the local Katzie First Nation longhouse tradition. Situated on a promontory above North Beach, the centre has a commanding view of the lake.

Within an hour of leaving the dock at North Beach you can land at a variety of small beaches. There's plenty of driftwood on which to spread out a towel or tablecloth. The hills behind are thick with evergreens, but exploration is remarkably easy as there is only light undergrowth. Alouette Lake warms up in summer to provide some of the best freshwater swimming in the Lower Mainland. You can also explore Moyer Creek, whose boulder-filled course leads back into the hillside. There is a good view of the Golden Ears from this northern section of the lake.

Alouette Lake is long enough that it presents an opportunity to do some serious paddling. Beware the winds that rise around noon and blow from the south throughout the afternoon; don't expect to make very good time heading back towards the boat launch during this period. The best times to be out on the water are in the morning and in the late afternoon, when the lake is still.

GOLD CREEK TRAILS In addition to the short trail to lakeside described above, Lower Falls Trail runs beside Gold Creek as it flows downstream from the upper and lower falls. The falls on Gold Creek descend through a canyon, twisting over a set of rock staircases. The best viewpoints are at the top and bottom of the falls. There are two approaches to these spots. You will find both trails outlined on the large map located near the entrance to the Gold Creek parking lot.

Gold Creek originates far to the north in Golden Ears Park. For most of its course it is wide and fairly straightforward. As it nears the lake, it's suddenly confined by an imposing rock face, part of which has fallen away. At the upper falls you can observe the most dramatic descent of the creek—and at as close a range as your nerve will allow. The rock shelf through which the creek falls is flat enough in places to permit a daring observer to venture out for a close inspection of the volume of water tumbling by. The waterfall reflects the hues of the sky and the green of the trees, but the most entrancing colours come from the golden boulders and bluish stones in the creekbed.

Lower Falls Trail heads upstream at a gentle grade. At first you pass through a stand of second-growth western hemlock and vine maple. Just past the "1 km" marker the forest suddenly gives way to alder and cottonwood trees. Views of the mountains open up to the west. Alouette Mountain stands tall above Evans Peak, which is closer in the foreground. On high, those small patches of white may be snow or mountain goats; it's hard to tell at this distance, even with the help of binoculars. The closer you get to the falls, the more other peaks across the valley reveal themselves. The Blanshard Needle, Edge Peak and the twin Golden Ears stand grouped in profile. Even if this is your first visit to the park, you'll find the mountains look familiar because of their visibility on the horizon east of Vancouver.

This is a pleasant area and quite popular on weekends. The 3-km (1.9-mi.) Lower Falls Trail is a wide bed of cedar bark and makes for easy walking. Along the way there are several good picnic spots, quite accessible to the creek for swimming in the fresh soft water. There are campsites at places on the other side of the creek, reached via the West Canyon Trail. Walking time to the falls is an easy hour or less one way.

Short of an arduous climb to their peaks, one of the best views of the Golden Ears appears as you walk along the East Canyon Trail. This trail runs along the canyon above the creek and goes directly to the upper falls and beyond for a short distance. It begins uphill towards the North Beach campground from the Gold Creek parking lot. Longer than the Lower Falls Trail by approximately 1 km (0.6 mi.), this route takes twice as much time to complete because of its rolling course. Small orange distance markers show up with regularity along the way. This is a good workout for those on mountain bikes.

The trail climbs gradually uphill as the voice of Gold Creek rises through the forest from below. At the "2.5 km" sign lies the wreckage of an old log bridge that has been swept aside. An old metal gate stands partially covered by rocks. From here the trail climbs somewhat more steeply. After another 0.5 km (0.3 mi.), watch for orange ribbons on the left, which mark the turnoff to the upper falls. A rough trail, part of which is a broad, dry creekbed, leads downhill a short distance to a good viewpoint. The sound of Gold Creek as it plunges over the falls is relentless, overwhelming and hypnotic. Approach with extreme care.

WEST CANYON AND GOLDEN EARS TRAILS The several routes to the falls on Gold Creek are part of a dozen hiking, cycling, walking and riding trails within the park. Golden Ears Park is 55 km (34 mi.) long from its southern border to its northern boundary, where it connects with Garibaldi Park, of which it was once part. The Coast Mountains within which the park lies form a rugged and often impenetrable barrier of peaks and valleys. Weather conditions can change quickly in this region. Be prepared for any eventuality.

West Canyon Trail is one approach to the lower falls. This trail connects with Golden Ears Trail and eventually leads up to the Golden Ears themselves, a 12-km (7.4-mi.), seven-hour trip one way. At first the West Canyon Trail leads above and away from Gold Creek. There is evidence of the old logging railway that once ran through the canyon along the way to Alder Flats. After 5 km (3.1 mi.), you'll reach a sign pointing down a branch trail to the lower falls. At low-water seasons it's possible to ford the creek below the falls, provided you're prepared to roll your pant legs way up.

The hike to the top of Panorama Ridge is best kept for summer, when daylight hours are longest. Plan to be on the West Canyon Trail by 9 A.M. if you hope to reach the Golden Ears and return in the same day. Even if you walk only partway, there are still many rewards. The first 3 hours on the West Canyon Trail are the easiest, as there is very little elevation gain. A picnic in the Alder Flats area can offer views of the Golden Ears, Edge Peak and Blanshard Needle, as well as Gold Creek rushing down from the north. Seeing the peaks from this perspective is often accomplishment enough. *Note:* Biting insects can be a nuisance in this area in warmer months, so come prepared with repellent.

There are conflicting opinions as to the origin of the name Golden Ears. Veteran members of the Alpine Club of Canada and long-time residents of the Fraser Valley recall that the mountain was previously known as the Golden Eyries, nesting place of eagles.

20 KANAKA CREEK REGIONAL PARK

DISTANCE: About 30 km (18.6 mi.) east of Vancouver, in Maple Ridge

ACTIVITIES: Bird watching, fishing, hiking, nature observation, paddling, picnicking, swimming, viewpoints, walking

HIGHLIGHTS: Picnic beside a waterfall, paddle a creek, walk a forest pathway

ACCESS: Kanaka Creek Regional Park, located on the eastern outskirts of Maple Ridge, has three principal approaches, each offering different points of interest. To get to the rough launch site and creekside trails at the Fraser Riverfront section of Kanaka Park, take the Haney Bypass east from Highway 7 in downtown Maple Ridge and watch for green GVRD signs to the park as well as the creek itself, which passes under the road. There is a small CPR railway bridge here and a parking lot next to it on a service road. The two other entrances are off Highway 7 on the Dewdney Trunk Road at 252nd and 256th Streets. Both are well marked and lie 11 km (6.8 mi.) upstream from the Fraser.

In the building of the West, the Chinese were not the only labourers attracted from across the Pacific. Hawaiians also came to this region, where they established several small communities, intermarried with Natives on the North Shore and left their name, the Polynesian word for "man," to grace one of our regional district parks, Kanaka Creek. In the 1830s, preceding the arrival of the Hawaiians, Kwantlen Natives established a camp here under the guns of nearby Fort Langley, seeking protection from their marauding northern Native neighbours.

Although the entire area is a warren of well-used trails, you'll seldom meet many people in this park, which comprises about 405 ha

Kanaka Creek

(1000 acres) and runs along both sides of the creek. Golden Ears Park is the major draw in this area, and it siphons off most of the visitors.

LOWER REACHES Kanaka Creek flows into the Fraser River's north side, across the river and just east of Derby Reach (see map page 132). You can explore the marshlands at this junction with a light boat, launching from any of the Fraser Riverfront access points. The gently flowing creek makes a series of lazy backwater S-turns before reaching the faster-moving Fraser. Among the streams flowing into the lower Fraser, it is one of the few still in its natural state.

The banks of the creek are composed of slippery clay, so be careful when launching; rubber boots are recommended. The creek meanders through tall stands of bulrushes and past open fields bordered with graceful poplars as it approaches the Fraser. It's wide enough for two boats, though you're unlikely to encounter many.

These last bends in Kanaka Creek before it joins the Fraser are home to birds and fish, coyotes and rabbits, living undisturbed in their wildlife sanctuary except for the rumble of an occasional train passing nearby. Great blue herons often stalk fish from the riverbanks; they fly over from their colony in the woods of Derby Reach. If you're not in a boat, a three-storey observation tower above Kanaka Creek's sweeping oxbow lets you spy on them while they work.

A short walk or bike ride on the creekside trail past the tower

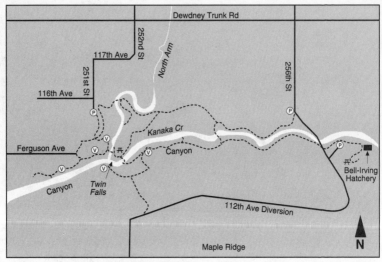

Kanaka Creek Regional Park

brings you to the Fraser, where you can head up or downstream. A small staircase descends to the river, an observation post gives broad views of the river, and a gracefully arched bridge spans the mouth of the creek. West to the heritage pier at old Port Haney, little about the Fraser has changed much in decades. There's always commercial and recreational boat traffic on the river.

CLIFF FALLS The entrance off 252nd takes you a short distance down the road to a parking lot beside a municipal playing field. From here a short, steep trail leads down to one of two bridges that span twin waterfalls created by the confluence of separate arms of Kanaka Creek. The north arm originates a short distance from the falls; the east arm begins farther back in the Blue Mountain Forest near Alouette Lake.

There are several picnic tables and a fire pit in a cleared area just above the falls, surrounded by signs emphasizing the danger of the cliffs. Numerous trails wind down to the creeks, and walking the streambed in either direction is not difficult once spring water levels have dropped and water temperatures have risen. Swimming is easy and you have your pick of a number of small pools, from ankle- to neck-deep.

Fossils in the stones by the sandstone canyon walls and the slippery grey clay along the banks are distinctive features of this area.

A woman who was a pioneer here in the early part of the 20th century told me that she used to make dolls with her friends by baking clay figures shaped from the Kanaka Creek clay.

The well-worn trails alongside the eastern arm of the creek make you realize how popular this area was with earlier inhabitants. Old wooden staircases, bridges and small dams lead through the forest, which rises and falls on each side of the creek in dramatic fashion. Salmonberry bushes are everywhere.

BELL-IRVING HATCHERY Use the 256th Street entrance to reach the Bell-Irving salmon hatchery, where you will also find a great deal of information on the park. Since the hatchery opened in 1983, more than two million salmon fry—most of them chum, with some coho—have been released. You may wish to witness the event, a spring ritual for local schoolchildren. Contact the hatchery at 604-462-8643 for information.

If you leave your car here it is a half-hour hike downstream to the falls. You can make a round trip of it by following the trail along the south side of Kanaka Creek. You'll find the trailhead directly across 256th Street from the hatchery. Another trail runs along the north bank. It is slightly overgrown at the outset but soon opens up to soft forest floor near the creek.

Along the way you'll discover many inviting approaches to the creek, especially on the north side, where you'll want to spend some quiet time. The trail that follows the south side of the creek involves more climbing through the sheltering forest. Despite extensive logging in earlier years, there are still some impressive-sized trees here.

21 ROLLEY LAKE PROVINCIAL PARK

DISTANCE: 70 km (43.5 mi.) east of Vancouver, in Ruskin

ACTIVITIES: Bird watching, camping, fishing, nature observation, paddling, picnicking, playground, swimming, walking

HIGHLIGHTS: A forested, family-oriented provincial park and campground

ACCESS: Via the Lougheed Highway (Highway 7) or the Trans-Canada Highway (Highway 1). Traffic on the Lougheed can be stop-and-go until it reaches the Pitt River; you can avoid this by using the Trans-Canada (Highway 1) to link up with the Lougheed at the Pitt River Bridge. Travelling east of Vancouver on the Trans-Canada, take Exit 44 just before the highway crosses the Port Mann Bridge, then head east on the Mary Hill Bypass towards Maple Ridge and Mission.

Once on Highway 7 you can save yourself a few more minutes by taking the Haney Bypass through Maple Ridge. Watch for the large overhead sign indicating a right turn off Highway 7 towards Mission. The bypass rejoins Highway 7 east of Maple Ridge, and you are well on your way to Rolley Lake and the Stave Lake region. The highway follows the curves of the Fraser River. East of Maple Ridge the countryside becomes noticeably less populated. The well-marked turnoff to Rolley Lake is at the mill town of Ruskin; the park lies 10 km (6 mi.) north of Highway 7. After turning off Highway 7 you will be driving uphill past the Ruskin Dam to an intersection with the Dewdney Trunk Road. At the sign here turn right and drive east to Bell Road, where a sign reads "Rolley Lake 2 km." Turn left here.

Trail beside Rolley Lake Falls

Rolley Lake Park is tucked away in the wooded hills of the Mission District east of Maple Ridge. At this point you are just east overland of Alouette Lake and the Blue Mountain Forest. Rolley Lake, which has been a provincial park since 1961, is a small lake with nothing hidden around its circumference except the 65 campsites (six of which are double-occupancy) in the nearby woods, several minutes' walk from the shoreline.

Settlers such as James and Fanny Rolley began arriving in the Mission District in the 1880s. The couple to whom the lake owes its name homesteaded here for a decade before moving to nearby Whonnock. Remains of the logging camps that took over and cleared off most of the cedar are still evident around the lake's western perimeter. The Japanese crew that worked much of the forest pulled out in the 1930s when the last of the red cedars and Douglas firs were gone. An ancient corduroy road, along which logs were hauled to old Port Haney, is in remarkably good condition considering the passage of time. You can see signs of the road when you

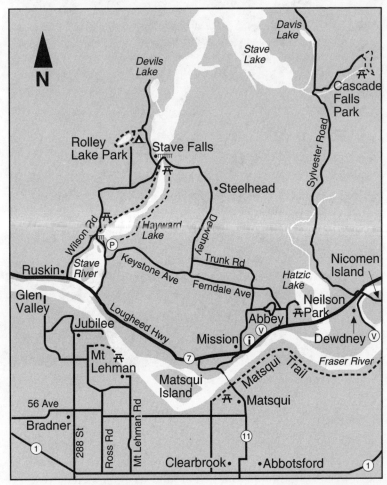

Fraser Valley

walk the trail that begins west of the day-use parking lot and leads past the outhouses set back in the woods behind the beach. This trail soon turns into the old corduroy road. Remains of rotting cedar shakes let you know you're in the right place.

In the 70 years since the loggers left, the forest around Rolley Lake has regrown amid what's left of the old growth. Fallen nurse logs, each supporting three or four offspring, are slowly repopulating the forest floor. A boardwalk trail leads across a wet zone at the southwestern end of the lake, away from a modest-sized beach and picnic area. Here, in the stillness, a practised eye can identify dozens of species of birds during the 90-minute walk around the lake. Pileated woodpeckers with their distinctive red heads (*pileated* is derived from the Latin *pileus,* meaning "felt cap") are among the winged residents often spotted.

A steep slope climbs above Rolley Lake's shady north side. Several small streams flow down off the hillside at wet times of the year. The water in the streams is a deeper red than a woodpecker's cap as it becomes tinted by the cedar mulch through which it runs. At intervals along this side of the lake, small wooden docks float under a canopy of long hemlock boughs, making ideal places to fish for rainbow and cutthroat trout or to use those binoculars to search out the profiles of herons standing sentinel in the marsh at the lake's northeastern corner. The catch allowance (for humans) is two per day; there is no limit on the amount of fun that young and old alike can share while tossing in a line. You can park yourself on one of the docks to enjoy the stillness, with no fear of being interrupted by the sounds of outboards—no motorized boats are allowed on the lake. For the best results, plan to fish here as early in the spring as possible while the lake is still well stocked with cutthroat and rainbow trout. Anglers 16 years of age and older must have a freshwater fishing licence.

The campsites at Rolley Lake seem exceptionally spacious compared to those at many other parks in B.C. Much of the surrounding forest is a mix of western hemlock and mature vine maple. The forest floor is open, and soft underfoot from centuries of cedar mulch. Children will find plenty of material for the construction of small forts and lean-tos in the underbrush. The vine maples naturally bend to form shelters that look surprisingly similar to the framework of Native sweat lodges. Note that the use of sticks and underbrush from campground and park areas for fires and tent structures is not permitted.

The camping season at Rolley Lake begins in early spring and lasts through midfall; a campsite costs $18.50 per day, with a limit of 14 days on occupancy. You can reserve a campsite here between March and September by calling 604-689-9025. This is an extremely popular park and space is at a premium during many weekends. But you will have the place practically to yourself at most other times, such as those special days in May and September before school ends or after it has reconvened. Each site comes furnished with a bright-yellow cedar picnic table and fire pit with cooking grill. The campsites are clean and there is plenty of water (though it's slightly sulphurous in smell) and firewood, with indoor toilets and tiled showers next to a children's adventure playground.

As you sit quietly, listen for the soft peeping of the bushtits, flocks of which come by to feed on insects. You'll hear them before you spot their dark shapes high in the boughs of the hemlocks. They drop from branch to branch, hanging upside down as easily as right side up, moving from bush to tree in straggling flocks. Another visitor, one of the early risers, is the Douglas squirrel, as black as the back of the Steller's jay, who'll be by later in the day to clean any leftover crumbs from your table.

In the mountains north of Rolley Lake are far larger species of wildlife, such as black bears, so be careful to pack all food away at night. On a large-scale map of the province you can see that a wilderness corridor, in which large and small animals have dominion, stretches from here north past Harrison Lake and all the way to Lillooet. When the end of summer signals the return of campers to the city, the woods and lakes here welcome the reappearance of wildlife that has spent the past few months in northern seclusion. Large birds such as eagles and Pacific loons are back with youngsters grown almost as big as their parents.

Follow the small stream that drains from the lake's northeastern end down into nearby Stave Lake. A waterfall drops away through the forest in several stages, each more dramatic than the one before. To find it, take the path from the lake to the camping area. The walk begins at campsite 27 and takes an easy 10 minutes. After crossing the stream below the first set of falls you enter a clear-cut area. Wild black and red raspberry, huckleberry and blueberry bushes choke the slope. Just 5 minutes farther downhill you have an even better view of the stream as it drops through the forest. Stave Lake glimmers below. In the sunlight of a late summer day the water in the lake is decidedly turquoise. The colour is the result of very fine sedimentation in the water, so fine that its reflection approaches the wavelength of visible light. Earlier in the summer the particles washing into the lake from winter snowmelt are larger, resulting in cloudier hues. Old stumps dot the surface of the dammed lake's west side like stubble on an unshaven face while its eastern shoreline is masked by driftwood. Rolley Lake looks mighty spiffy in comparison. Like the story of Goldilocks, it's not too big, not too small, just the right size indeed

For more information, contact BC Parks, 604-463-3513 or 604-924-2200. Maps are also available on-line at wlapwww.gov.bc.ca/bcparks.

22 RUSKIN & ENVIRONS

DISTANCE: About 60 km (37.3 mi.) east of Vancouver

ACTIVITIES: Boating, cycling, fishing, nature observation,
             paddling, picnicking, swimming, walking

HIGHLIGHTS: Old logging-railway line to walk or cycle as
             salmon spawn in the Stave River

ACCESS: Signs indicate the turnoff north to Hayward Lake
             from the Lougheed Highway (Highway 7). A
             parking lot is located at the south end of the
             Railway Trail beside the Ruskin Dam, about 4 km
             (2.5 mi.) from Highway 7 on Wilson Road. The
             south end of the Reservoir Trail and the Ruskin
             Recreation Area are located on the east side of
             Ruskin Dam. A single-lane road leads across the
             dam to them. (See Fraser Valley map, page 106.)

For a little backwoods town in the north Fraser Valley, Ruskin has a lot going for it. In the course of a day trip here visitors can walk or bike the 6-km (3.7-mi.) Railway Trail along the west side of Hayward Lake, hike sections of the recently completed 10-km (6.2-mi.) Reservoir Trail, picnic at the Ruskin Recreation Site while observing the annual salmon run in the nearby Stave River and, for the price of a saltwater-fishing licence, head home with a guaranteed catch. All in all, not too shabby a selection when you're in the mood for a simple outing.

In the late 1800s, Ruskin was one of several riverfront towns—Whonnock and Albion are two others along this stretch of the Fraser west of Mission—settled in what is traditional Kwantlen First Nation territory. By the light of kerosene lanterns, newcomers looked to electricity as leading-edge technology. To meet this need, a dam and hydro generating plant were constructed at Stave Falls, 10 km (6.2 mi.) upstream from the Fraser along the Stave River. In the early 1900s, the shortest incorporated railway in Canadian history ran from Ruskin to Stave Falls, carrying supplies for the dam and returning loaded with cedar logs, shakes and shingles. Cedar logging ended here a half-century ago. Today, most of the mills that line the Fraser River are quiet. In their place are new, value-added endeavours such as the log-hewn Shingle and Shake Pub on Wilson Road and a network of new and upgraded recreation trails around nearby Hayward Lake, built by a trail crew of ex-loggers with funding from BC Hydro and Forest Renewal BC.

RAILWAY AND RESERVOIR TRAILS Since BC Hydro opened the Railway Trail to the public for recreation in the 1980s, the former railbed has been widened in places and made smoother, particularly in the past several years. The trail runs 6 km (3.7 mi.) between the Ruskin Dam and a large picnic ground at North Beach beside the Stave Falls Dam.

For the most part, this is a gentle grade with a few steep sections that will get your heart rate up. Along the way it skirts the remains of seven partially submerged trestle bridges. Each trestle is a well-worn design piece—an arrangement of thick posts and cross-beams that serves to remind that architecture is a blend of both construction and art.

Overhung by a sheltering forest canopy, much of the Railway Trail is ideal for an outing in cloudy weather. Stately stands of second-growth Douglas fir rear skyward like sentinels. Several recently completed loop trails veer off from the Railway Trail and climb the steep hillside above Hayward Lake, in actuality a reservoir formed between the Ruskin and Stave Falls Dams. Benches are placed at each switchback so that visitors can catch their breath while enjoying a view deep into the nearby glens. In fall and winter months, ivy and fern glisten like malachite. Small streams lace the hillside and trill a soothing background accompaniment. A lengthy stretch of boardwalk, constructed by a crew from the nearby Elbow Lake correctional facility, winds across Bob Brook.

The Reservoir Trail links with the Railway Trail to provide a continuous 16-km (10-mi.) loop around the lake. Highlights along the Reservoir Trail include a 150-m (490-ft.) floating bridge near the Ruskin Dam and a viewpoint of Steelhead Falls near the Stave Falls Dam. All of the wood on the recently completed and upgraded sections of both the Railway and Reservoir Trails was milled from recycled hydro poles and log booms.

RUSKIN RECREATION AREA Although there is a picnic ground at the north end of Hayward Lake, in fall the best place to picnic either before or after a workout on the trails is at the Ruskin Recreation

Fishing the Stave River below the Ruskin Dam

Area, just below the Ruskin Dam. A short walk from the parking lot leads to a series of spawning channels on the Stave River. From October to December the river and channels are choked with hefty chum salmon, followed by a run of smaller coho salmon. The Stave is full of energy as thrashing salmon launch themselves into the air in the midstream current. Close to shore, schools of battered but still breathing chum, coloured like speckled marble, silently scull past the decomposing bodies of those who've finished their epic journey. An ecstatic chorus from circling flocks of gulls sings them homeward. Equally thrilled are the families who have come to snag a few fish for themselves.

Although wide spawning channels have been dug on each side of the river, the best viewing is from the Ruskin Recreation Area. To reach it, take single-lane Ruskin Road across the top of the dam from Wilson Road and descend the east side to the nearby site gates. A boat launch (also gated) is on your left as you enter. Several picnic tables are located on a benchland above the Stave River. A short trail descends to the river, with a bridge crossing the spawning channel and leading out onto the banks of the river itself. Downstream from the recreation site you can see Ruskin and the wide expanse of the Fraser River.

STAVE LAKE AND NORTH BEACH Two more recreation sites are located at the north end of Hayward Lake, reached by driving up Wilson Road to the Dewdney Trunk Road and proceeding east to the small settlement of Stave Falls (a community of a hundred homes at the time of the dams' construction). One is a boat launch on Stave Lake; the other is the recreation area at North Beach on Hayward Lake. The two lakes are separated by the Stave Falls Dam. North Beach is dotted with picnic tables and is a busy place in good weather. At other times it can be so deserted that it's almost spooky. Only hand-powered boats or boats with electric motors are permitted on Hayward Lake. (Canoe rentals are available on a seasonal basis from Clarks Estate General Store in Stave Falls.) Larger, more powerful boats should launch on Stave Lake at a site 1 km (0.6 mi.) north of the North Beach turnoff.

As you enter the North Beach recreation area, you will see the beach and picnic area just beyond the parking lot. The boat launch for Hayward Lake is just beside the parking lot. Although a paddle on the lake can be enjoyable, there are almost no places along the shore line to stop.

A charming gazebo graces the grass lawns surrounding the beach. The history of the Stave Falls Dam project is depicted in archival photographs at an interpretive display nearby. If you're in the mood for a short walk, take the Pond Loop Trail to a bluff overlooking the reservoir. The trail begins at the south end of the beach, where the north end of the Railway Trail is also located.

23 MISSION & ENVIRONS

DISTANCE: 80 km (50 mi.) east of Vancouver

ACTIVITIES: Boating, cycling, driving, fishing, historic sites, nature observation, paddling, picnicking, swimming, viewpoints, walking

HIGHLIGHTS: Fields of irises and dahlias bloom on benchlands above the Fraser River; sweeping valley views from a heritage park or monastery

ACCESS: Take the Lougheed Highway (Highway 7) east to Mission. Watch for the Travel Info Centre, located on the north side of the highway just past Mary Street, where you can obtain a Mission Visitors' Guide with detailed street maps of the area. (See Fraser Valley map, page 106.)

To find Fraser River Heritage Park, turn north off Highway 7 on Third Avenue at its convergence with Mary Street. The park entrance is at Mary and Fifth.

To get to Westminster Abbey from Highway 7, take Stave Lake Road to the Dewdney Trunk Road. Turn right and go east along Dewdney. Watch for the abbey on your right just past the intersection of Dewdney and Goundrey Street.

To find Ferncliff Gardens, turn north off Highway 7 onto the Dewdney Trunk Road, drive three blocks, then turn right on Henry Street. Continue down Henry to its end, where it turns into McTaggart Street (which becomes a dirt lane), then turn right at the Ferncliff Gardens sign. A lovely Tudor-style farmhouse sits sheltered behind a cedar hedge; the main barn and garden office lie just beyond at road's end.

To reach Neilson Park, drive north from Ferncliff Gardens on McTaggart, turn left on McEwen, then turn immediately right on Edwards Street and follow the signs to the park from here.

Dahlias at Ferncliff Gardens

Imagine being lucky enough to live on a ridge on the north side of the mighty Fraser River, overlooking the Matsqui Prairie, with towering Mount Baker as the centrepiece of your view. Residents of Mission enjoy this natural spectacle every day, weather permitting. You can, too, when you visit Westminster Abbey, any of several well-kept parks or, best of all, hidden Ferncliff Gardens. There's also much to choose from in the vicinity of Mission, including a drive to Cascade Falls Regional Park (built with access for the handicapped in mind) or a cycle tour of Nicomen Island.

FRASER RIVER HERITAGE PARK Located at an important geographical point where the Fraser River makes an elbow turn on its way to the Pacific, Mission is tied historically to the Cariboo gold rush of the 1850s, but with a slightly different twist. With the influx of tens of thousands of miners pursuing gold came grief for the First Nations people through whose lands the prospectors travelled. In 1860 Father Fouquet, a French priest with the Oblates of Mary

Immaculate, founded St. Mary's Mission to provide shelter, counselling and schooling for Native people. It was the first and largest residential school of its kind in the Pacific Northwest. In 1959, the federal government rebuilt the school 3 km (1.8 mi.) east of the old site. Each year in July the Mission Powwow draws participants and spectators to a three-day festival of Native singing, drumming and dancing held on the grounds of the new school, off the Lougheed Highway just east of the Travel Info Centre.

The remains of the old mission were cleared in 1965, and in its place is the expansive Fraser River Heritage Park. You can still see footprints of the old buildings near the bandshell. On the east side of the park is a small cemetery surrounded by a grove of tall, sturdy hemlocks. Father Fouquet is buried here in a section set aside for Oblate priests.

A log chalet, the Norma Kenney House, is located at the park entrance. It serves as a reception centre and is home to the Blackberry Kitchen, a good place to pause for refreshment in summer, and the Valley Treasures gift shop, which features work by local craftspeople. Fraser River Heritage Park is also the site of the annual Mission Folk Festival.

WESTMINSTER ABBEY Westminster Abbey, home to a Benedictine monastery and Mission's most imposing landmark, was completed in 1982. The abbey stands atop a ridge overlooking the Fraser River valley. Treat yourself to a visit for the view—even better than at Fraser River Heritage Park—and a choral vespers service in the abbey. The simplicity of the unaccompanied chanting stands in remarkable contrast to the imposing character of the abbey itself, designed by Vancouver architect Asbjorn Gathe. In late afternoon, when the slanting rays of the sun shine through the modern stained-glass windows, the abbey's interior is bathed in shades of burnt orange and cool blues, highlighting a series of 21 bas-reliefs mounted on the walls. Visiting hours at the monastery, where the ancient Benedictine credo has always been to show hospitality to guests of all faiths, are weekday afternoons from 1:30 to 4:30, and 2 to 4 on Sundays. The 30-minute vespers service begins at 5:30 on weekdays and 4:30 on Sundays.

If you are here just to visit the grounds, formerly a family farm and still operated by the self-sufficient monks, make your way along the path that leads south from the abbey's parking lot. It gently winds up to one of the most commanding viewpoints found anywhere in the

Fraser Valley, a must-see for visitors. Large knolls thrust up from the valley floor to the east; across the wide Fraser from the agricultural lands of Hatzic and Nicomen Island, the well-ordered Matsqui Prairie lies before you to the south, surmounted by Sumas Mountain and Mount Baker.

FERNCLIFF GARDENS At certain times of the year, from the abbey viewpoint you can see a small but intense patch of colour on the eastern slopes below: Ferncliff Gardens. After the tulips and daffodils have finished blooming in the nearby Bradner region (see chapter 28), nature goes into a bit of a lull. But not for long. Across the river, Ferncliff Gardens provides one of the most beautiful floral displays in the valley, especially from May to October. Not only is the variety of blooms awesome to see, but the setting is second to none.

Ferncliff Gardens was started in 1920 in Hatzic, 3 km (1.8 mi.) east of downtown Mission. Once a thriving commercial berry-growing centre, Hatzic today more closely resembles a bedroom community. Signs of redevelopment are already everywhere around Ferncliff, and as the years go by it will become even more of an oasis.

Specializing in irises, peonies and dahlias, current owner David Jack has an open-door policy for visitors, who are invited to drop in anytime. Easily more than a hundred varieties of irises and nearly that many peonies bathe the landscape with a spectrum of brilliant hues in May and June. Flowering continues, row upon row, until the end of June, then the fields lie fallow for a short while before acres of dahlia blossoms open between early August and mid-October. During these times many gardeners visit Ferncliff to make their selections. When blossoming finishes, the bulbs, tubers and rhizomes are harvested and shipped out to buyers. The challenge faced by anyone who visits here is to come away without dreaming—in Technicolor, of course—of creating their own backyard Ferncliff. For more information on Ferncliff, call (604) 826-2447.

HATZIC AND NEILSON PARKS Photographers will enjoy the views of Ferncliff from the open slopes of nearby Hatzic Park (its entrance is off Draper Street). This is also a good place to picnic after a visit to the gardens. Another spot suited to this same purpose is nearby Neilson Regional Park, located on the west side of Hatzic Lake and an easy 5-minute drive from Ferncliff. Open fields slope down to the shore of Hatzic Lake from the parking lot. There are numerous picnic tables, a swimming beach and a salmon spawning channel on Draper Creek that teems with activity come October. (*Note:* No domestic pets are allowed in Neilson Park.) You can launch a hand-carried boat here and spend some leisure time exploring Hatzic Lake. From out on the water, Westminster Abbey's bell tower appears on the skyline.

CASCADE FALLS REGIONAL PARK For an extensive look at the region around Mission, drive a short distance east of Hatzic Lake on Highway 7 to Sylvester Road and turn left. The rural setting along the road makes for a pleasant drive north as you head towards Stave Lake through the Hatzic Prairie and Miracle Valley. This is definitely backwoods country; suddenly the hustle and bustle of the Fraser Valley seem distant. You may not wish to drive the entire 35 km (21.7 mi.) to Stave Lake—access to the lake is better from the boat launch at Stave Falls (see previous chapter)—but 15 km (9.3 mi.) along is Cascade Falls Regional Park, a satisfying enough destination.

At Cascade Falls Park, wide trails and a footbridge allow everyone an approach to the soothing waterfall, where visitors receive an ear massage from the music of its tumbling passage. Split logs serve as both benches and picnic tables. In wet months the water in Cascade Creek runs at full bore, first dropping through a narrow chute at the top of the falls into a large pool, then making another long drop to the valley floor, a total of 50 m (164 ft.) in all. A dike trail runs along Cascade Creek as it flows west of the falls into Stave Lake. Much of the land on which the dike is built is private, but there are opportunities for cycling in places.

NICOMEN ISLAND An even better venue for cycling is a short distance farther east of Hatzic on level-surfaced Nicomen Island. Entirely rural, this countryside is as sleepy as it gets out here in the Fraser Valley. After the Lougheed Highway passes Hatzic Lake, it runs through the small town of Dewdney, then crosses a bridge onto Nicomen Island. (Just before the bridge, River Road leads off to the right and follows the shoreline of Nicomen Slough past a pub and a number of wharves to Dewdney Nature Park, where there's a boat launch.) You may wish to leave your vehicle beside the bridge at Dewdney and use your bicycle to explore the dike trails around the perimeter of Nicomen Island as far east as the rustic town of Deroche, located where Highway 7 crosses from Nicomen back onto the mainland.

24 SASQUATCH PROVINCIAL PARK

DISTANCE: 125 km (78 mi.) east of Vancouver, near Harrison Hot Springs

ACTIVITIES: Boating, camping, cycling, fishing, paddling, picnicking, playgrounds, swimming, walking

HIGHLIGHTS: Sandy beaches beside a mountain fiord

ACCESS: Sasquatch Park is on the east side of Harrison Lake, 6 km (3.7 mi.) north of Harrison Hot Springs, and is accessible from either the Trans-Canada Highway (Highway 1) or the Lougheed Highway (Highway 7).

Since Sasquatch Park first opened to the public in 1968, thousands of holidayers have been drawn to the three provincial campgrounds nestled beside two of the four lakes within the park. There's ample room for overnighters at the 177 campsites, and there's enough recreational diversity spread over its 1220 ha (3013 acres) to satisfy the choosiest of day trippers.

At the entrance to the park is the grassy Green Point picnic area, beside the shores of Harrison Lake, which features dozens of wooden tables stained honey gold, many with barbecues; an open play area; and a beach with great exposure to the afternoon sun. This is important, as the waters of Harrison Lake, a deep fiord, are cold year round.

East of Green Point the park road turns from pavement to gravel as it passes beside small Trout Lake, entirely surrounded by thick green growth. About 3 km (1.9 mi.) farther east the park road divides, with one branch leading 2 km (1.2 mi.) south to Hicks Lake, the other the same distance east to Deer Lake. Gates restrict motorized vehicles to the main road, but several old logging roads leading off through the park are perfectly suited for exploration by bicycle. The road to the lakes climbs through a saddle in the slope of the modest-sized mountains surrounding Harrison Lake, where the Cascade and Coast ranges merge.

Judging from the old stumps that still populate the forest, Sasquatch Park was logged many years ago. Today the sheltering forest is more deciduous than evergreen. Broadleaf maple, white birch and poplar present an alluring sight in autumn when the leaves

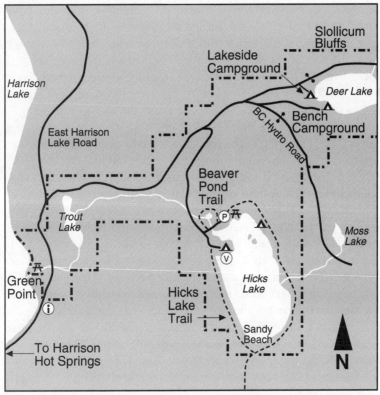

Sasquatch Provincial Park

change colour. From spring through early fall birdsongs fill the air and mingle with a chorus of frogs until late evening.

Deer Lake is a rather simple body of water that reveals itself from a vantage point on the beach at its western end. There's a children's play area just uphill from lakeside with slides and a jungle-gym setup. Only quiet electric motors are allowed on boats that put in here, whereas on nearby Hicks Lake gas-driven motors up to 10 horsepower can be used. Other than on long weekends, visitors with small boats will usually have the lakes to themselves. You can launch from the beach, where in the morning the aromas of smoke and fresh coffee are carried on the breeze from nearby campsites, or you can drive your car down to a small dock tethered at the south end of the beach.

The circumference of Deer Lake can be easily paddled in an hour without rushing. From the beach you can also walk a lakeside trail

119

out to a sandy point where fishing or swimming may suit your mood. Or you can cycle the fire and service roads that run well back into the surrounding mountains. For those who wish to get away from the beaches beside the campgrounds, there are more isolated sandy stretches at the far end of either lake that can be reached by boat. Watch for mountain goats in the early-morning light on the slopes of Slollicum Bluffs, which rise above the lake's north side.

You could spend a morning on Deer Lake, then explore nearby Hicks Lake, 4 km (2.5 mi.) away and twice as large. It's not as open as Deer Lake, with several points of land jutting out into the lake from which to fish or catch a view of the Cascade Mountains rising on the southern horizon. As you approach Hicks you'll see signs pointing in several different directions. Decide whether you want to head over to the day-use parking lot next to a boat launch and picnic area or proceed to the campground, where there is also a beach and picnic area. Trails link all the areas together, and it's only a few minutes' walk between the day-use area and the campground. However, when you're packing coolers and beach equipment, you don't want to lug it too far from the car. For the best views, check out the beach beside the campground amphitheatre: the peaks of the Skagit Range near Chilliwack Lake stand out on the southern horizon. There are also some good fishing spots here on a point of land in front of campsites 2 to 17 (some of the most desirable locations, along with sites 36 to 41).

For a short but nonetheless interesting walk, check out the Beaver Pond Trail, which leads around a marshy area near the day-use parking lot. Boardwalks and bridges take you past a small creek flowing west from Hicks Lake, part of which has been diverted by a beaver dam into a small pond. (The creek flows next into Trout Lake and eventually finds its way into Harrison Lake.)

Put your boat in at the Hicks Lake launch site or walk or cycle the trail ringing the lake to Sandy Beach at the south end, perhaps targeting it as your picnic destination if you're travelling light. You'll reach the beach in 1 hour after a stroll in the shade along an old logging road. Partway around is the group campsite, in front of which is a good beach. An easy swim offshore are two small forested islands, perfectly sized for adventure exploration with children and a good place to cast in a fishing line. Rainbow trout thrive in these waters, as the sight of ospreys attests.

Campsites at Sasquatch may be reserved in advance by calling 604-689-9025. For more information, call BC Parks' Fraser Valley office, (604) 463-3513.

SOUTH OF THE FRASER

25 REDWOOD & PEACE ARCH PARKS

DISTANCE: 35 km (20.2 mi.) south of Vancouver, in South Surrey

ACTIVITIES: Cycling, group functions, historic sites, paddling, picnicking, playground, tobogganing, viewpoints, walking

HIGHLIGHTS: A tree house and a cross-border stroll

ACCESS: For Redwood Park, follow Highway 99 south from Vancouver to the King George Highway (Exit 10) in Surrey. Go south on King George to 20th Avenue, then east to 180th Street, and south two blocks to the park's main entrance. Alternatively, enter at the trailhead and small parking area on the north side of 16th Avenue just east of 177th Street.

To reach Peace Arch Park, follow Highway 99 south almost to the Canada Customs and Immigration Building, then turn west (right) onto Beach Road. Watch for a sign pointing the way to Peace Arch Park. Follow Beach Road a short distance towards Semiahmoo Bay, then turn south (left) off Beach to reach the park entrance.

Here are two special parks in South Surrey practically within sight of each other. Redwood Park is operated by the City of Surrey, and Peace Arch Park is administered by BC Parks.

REDWOOD PARK Tucked on a hillside in South Surrey's Hazelmere Valley, this small park is a quiet little morning or afternoon getaway. Trails run through the shaded forest on a bluff overlooking farmland on both sides of the border, and there are picnic tables and a children's playground next to the main entrance.

Redwood Park was the home of twin brothers, David and Peter Brown, who arrived in South Surrey in the late 1870s. They bought farmland in the Hazelmere Valley in 1893 and lived there until 1958.

Peace Arch Park

Trees were as much a part of their lives as the open fields that ran along the ridge of their property on North Bluff Road (now 16th Avenue). The brothers planted 32 species of trees native to Europe, Asia and North America. The most successful of all, the tall redwoods bordering the fields, tower above the rest.

The Browns' redwoods have found a home from which they can look south towards distant Humboldt County in northern California, where their cousins attain greater heights than any other tree species in the world. Four adult humans holding hands can just encircle the biggest redwood in the park. And these are only young trees—imagine how much bigger they'll be this time next century!

Carved on a sheltered sign at the beginning of the trail through Redwood Park is the Prayer of the Woods, setting a tone for the rest of your visit.

> I am the heat of your hearth on the cold winter nights, the friendly shade screening you from the summer sun, and my fruits are refreshing draughts quenching your thirst as you journey. I am the beam that holds your house, the board of your table, the bed on which you lie, and the timber that builds your boat. I am the handle of your hoe, the door of your homestead, the wood of your cradle, and the shell of your coffin. I am the bread of kindness and the flower of beauty. Ye who pass by, listen to my prayer. Harm me not.

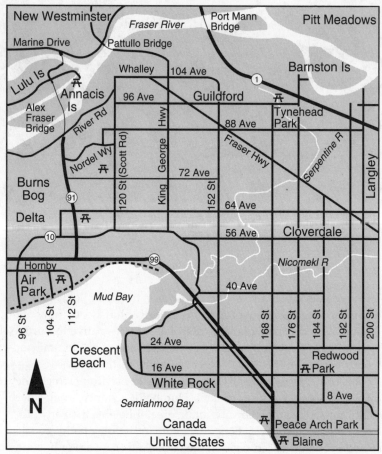

Surrey and Delta

Over the years the Browns had several different homes on the property, each of which was destroyed by fire. Finally they built a tree house in the middle of the forest. This one lasted. A long ramp led up to the door of their home, which was sturdily perched a storey above the forest floor. The original was taken down in 1986, but a replica has been installed in its place and is available for use by groups. If you'd like to plan a school, Boy Scout or Girl Guide party here, call the Surrey Parks and Recreation office, 604-501-5174, to get the key. There is no charge for the use of the tree house.

Other tall evergreens add to the park's green mosaic. From November through March, when most of the deciduous trees have shed their leaves and the gnarled branches dance and sway like many-armed Shivas in the wind, Redwood Park is a pleasant stop on a cold day, sheltering visitors from wind and rain. After a snowfall, the open ridges beside the forest will be thrilling to ride on a toboggan. Sheltered barbecues and a secluded campfire area—an unusual feature in a suburban park—are among the other attractions here. *Note:* Bring your own firewood.

If you're looking to take some produce home, a good place to stop is at the Hazelmere Organic Farm, open to the public from 9 A.M. to 5 P.M. Saturdays, on the west side of 184th Street just north of 16th Avenue beside Redwood Park.

PEACE ARCH PARK Imagine heading for the Canada-U.S. border without actually intending to go any farther. Peace Arch Park is ideal for strolling with the family pet past the extensive flower beds, for gathering the clan for a picnic barbecue at the beautifully maintained shelter on the Canadian side, or for just having your picture taken in front of the park's gazebo beside the lily pond. (When you visit the gazebo, be sure to look up at the interior ceiling. The sectioned roof is constructed of wood from eight different native B.C. trees, beautifully lacquered. The patterns made by the various grains make for interesting comparisons.)

Scattered about the park are 41 picnic tables. The large picnic shelter, open to all, is available for groups of 20 or more and has a kitchen equipped with hotplates and sinks. It's open from 8 A.M. to 9:45 P.M. daily. No reservations for its use are accepted and no group has exclusive use of the shelter. However, it is advisable for large groups to notify the park office in advance. Contact the park supervisor at 604-531-3068 between 9 and 10 A.M. Outside the shelter is a children's adventure playground. There is another playground on the American side next to 0 Avenue.

Once you begin to explore Peace Arch Park, you'll understand why it's a favourite photo site for wedding parties on a sunny afternoon. The lovingly tended flower beds provide a colourful backdrop. And there's a certain giddy feeling one gets in walking back and forth across the border—officially, a strip 12 m (40 ft.) wide, originally cleared in 1857—that's difficult to describe. Perhaps it's the ease with which you can wander between the two countries on foot, compared to crossing by car.

While the ambience of Peace Arch Park is a major part of its attraction, especially during months when the flowers are at their peak and a cooling breeze wafts in from Semiahmoo Bay, the centrepiece, the Peace Arch itself, is impossible to ignore. Tourists from outside North America have a special fascination with the monument when it comes to taking pictures. Yet many passers-by who call Vancouver home may not be aware of the true worth and significance of the imposing white monument, the only symbol of its kind erected at any border crossing in the world.

Informative displays mounted throughout the park on both sides of the border acquaint visitors with the arch's history. (British Columbia maintains 9 ha/22 acres of park north of the 49th parallel, while Washington state takes responsibility for 7 ha/17 acres on the southern side.)

One important fact about the creation of Peace Arch Park should not be overlooked: donations from schoolchildren on both sides of the border raised most of the funds required to purchase land for the park. Each year on the second Sunday in June, thousands of children and adults gather in the park for a Hands Across the Border celebration.

Use the parking lot at Peace Arch Park as your staging area whether you plan to explore on foot or by bike. Large picnic shelters are located in both the Canadian and American sides of the park. The one on the Canadian side is most visible; the American shelter is concealed behind the flower beds on the hill to the east of the Peace Arch and Highway 99.

Adjacent to the park, Beach Road runs north beside Semiahmoo Bay and its confluence with the Campbell River, through the private Semiahmoo Indian Reserve. Explore the Campbell River estuary, a site rich in wildlife sequestered behind the sheltering banks that support the Burlington Northern Railroad tracks. A wooden pedestrian bridge crosses Campbell River from the reserve and links with a boardwalk that leads through the estuary to White Rock's Semiahmoo Park and municipal seawall, complete with picnic grounds. Tie this in with a visit to Peace Arch Park and you'll have a very full day's worth of exploration on your hands. *Note:* There is no access to the beach on Semiahmoo Bay from Peace Arch Park.

26 TYNEHEAD REGIONAL PARK

DISTANCE: About 30 km (18 mi.) southeast of Vancouver, in Surrey

ACTIVITIES: Bird watching, nature observation, picnicking, walking

HIGHLIGHTS: Wildlife viewing, from salmon spawning in the Serpentine River to butterflies fluttering in a garden built especially for them

ACCESS: Take Exit 53 south on 176th Street from the Trans-Canada Highway (Highway 1) and make the first turn west on 96th Avenue. From here you have a choice of two approaches. Either turn right at the next major intersection, 168th Street, and drive to an entrance at the road's north end, or continue west to the park's main entrance beside the Tynehead Hatchery. (See Surrey and Delta map, page 124.)

Home to the headwaters of the Serpentine River, Tynehead Regional Park is a sheltering place for wildlife in the midst of Surrey. The park also provides its human neighbours sanctuary from the same threat faced by the area's fish, game and birdlife: the overpowering forces of development. Bordered as it is by the Trans-Canada Highway, it's a miracle that Tynehead can offer both serenity and quietude in its 260 ha (642 acres) of grassy meadows and second-growth cedar, hemlock, ash and maple.

If you want to delve straight into Tynehead's wild side, head to the park's 168th Street entrance. From here you can easily connect with the park's main trail—the Serpentine Loop Trail—that leads to the Serpentine Hollow Picnic Area. To reach it requires a pleasant 10-minute walk from the parking lot and information kiosk across a meadow and past some big cedars. There's nothing to stop you from heading off towards a quiet part of the park away from trails and roads. Look for a sunny sheltered spot by the hedgerows if that suits your mood. *Note:* A portion of the meadow is a dog off-leash area.

The Serpentine River flows west into Mud Bay through the Surrey flood plain from its headwaters in Tynehead Park, fed by

Trail through the Tynehead woods

several creeks and a natural spring. In springtime and after rain-storms, when the river runs faster than you might expect, high water cuts into the sandy banks, regularly bringing cedar and poplar trees down across the river. These make good bridges for explorers during drier, warmer weather. Kids will enjoy spending time by the river searching for tadpoles, so bring their rubber boots and pails .

Several viewing platforms, well situated for birding, are perched above the river, as well as two small bridges that take walkers across sections. In most places the trail is hard-packed, suitable for wheelchairs and strollers. Close to the river, the forest is predominantly second-growth cedar and mature vine maple. Thick bramble bushes, matted down by snowfalls during parts of the year, skirt the cedars' low-lying branches, and a thin, hard layer of packed snow can persist on sheltered stretches of the trail long after a storm. Dried berries from each year's abundant crop help birds in the area survive these hard times.

Near the park's southern boundary where the Serpentine flows out of the park is the Tynehead Hatchery. Run by a volunteer organization, the Serpentine Enhancement Society, this is the site of a fish release each spring as part of the salmonid enhancement program. (For information on the dates of the release, to which the public is invited, call 604-589-9127.) Come fall, you can see salmon migrating to the spawning grounds in the park. Because the Serpentine River becomes quite silty at times, a well has been drilled near the hatchery to provide a source of clean water for the fish tanks during the earliest stages of roe development.

The sound of the water in the river effectively camouflages the rumble of highway traffic. A profusion of cedar stumps throughout the park, some of them hollow, are reminders of the extensive grove that once stood here. Some stumps act as nurse logs, supporting as many as eight tall young hemlocks intent on taking their place in the sun.

Walk west of the Serpentine Loop Trail to Serpentine Hollow. Take the Trillium Trail to a viewpoint of the Butterfly Garden, which has been specifically planted to attract members of this insect order. Well-spaced cedars dot the lawn beside the garden, with several picnic tables strategically placed to catch sunlight. A viewing platform overlooks the picnic area. The trunk of a giant fir thrusts up through the middle of the platform, giving it a tree house quality. Water music from the Serpentine's tributaries fills the air here.

27 FORT LANGLEY & ENVIRONS

DISTANCE: 56 km (35 mi.) east of Vancouver

ACTIVITIES: Boating, camping, cycling, fishing, historic sites, paddling, picnicking, viewpoints, walking

HIGHLIGHTS: A lovingly preserved national historic site presides over picnickers and anglers on Fraser River sandbars

ACCESS: Take the Trans-Canada Highway (Highway 1) east to either the 200th Street or 232nd Street exit and follow the signs north to Fort Langley. If you are coming from the north side of the Fraser River, take the ferry from Albion, located on the Lougheed Highway (Highway 7) just east of Maple Ridge. The fort is situated on Mavis Street, two blocks east of Glover Road, Fort Langley's main street.

To reach Derby Reach Regional Park from Fort Langley, head south on Glover to 96th Avenue. Turn west on 96th and follow it to where it joins McKinnon Crescent. Follow McKinnon to Allard Crescent, where you turn right to Derby Reach Park.

There are several approaches to Glen Valley Regional Park. Two-Bit Bar is located at the intersection of 88th Avenue and 272nd Street. Follow River Road east of Two-Bit Bar to reach Poplar and Duncan Bars, a total distance one way of about 4 km (2.5 mi.) between the three sites.

Several historic 19th-century forts have been preserved in British Columbia as reminders of how the West was originally colonized. Fort Steele Heritage Town, near Cranbrook in the East Kootenays, is the best example. Much closer to home is Fort Langley, a restored Hudson's Bay Company post that is open year round. It, too, is a delightful reminder of yesteryear, and much easier to reach from Vancouver. As part of a visit to Fort Langley, picnic here or at either of two nearby regional parks.

Derby Reach Regional Park

FORT LANGLEY NATIONAL HISTORIC SITE Not only will you enjoy the natural setting of this unique frontier site next to the Fraser River, you'll also get a better idea of how life was lived 150 years ago. Construction of a fort at the present site of Fort Langley began in 1839. The next year, fire reduced everything to ashes. Undeterred, the Hudson's Bay Company rebuilt the fort, which continued to prosper as newly arrived settlers began working the rich Fraser Valley farmland that surrounds the fort. Fort Langley reached the height of its commercial importance in the 1850s, when it provisioned miners for their journey up the Fraser River to the Cariboo gold fields.

The fort flourished for several decades after the gold rush, until the company opened a sales shop in town in 1886. By this time the palisade had been dismantled, and many of the fort's buildings had either been pulled down or converted to other uses. Restoration work began in earnest in the late 1950s. Today, visiting the reconstructed Fort Langley is like stepping back inside the walls of time.

As you enter the fort, one of the first things you'll want to do is explore the ramparts and peek over the tops of the walls onto the

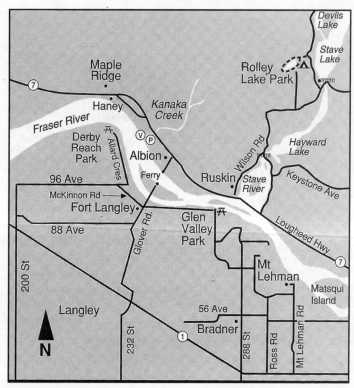

Fort Langley and area

river below. This is also a good place to survey the spacious grounds inside the fort. The buildings spread around the grounds include the aptly named Big House, an artisan's cottage, a cooperage where the craft of barrel making is displayed, a blacksmith's shop and the trading post's storehouse, located in the oldest building on the grounds. Knowledgeable park employees in heritage garb put on daily presentations of spinning, smithing and other activities related to life at the fort. They will answer any of your questions and may even invite you to participate. Next to the artisan's cottage is a replica of a large Columbia River skiff that is refloated each year on Brigade Days, held on the August long weekend. For information on special events, school programs or hours of operation at the fort, call 604-513-4777, or visit the Web site www.parkscan.harbour.com/fl/.

From the fort's ramparts you have a good view out over the Fraser River's Bedford Channel across to small Brae and McMillan Islands, now joined as one, from which the Albion ferry sails. Much of the island is a Kwantlen Indian reserve, and the remainder has been acquired for a park by the Greater Vancouver Regional District. For a treat afterwards, drive out onto the island to the Fort Langley Seafood Café ("Home of the Famous Fries"), located on the east side of Glover, where traffic waits for the Albion ferry.

Train tracks run along the riverbank below the fort. Nearby is the Fort Langley Railroad Museum on Glover Road, which includes a restored station from the 1920s, a CNR caboose and an operating model railway. The museum is well worth a visit as you explore the town in the vicinity of the fort. A large interpretive map of Fort Langley, displayed at the railroad historical site, outlines a heritage walking tour of the town.

DERBY REACH REGIONAL PARK The countryside around Fort Langley is mostly level, making for a quick 10-minute drive or an easy 30-minute bike ride between here and either of two GVRD parks, Derby Reach and Glen Valley.

As you approach Derby Reach's Edgewater Bar entrance you will pass the Houston House and nearby Karr/Mercer historic barn. The Fort-to-Fort riverside trail begins across the road from the farmhouse. Trails through the wooded countryside to the west of the Houston House are for hikers and horseback riders only.

Derby Reach is a site on the Fraser with both historic and sporting importance. The GVRD owns 165 ha (407 acres) along 3 km (1.9 mi.) of the south shore of the Fraser River. The park includes Edgewater Bar, one of the best fishing bars on the river and the original location of Fort Langley and Derby Townsite. Derby Reach represents the last surviving use of a name that was once applied to old Fort Langley. The town was renamed Derby in 1858, when it was expected to become the capital of British Columbia. (The Earl of Derby was the British prime minister at the time.)

Located just east of Barnston Island and across the river from the entrance of Kanaka Creek (see chapter 20), Derby Reach is of principal interest to anglers. Among local parks it has the unique feature of providing overnight camping space for vans or tents. The 38 sites are allocated on a first-come, first-served basis. There is a fee of about $11 per night, with a maximum stay of three nights.

The pace of life at Derby is measured by the willingness of fish to bite. Edgewater Bar not only has a riverside setting that draws anglers year round, it also has the most thoughtfully designed picnic tables. Each comes complete with a square of Arborite sunk into its corner, *the* designated place to filet your catch without making a mess of your picnic.

Derby Reach is a great place to be whether or not the fish are biting. A hush hangs over the assembled hopefuls as long lines are strung out into the river in front of lawn chairs and there's nothing to do except watch Big Muddy roll by. Bring along rubber boots for your kids. Although most visitors sit with their feet up and their lines strung out, there is an open playing field next to the picnic area where you can toss a Frisbee or a baseball. A nature trails runs through the woods behind the reach to a marshy area. Great blue herons nest in the tall cottonwoods that line the trail. In winter, when the trees have dropped their leaves, look for their massive nests high in the branches above.

GLEN VALLEY REGIONAL PARK Glen Valley Park features three fishing bars: Two-Bit, Poplar and Duncan. Of the three, Poplar Bar is the largest and offers the most interesting options. You can fish, launch a hand-carried boat, and walk or cycle several riverside trails. Crescent Island lies a short distance offshore from Poplar Bar in the Fraser River. The island forms a natural breakwater for canoes and kayaks, away from the wake created by larger boats, which stick to the Fraser's main channel. The Stave River enters the Fraser's north side, just east of Crescent Island (see chapter 22). If you are feeling adventuresome, you can explore both waterways in the course of a day trip here.

Glen Valley is a traditional agricultural setting located between the Fraser River and a high bluff. It's quite a puff to cycle up to the small community of Bradner (see next chapter), located on the bluff, but it does make for an interesting drive. In March and April, the fields are bright with daffodils. You may choose to drive the 7 km (4.3 mi.) to Glen Valley from Fort Langley, or you may wish to leave your vehicle near the fort and bicycle east along 88th Avenue. The road is wide, largely untravelled and signed as part of the Langley bicycle trail network.

28 BRADNER, MOUNT LEHMAN & MATSQUI TRAIL REGIONAL PARK

DISTANCE:	75 km (46.6 mi.) east of Vancouver
ACTIVITIES:	Camping, cycling, fishing, nature observation, picnicking, walking
HIGHLIGHTS:	Daffodils and dairy farms arranged beside the Fraser
ACCESS:	To get to Bradner, take the Trans-Canada Highway (Highway 1) east to the 264th Street North exit (#73). Turn east on 56th Avenue (Interprovincial Way) to Bradner Road, then south (right) on 288th Street to enter Bradner.

To reach Matsqui Trail Regional Park, take Highway 1 to Abbotsford, then head north on Highway 11 towards Mission. Watch for the green GVRD signs that point the way to the park near the south end of the Mission Bridge. (See Fraser Valley map, page 106, and Fort Langley and area map, page 132.)

In the gently rolling hills east of Vancouver the spring equinox signals the start of a festive season. Everyone keeps one eye out for the first robin, the other for the first daffodil. Both are harbingers of winter's true end. Whether you're wanting to celebrate spring, looking to shake off cabin fever after a winter indoors or just seeking an opportunity to dig your bicycle out of the garage, the Bradner and Mount Lehman region has a welcome ready for you. Even if the spring breeze still has a chill edge to it, pack a lunch, as there are sheltered spots beside the nearby Fraser River for picnicking. If you time your arrival close to the Easter weekend, plan to attend the Bradner Daffodil Festival, held here annually since 1928.

The daffodil festival, complete with its legendary bake sale, is held in the Bradner Community Hall. A small park with a gazebo across the road from the Bradner General Store is one potential picnic location.

In 1906, an English gardener, recently arrived in Vancouver, spotted a stump full of blooming daffodils. Fenwick Fatkin instantly knew that he'd found his calling in the New World. He bought property in Bradner, a small farming town in the Fraser Valley, and set about cultivating several varieties of this popular member of the amaryllis family. In 1928, Fatkin held a "parlour show" in his home, featuring 14 varieties of daffs.

These days more than 400 varieties of daffodils bloom in the area's fields. In spring, the sight of daffodils and narcissi poking their yellow or white heads above the ditches is your first clue that you're close to Bradner. You'll soon start to come across roadside stands with bunches of daffodils for sale. Many of the stands operate on the honour system: just choose your blooms and leave your money.

Many back roads crisscross this plateau atop the Pemberton Hills bordering the Fraser River. No matter what your vantage point, you'll find yourself lifting your eyes north to one of the best full-face views of the Golden Ears and south to broad, glaciated Mount Baker. As you drive east or west of Bradner, you drop down into prairie land, with Fort Langley to the west and Matsqui to the east. The area around Bradner is perfect for either a leisurely inspection by car or an energetic bicycle ride. Many of the roads on the plateau are flat, and traffic is generally light. One caution: the shoulders of most roads are narrow.

If you drive out with bikes on board and are wondering where to leave your car, try the large parking area beside the Bradner schoolhouse or a second one at the north end of Bradner Road beside Jubilee Hall, several miles north of town. Just beyond the hall the pavement narrows, then becomes gravel for an exciting descent on the Langley side into Glen Valley below (see chapter 27). Travelling north from Bradner to Jubilee you'll pass well-kept homes, some with daffodils for sale in spring. One farm in particular has hundreds of varieties of daffodils under cultivation. The owners here welcome visitors and encourage them to walk out into the field for a closer look at the many types, with their different colouring and form.

Around Bradner are a dozen roads to choose from, most of which feed into each other at one point or another. An occasional heritage marker will help direct you to some interesting vistas, but otherwise finding your way around this small region can be rather haphazard. A helpful map of the Fraser Valley is available from ITMB Publishing, 530 West Broadway, Vancouver, B.C. v5z 4A5, 604-879-3621, or from the Web site www.itmb.com.

Matsqui Trail Regional Park

A century ago, riverboats served the fledgling community of nearby Mount Lehman, an early port of entry to Matsqui, taking produce from local farms to the city dwellers of New Westminster. By 1908, the B.C. Electric Railway Company had laid tracks along this stretch of the Fraser River. (The route was later taken over by

Canadian National Railways.) In 1992, as part of Matsqui's centennial celebrations, several trails were revitalized, among them the Landing Road Heritage Trail. Not long, it leads down through the forest to an old railway siding and log pilings beside the Fraser, reminders of earlier times. Several picnic tables are set beside the trail. Follow the roadside markers east of Jubilee Hall to reach the Landing Road Heritage Trail at road's end.

MATSQUI TRAIL REGIONAL PARK Harris Road leads east of Mount Lehman and links up with the Matsqui Trail. This dike trail was once part of a route from Horseshoe Bay to Hope. Now a Greater Vancouver Regional District park, it extends a level 14 km (8.7 mi.) along a series of dikes, past the Mission Bridge and open fields with grazing cattle to the slopes of Sumas Mountain.

The trails are built atop the dikes that deflect the Fraser's westbound flow and prevent the river from inundating the broad prairie south of Mission. As you look around you'll easily spot the peaks of Mount Baker and Mount Shuksan to the south as well as Mount Cheam to the east.

Matsqui Trail Regional Park is the most easterly of the GVRD's 22 parks, a network that stretches as far north as Howe Sound. As at Derby Reach Regional Park downstream in Fort Langley (see chapter 27), you can overnight here if you wish. After its annual winter closure, Matsqui Trail's campground—composed of four spacious but plain campsites overhung by tall black cottonwood trees—reopens at the beginning of March. Although the sites are favoured by anglers who cast for cutthroat trout and steelhead salmon, anyone who enjoys the company of a river will find this an attractive place to spend an evening, especially if you're fond of soulful train whistles. Both the CPR and CNR main lines pass nearby. In fact, don't be surprised on your approach or departure if a rolling freight train temporarily blocks the entrance to the park. In time-honoured fashion, just start counting boxcars.

Railways long played a key role in moving people and produce through Matsqui. The notorious Billy Miner even held up a train here, as you'll learn if you join a guided cycle tour occasionally offered at the park. Billed as "Rolling Through Time," the 2-hour ramble is led by a park interpreter who will not only point out the site of the heist but also delve into the history of the biblical Fraser River flood of 1948. As a result of that devastation, sturdier fortifications were built inland. Today you can not only explore that dike's hard-packed gravel surface—wide enough for farm equipment to use at harvest—but also ramble along an older, rougher dike closer to the river. For much of the distance between Mount Lehman and Sumas Mountain these twin dikes ring the Matsqui Prairie. A wide gap separates them. Local farmers cultivate hay in the more protected stretches.

The CPR Bridge that links Matsqui with Mission marks an important boundary on the Fraser. This is judged to be the point east of which the intertidal impact of the Pacific ceases to register in a significant way. Hence anglers who dip their lines west of the bridge must possess a federal saltwater fishing licence, while those casting to the east need a provincial freshwater permit. The bridge itself is a sturdy cat's cradle of riveted black-iron trusses and braces.

In stark architectural contrast to the railway bridge's low profile stands the modern Mission Bridge across which traffic flows on Highway 11. Its forked concrete columns support a bridge deck that curves high above the river. When the river is calm at sunset, the reflection of the columns on the surface produces an interesting *trompe l'oeil* that makes the bridge appear twice as tall as it actually is.

Some of the best points of access to the river are near the two bridges. As the main dike trail heads east of here it curves inland, allowing only one or two opportunities to watch the river at close range. Stick to the rougher trail for the best viewing spots. Bring along a pair of binoculars. The farther east you go, the wilder the countryside becomes. This is especially noticeable as the dikes near Sumas Mountain, much of which is now a provincial park. On the opposite bank of the Fraser stands Strawberry Island. Hundreds of gulls gather here near sunset, strung out in a long row along the beach like linen on a clothesline.

For more information on Matsqui Trail Park, call the GVRD's East Area office, 604-530-4983, or visit their Web site: www.gvrd.bc.ca/services/parks/.

29 CAMPBELL VALLEY REGIONAL PARK

DISTANCE:	55 km (34 mi.) east of Vancouver, in Langley
ACTIVITIES:	Historic site, horseback riding, nature observation, picnicking, walking
HIGHLIGHTS:	Boardwalks and valley trails connect with open farm fields
ACCESS:	Follow Highway 1 southeast to the 200th Street exit and drive 14.5 km (9 mi.) south to either the park's 16th or 8th Avenue entrances. Or from Highway 99 South take the 8th Avenue East exit and travel 7.5 km (4.7 mi.) to the South Valley entrance on 200th Street.

In 1898, when Alexander Annand left Port Moody to take up farming in southwestern Langley Township, he had no greater intention than to homestead. Much of the better land from here north to Fort Langley on the Fraser River had already been claimed. But he must have been happy to have had water in the small wetland valley above which he cleared forest for pasture. Home, barn and sheds went up, an orchard grew, time went by.

Annand eventually passed the farm into other hands, but his imprint is still visible in the hand-hewn lumber of the farmhouse and on the smooth surface of the surrounding fields. Below, where Little Campbell River seeps in, a trail leads to several level meadows from which wagons once hauled out hay to feed the livestock. Half forest and half marsh, the valley is a quiet haven for birds and rich with berries.

This gently rolling region just north of the Canada-U.S. border lends itself to exploration on foot or horseback. Over the years Langley riders have kept open the trails that run east to Aldergrove. Since September 1979, when the GVRD took control of more than 535 ha (1320 acres) of the Campbell Valley, including the Annand farm, these trails have come into greater public use.

Campbell Valley Regional Park attracts more than 200,000 visitors annually, and although not all of them are on horseback, the flavour of the area is contagious enough to make anyone want to

Campbell Valley

mount up. The Shaggy Mane Trail, which rings the park, runs 11 km
(6.8. mi.), quite a distance on foot but an easy 2-hour ride. Two stables near the park equestrian centre at Campbell Downs provide
horses and guided tours of the trail on a one- or two-hour basis. For
information, contact Back in the Saddle Again Stables, 604-534-3264,
or Langley 204 Riding Stables, 604-533-7978.

While the Shaggy Mane Trail runs around the perimeter, the valley itself is interlaced with trails of varying length, including several
stretches of boardwalk over marshy sections. The trails are mostly
level and scenic, especially the 2.3-km (1.4-mi.) Little River Loop
Trail, which is also suitable for wheelchairs. (Many features in this
park, including specially adapted picnic tables, have been designed
for people with disabilities.) The park's groomed trails also provide
a great advantage for parents with young children in strollers.

This is picnic country in summer. The perfume of wild roses and
fireweed, blackberries and salal, distilled over the course of a hot
day, carries down off the hillside between the Annand/Rowlatt
Farmstead and the marsh. Most of the historic farm buildings have
been restored, including two barns that date from 1903 and 1937.
Visitors are welcome to explore them, although care must be taken
not to disturb the privacy of the caretaker's family who live in the
1898 farmhouse.

Adjacent to the farmstead is the Lochiel Schoolhouse, built in 1924

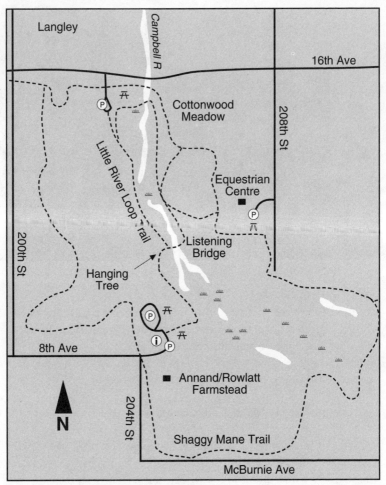

Campbell Valley Regional Park

and relocated to the park in 1988. Peer in the windows for a nostalgic glimpse of desks arranged in neat rows with a map of the Dominion of Canada prominently displayed on one wall. The brightly lit school has a remarkable number of windowpanes. The Langley Centennial Museum offers demonstration one-room schoolhouse programs to students throughout the GVRD. For information, call 604-888-3922.

Near the farm are a dozen tables, each with its own hibachi, arranged around the visitors' centre and garden at the 8th Avenue entrance. Directly below, but hidden by dense growth in summer, are the boardwalk and trails that run north to another picnic area at the

16th Avenue entrance. A Demonstration Wildlife Garden is planted beside the visitors' centre. The garden is ingeniously planted with trees, shrubs and small plants that attract wildlife such as butterflies. Ponds and hedgerows provide refuge for larger animals. Hands-on educational displays in the centre assist visitors to discover the park's rich natural and cultural heritage.

If you'd prefer to take a picnic basket on your walk into the park, head towards the Listening Bridge on the Little River Loop Trail. The bridge is easily located to the east of a clearing dominated by a large maple known ominously as the Hanging Tree. (There is no evidence that it was ever used to dispense vigilante justice.) Although there are several open areas along the western side of this valley trail, there are none on the east side, much of which is covered with boardwalk. The hillside is steepest on the east side beyond the bridge, where at one point a wide pathway leads off to the Cottonwood Meadow and the equestrian centre. Watch for comfortable benches on the board-walk from which you can look back down the valley through tall stands of bulrushes. Don't let the number of visitors to Campbell Valley Park dissuade you from coming. Thick summer growth provides a sense of privacy with every bend in the trail.

Several times each year special events are held at the park. The themes vary; one of the more popular is a guided exploration of the park in search of ripe berries and ingredients for wild teas. Sampling always happens afterwards back at the visitors' centre. There is no charge for these events or for the annual Celebration of Nature, held on the first weekend in October. For further information on these programs, call the park at 604-530-4983, or visit their Web site: www.gvrd.bc.ca/services/parks/.

30 ALDERGROVE LAKE REGIONAL PARK

DISTANCE:	70 km (43.5 miles) southeast of Vancouver
ACTIVITIES:	Bird watching, cross-country skiing, cycling, group functions, in-line skating, paddling, picnicking, stargazing, swimming, tobogganing, viewpoints, walking
HIGHLIGHTS:	Gently rolling hills, fall colours, roadside stands
ACCESS:	Take the Trans-Canada Highway (Highway 1) east to the 264th Street exit (#73). Head south to 8th Avenue (Huntington Road), then turn east to reach the main park entrance at the intersection of 8th Avenue and 272nd Street. (There are equestrian and pedestrian entrances on the west and east sides of the park, 272nd Street and Lefeuvre Road, respectively.)

For one season of the year—summer—Aldergrove Lake is a magnet for overheated kids on vacation. The rest of the time, it's a quiet corner tucked away on the border between Langley and Matsqui in the southern Fraser Valley. Two main trails loop and interconnect as they thread through a tall, dense forest, eventually leading out into the brightness of an open meadow surrounding Aldergrove Bowl, a former gravel quarry that has now been successfully restored to green space, with a small pond. You can walk or cycle these inviting trails over the course of several hours or even cross-country ski them when conditions are right.

The rolling countryside around Aldergrove Lake is largely under cultivation, taken up by berry and dairy farms and plant nurseries. Little creeks crisscross the fields, culverted under roadways and bridged where they really display their girth. Salmon spawn in some, especially when the creeks are running high after a fall rainstorm. Endangered species, such as the Salish Sucker and the Nooksack Dace, return in smaller streams, such as Pepin Brook, which flows through the park on its way to join the Nooksack River in nearby Washington state.

If you pull in here with high hopes that water levels in Aldergrove

Aldergrove Lake

Lake have benefited from rainstorms too, think again. Imagine an enormous bathtub with the plug pulled: this is Aldergrove Lake in the off-season, from Labour Day to Victoria Day. Entirely artificial, shaped like a sandy racing oval with a concrete pad on its bottom, the lake can be bone dry. That doesn't deter kids from building sand-castles on the shoreline year round. The size of the parking lot confirms that the lake is very popular in summer, but most times the lot is as empty as the basin. A stone's throw from the lake on the north side of Pepin Brook is a large playing field and the Blacktail group picnic area with a covered barbecue shelter. (You can reserve the latter by calling 604-432-6352.) Fringed with young maple trees, come October this is a colourful locale.

There's much more to Aldergrove Lake Park than first meets the eye. Set out along the pedestrian-only 4-km (2.5-mi.) Pepin Brook Trail, which mostly follows a ridge along the park's northern perimeter. The surface of this quiet woodland trail has a pleasant spring underfoot. On summer nights in August, stargazers gather in an

Rock n' Horse Trail, Aldergrove Lake

open field beside the trail for astronomy programs provided by the park in cooperation with the Royal Astronomical Society and the Pacific Space Centre.

Walk or cycle the 7-km (4.3-mile) Rock n' Horse Trail, which intertwines with Pepin Brook Trail in places. You can usually expect to encounter horseback riders on this aptly named route. A Trail Users Courtesy Code posted at intervals reminds everyone of the procedures to avoid conflict: cyclists yield to pedestrians and equestrians, while pedestrians yield to equestrians. Take care not to spook any horses you may meet; slow down when approaching them and stand aside on the down side of the trail while they pass.

You won't need any prompting to mount a bicycle saddle and pedal off through the sheltering forest along this easygoing trail, suited to beginner- and intermediate-level cyclists who like to enjoy a view and a challenge at the same time. The farther you cycle, the better the trail gets. Just when it looks as if you'll spend your visit marvelling at tall broafleaf maple and cedar trees, suddenly the forest opens up and you're riding over hills beside farmland where berry bushes colour the horizon. Continue up and down, back and forth along the trail, enjoying views of Mount Baker's snowcap (cloud cover permitting). At sunset you can watch it turn shades of pink and red.

A massive erratic boulder, a leftover from glacial times, is nestled in the woods near Lefeuvre Road. The Transformer, a supernatural character from Native mythology who went about changing animate beings into inanimate objects, might just have had a hand in this one. Transformations of other kinds have influenced the park since it was created in 1970. The recycled timbers used to build Hunt Bridge, located close to the pedestrian entrance on 272nd Street, came from Vancouver's old Cambie Street Bridge in 1985. More recently, a gravel mine near the southeast corner of the park has been greened up and restored as a small lake and marsh/pond. Unlike those in Aldergrove Lake, water levels in Aldergrove Bowl are stable year round—good news for canoeists and kayakers. Plans call for the creation of a beach volleyball zone over the next few years for teenagers to enjoy. For information on activities, plus updates on Aldergrove Lake Park's development, call 604-530-4983 or visit the GVRD's Web site: www. gvrd.bc.ca/services/parks.

Should your park outing leave you wanting more, paved shoulders on the Langley back roads around the park provide ideal routes for extended cycling and in-line skating excursions. They are wide and smooth, and best of all there is only a hint of traffic along most of the routes. Enjoy rural scenes as you ride or skate along. Mount Baker seems astonishingly close at hand. For quick access to the back roads, park at the entrance to Aldergrove Lake Park at 8th Avenue and 272nd Street and begin from here. The paved shoulders nearby on 272nd Street were developed for cyclists and in-line skaters. Signs posted by the Township of Langley point out the route to follow. A note of caution: Although you can in-line skate on the roadway that leads into Aldergrove Lake Park, a steep hill that drops down to the main parking areas and the lake will probably prove too challenging for novice skaters. Always wear a helmet and protective padding just in case.

Explore the region at your leisure as you make your way to and from the park by following the back roads south of Highway 1. The drive along the country roads of Surrey and Langley is a reward in itself. In autumn, front porches and roadside stands brim with colourful squashes and mound upon mound of pumpkins, the harvest from nearby fields.

31 CULTUS LAKE

DISTANCE: 100 km (60 mi.) southeast of Vancouver

ACTIVITIES: Boating, camping, cycling, hiking, horseback riding, paddling, picnicking, playground, swimming, viewpoints, walking, windsurfing

HIGHLIGHTS: A warm, inviting freshwater lake

ACCESS: Follow the Trans-Canada Highway (Highway 1) for 90 km (56 mi.) almost to Chilliwack. Watch for signs indicating Exit 104 to Yarrow and the provincial parks at Cultus and Chilliwack Lakes. Once you've left the highway, you are on No. 3 Road. East of Yarrow, Vedder Mountain Road skirts the base of Vedder Mountain. Just before the bridge over the Chilliwack/Vedder River, turn uphill (south), following the provincial-park signs. Cultus Lake is 4 km (2.5 mi.) from this point.

Mention Cultus Lake to many people and what immediately come to mind are images of speedboats, summer parties, water slides and, above all, crowds of campers. While these impressions are certainly accurate during the hottest days of summer, there is a quieter side to the lake and its environs at most other seasons.

Natives once believed that supernatural creatures lived in Cultus Lake and manifested themselves as dirty swirlings in the water. These days you could be excused for thinking that the name is a direct reference to the jet-skiers who buzz along the shoreline, whipping the waters into a frenzy. Natives called the lake *Tso-wallie*; the modern name comes from a Chinook word meaning "worthless" or "bad," perhaps because of a taboo or in reference to the squall-plagued waters.

Cultus Lake has limited drainage aside from the Sweltzer River, which flows out the north end. A small creek enters at the south end, but otherwise there is no source of fresh cold water to feed the lake once the snowpack has melted from the surrounding slopes. In comparison to the frigid waters of nearby Chilliwack and Harrison

Cultus Lake

Lakes, Cultus is a bathtub, which surely accounts for its popularity among visitors for almost a century. Because of the warm water, too, fishing in the park is good, with rainbow and cutthroat trout and Dolly Varden char to be hooked.

Cultus Lake was originally settled at its north end. There is still a small community of year-round residents here and another at Lindell Beach at the lake's south end, though most cottages are used only on a seasonal basis. Row upon row of small, well-kept cabins, built close together, ring the shores at both ends of the lake.

CULTUS MUNICIPAL BEACH Although much of the summer activity has expanded along the east side of the lake, it is at Cultus's north end that you will find some of the best swimming, especially if you have smaller children in tow. There is a playground and a maze of docks, complete with a small slide, on which to sun while keeping an eye on young bathers. On the nearby lawns of the municipal park you'll find plenty of room to hold barbecues, with a picnic gazebo, tennis courts and washroom facilities close at hand. Beach Buoy Leisure Rentals, (604) 858-8841, housed in an old wood-frame

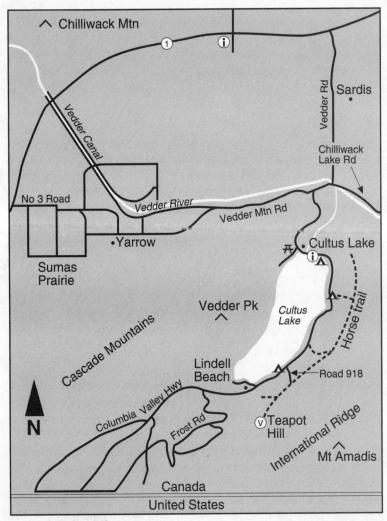

Cultus Lake

building set back above the water, rents out canoes, rowboats and paddlewheelers.

To reach the municipal beach, turn right at the large wooden public-parking sign as you enter the town of Cultus Lake and drive the short distance to lakeside. Even if your destination is the nearby provincial park, this is an interesting location through which to stroll and admire the cottages. Some sport quaint names—Bide-a-wee, Laffalot, Dunroamin—and mounted atop one beachfront cabin are several pairs of ancient homemade water skis equipped with cut-off rubber boots, signs of earlier, more ingenious times.

CULTUS LAKE PROVINCIAL PARK Once past the mall, the go-kart track, the commercial water slides and the stable where trail rides may be arranged, Columbia Valley Highway, the main road around the lake, heads south for 4 km (2.5 mi.) towards the provincial park. Just past privately operated Sunnyside Campground is the park headquarters, (604) 858-7161, where well-informed staff can answer questions on recreational options in the surrounding district. You can reserve a site here by calling 604-689-9025 in Greater Vancouver. For more information, call (604) 824-2300.

There are four campgrounds within the park, as well as three large picnic grounds. During summer months the gatehouse at the entrance to the park is open 24 hours a day. If you are seeking camping space, this is the place to register. An overnight camping fee of $18.50 is charged from April to Thanksgiving weekend in October. Both Entrance Bay and Maple Bay have a boat launch, beach and picnic day-use area.

The boundaries of the park encompass both sides of Cultus Lake, but only the southeast side is developed for recreation. To the northwest is open countryside where second-growth forest is beginning to establish itself. Much of the northwest side of the lake is made inaccessible by cliffs that plummet to the water's edge.

International Ridge rises steeply above the campsites and day-use areas on the southeast side of the lake. Several trails traverse the ridge. One particularly popular one leads to a viewpoint on Teapot Hill, named by two surveyors in the early 1950s. While laying out boundaries for the 658-ha (1626-acre) park, they found an abandoned teapot on the open face of the knoll that rises 750 m (2460 ft.) above the lake, affording good views to the south, west and north.

Of the several approaches to Teapot Hill, the easiest begins on the east side of the road between Delta Grove and Honeymoon Bay. The entrance is marked by a gate and signposts. One sign reads "Road 918"; its companion points the way uphill to Teapot Hill. There is limited parking next to the trailhead. Interpretive signs are situated at various places along wide, well-worn Road 918. Near the top the road forks right while the well-marked trail to Teapot Hill leads uphill to the left.

The forest through which the road and trail run is made up largely of second-growth western hemlock and tall broadleaf maple. In autumn, as the maple leaves turn golden with the change in seasons, the forest around Cultus Lake is bright and colourful. The air is rich with the smell of humus, and the dry leaves crunch underfoot as you walk along. Total walking time one way from the road to the top of Teapot Hill is less than 1 hour.

From the top, the most interesting views are of Lindell Beach and south to the Columbia Valley, which opens and then narrows on its way into the United States, with several peaks of the Cascade Mountains rising in the distance.

A horse trail runs much of the way along International Ridge. It joins Road 918 near Honeymoon Bay. Feeder trails lead from both the Entrance Bay and Clear Creek campgrounds to the horse trail, providing a pleasant alternative to the more straightforward approach to Teapot Hill via Road 918 mentioned above. The walk one way from Entrance Bay to Teapot Hill is less than 2 hours; from Clear Creek it's 90 minutes one way. The horse trail offers more variety than Road 918 as it rises and falls along the hillside below International Ridge.

COLUMBIA VALLEY The Columbia Valley Highway leads south from the park onto the benchland above the town of Lindell Beach. Lindell Beach is similar in flavour to the community at the north end of Cultus Lake and offers a variety of commercial services. From here you may choose to drive through the Columbia Valley, an enjoyable 1-hour jaunt, or to explore the area by bicycle. In contrast to the narrow shoulders and highway traffic running the length of Cultus Lake, the roads south of Lindell Beach are far less busy, making them ideal for cycling.

Columbia Valley Highway divides just south of the Cultus Golf Park. It really doesn't matter which of the two forks, Frost Road or Columbia Valley, you choose to follow, as one feeds into the other near the international border, creating a loop through the valley. Both major roads level out soon after cresting on the benchland above Lindell Beach and run 12 km (7.4 mi.) to the border, which is marked by one small obelisk and a narrow 12-m (40-foot) cut visible on the hillside above the valley. Avoid side roads that are posted "No Exit" and you will have no trouble wending your way along. Whether you drive or cycle, your reward may be a sample of berry wine from Columbia Valley Classic's vineyard along the way.

32 CHILLIWACK LAKE

DISTANCE: 141 km (87.5 mi.) southeast of Vancouver

ACTIVITIES: Boating, camping, cross-country skiing, cycling, fishing, hiking, nature observation, picnicking, swimming, viewpoints, walking, windsurfing

HIGHLIGHTS: Big peaks and big trees

ACCESS: Travel 85 km (52.8 mi.) east along the Trans-Canada Highway (Highway 1) to the Chilliwack Lake exit (#104), then east on No. 3 Road. You'll pass through the rural community of Yarrow. Continue east along Vedder Mountain Road. Just over the Vedder Bridge, turn south (right) onto Chilliwack Lake Road at a well-marked intersection. Drive another 42 km (26 mi.) to the lake, an easy 2-hour drive from Vancouver. (The pavement gives way to a well-maintained gravel road for the last 12 km/7.4 mi.)

All it takes is one trip to an exotic locale like the Carmanah Valley on the west coast of Vancouver Island to make you fall in love with the sight of very large trees. There are other locations closer to Vancouver where small groups of these gnarly giants still flourish—for example, Lighthouse Park (see chapter 2) in West Vancouver. Once you've caught the bug, you'll be driven to find whole hillsides and valley bottoms full of these huggable hulks. Perhaps it's their serene nature: all that biomass in motion without so much as a gurgle to be heard, just a sighing from high above.

If you've got the itch, head for Chilliwack Lake, where you can enjoy the company of some big trees with much, little or no effort—take your pick. Walk the provincial-park trail up Post Creek to Greendrop and Lindeman Lakes near the north end of Chilliwack Lake, or ramble through the ecological reserve of old-growth cedars beside the upper Chilliwack River at the lake's south end.

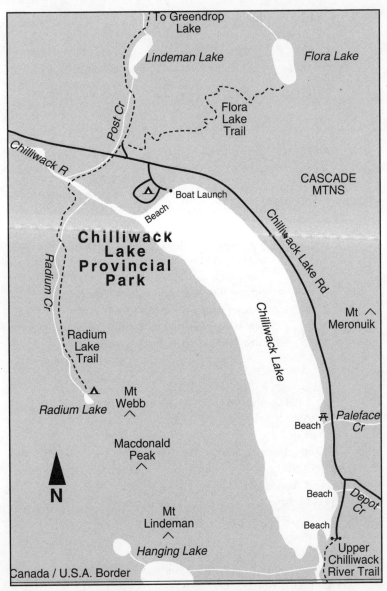

Chilliwack Lake

CHILLIWACK LAKE PROVINCIAL PARK In late 1997, the borders of Chilliwack Lake Park expanded dramatically. BC Parks' original 162-ha (400-acre) toehold at the north end of the lake mushroomed when the provincial government added a further 8960 ha (22,140

Chilliwack River

acres). Today, most of the Chilliwack River drainage north of the Canada-U.S. border is protected, as are the Post Creek and Radium Creek drainages. This is exciting news for Lower Mainland day trippers who have explored this area's trails and waters for decades. It's also beneficial to wildlife populations of grizzly bear, spotted owl and amphibians such as the Pacific giant salamander. The latter is no Komodo dragon, but at 30 cm (12 inches), two-thirds of which is tail, the province's largest salamander is as startling to encounter as a large mammal. Just as arresting is the sight of the rugged peaks that rise on all sides of Chilliwack Lake. The urge to get close to them is hard to suppress.

If you decide to camp at Chilliwack Lake Park, you may be lucky enough to find room beneath some large ponderosa pines at lakeside. There are 146 campsites in all. The best ones are situated on a bluff overlooking the lake, with a wide sandy beach below. A fee of $12 is charged when the campground is open from April to October. There's also a boat launch here suited to large watercraft.

POST CREEK–GREENDROP LAKE TRAIL The Post Creek trailhead lies just north of the provincial campground. What makes this such a desirable destination for day trippers is that along much of the 6-km (3.7-mi.) trail up Post Creek to Lindeman and Greendrop

Lakes are some of the largest stands of old-growth trees in the Lower Mainland. Within minutes after starting up the trail the first giant firs appear and you will know you're on the right track.

The steepest part of the trail, at the very beginning, is hardly daunting, even from the pint-size perspective of a youngster. In half an hour you reach turquoise-tinted Lindeman Lake, where rainbow trout play. Around the lake's east end a boardwalk staircase helps surmount a stretch of scree. Above, some classic craggy ridges—characteristic of the Cascade Mountains, which under one name or another run from here to the Mexican border—ring the lake.

For many visitors, the sight of Lindeman Lake will be rewarding enough. However, should you persevere for a further 2 hours, there is an extraordinary sight waiting at Greendrop Lake. Giant red cedars sink their roots into the mountain slope above the lake. In places, the massed roots feed right out of the lake. Reminiscent of mangroves in a bayou swamp or the giants at Carmanah, these trees taper skyward 50 m (nearly 200 ft.) or more in many instances.

Along the way to Greendrop Lake the trail passes through a rain forest environment. Patches of prickly devil's club occur frequently beside the open, well-marked trail. There's always the sound of rushing water at hand. Occasionally some snow lingers even in summer, camouflaged by a layer of fallen needles. The Skagit Valley lies just below Greendrop's eastern end.

CHILLIWACK LAKE The peaks of the Cascade Mountains' Skagit Range surround the shores of Chilliwack Lake. It's 14 km (8.7 mi.) from the north end of Chilliwack Lake to its south end. For much of the way the two-lane gravel road is level and runs alongside or just above the lake, turning away briefly to cross bridges over Paleface and Depot Creeks. There is a wide, sandy beach at the mouths of both Paleface and Depot Creeks. Paleface is the easier of the two to access, particularly for windsurfers. An old road into Depot Creek has been closed, but it only takes a few minutes to walk downhill onto Depot's sandy delta.

Paleface Creek is an ideal staging area if you bring bicycles, boats or even horses, as some folks do. Windsurfers love the winds that are almost guaranteed to blow across the lake daily. The lake is often whipped up by winds funnelling out to the coast, so be cautious when out in a small boat.

There is a sandy beach at Chilliwack Lake's south end as well. The Chilliwack River has been depositing fine sand here for as long as it has run into the lake. This is one beautiful beach, especially with the views of Mount Lindeman directly to the west and, farther north, Macdonald Peak and Mount Webb. Suddenly, Vancouver feels very far away. These peaks have a distinct geological history, and it shows in their cragginess. Get out the binoculars for a close-up look at the crenellated ridges.

UPPER CHILLIWACK RIVER TRAIL Follow the well-worn track that leads behind the beach at the lake's south end to where the upper Chilliwack River, which originates on the American side of the border, flows into the lake. The Upper Chilliwack River Trail is clearly marked by a large brown wooden stake on the left side of an old road, about 100 m (just over 300 ft.) before the bank of the river. It leads into an ecologically sensitive area, and visitors are reminded to stick to the trail, as footprints kill tender roots.

Enormous old-growth cedars surround you almost as soon as you begin walking the well-maintained pathway. Groves of these giants, some of them 3 to 4 m (10 to 13 ft.) in diameter, feed on the steady supply of water from the nearby river. The upper Chilliwack River usually crests in late June, then drops during the summer. Wide sandbars lie exposed in many places until autumn rains bring water levels up once more. The river gurgles along past the ecological reserve, where most of the riparian forest is preserved. Signs posted high on several behemoths mark the boundaries of the reserve, which covers an area approximately 3 km (1.9 mi.) long, stretching to the Canada-U.S. border.

Amble upstream in search of a perfect picnic spot. If you're careful, you can cross the river atop several large blowdowns early on where the trail divides. A large sandbar stands exposed here, one of the few open places where light penetrates the wide overhanging limbs of the forest.

Press on along the main trail to the international border, a clearing 12 m (40 ft.) wide running up the slope on the west side of the river. Fortunately, the clearing that marks the 49th parallel doesn't extend right down to the river, so the forest next to the river remains undisturbed. South of the border, the trail begins to deteriorate as it passes through marshier sections, a good place to turn back to the lake.

33 SKAGIT VALLEY

DISTANCE: 210 km (130 mi.) east and south of Vancouver

ACTIVITIES: Bird watching, boating, camping, cycling, fishing, hiking, picnicking, playground, nature observation, stargazing, swimming, walking, windsurfing

HIGHLIGHTS: Wide, wild jewel of a valley

ACCESS: The road into the Skagit Valley begins off the Trans-Canada Highway (Highway 1) on the western outskirts of Hope, about 150 km (93 mi.) east of Vancouver. Leave the Trans-Canada at Exit 165. Drive a short distance to the well-marked Silver/Skagit Road turnoff in the settlement of Silver Creek. A sign at the start of the road, posted for the benefit of American visitors headed for an outpost of their country at the road's southern end, announces "Hozomeen 38 miles" (or 61 km). There are no services along this wide and well-maintained road, so make sure to fill your tank at one of the local service stations in or near Hope.

Come sit beside the crystal-clear waters of the Skagit River, deep within a long valley that stretches 70 km (43.5 mi.) south from the eastern Fraser Valley town of Hope to the Canada-U.S. border. Here's a place where you can follow the changing seasons: smell the rich humus as the earth begins to warm in spring, or listen to the wind in the dry leaves of the trembling aspen trees above, whispering that nature has entered the transition zone between summer and autumn. Walk or cycle the network of roads and trails, or paddle a boat to a wilderness site on Ross Lake for a picnic. Fishing for rainbow trout in the Skagit's waters is still one of the biggest drawing cards here. Come the end of the day, there are plenty of camping spots from which to choose, should you be fortunate enough to have time to spend a night or two. On clear evenings the Milky Way pours out across the open sky above you. By comparison, what we see in the city starscape are, indeed, *skim* pickings.

Skagit River with Silvertip Mountain above

In spring and fall, this important migration corridor fills with
dozens of species of birds and mammals on the move. Year-round,
its vastness is inhabited by hundreds of species of birds, reptiles,
amphibians and most of the common B.C. mammals. Elk and
mountain goats frequent the higher mountains. Several ecological
reserves in the valley feature virgin stands of Douglas fir, western
red cedar and ponderosa pine.

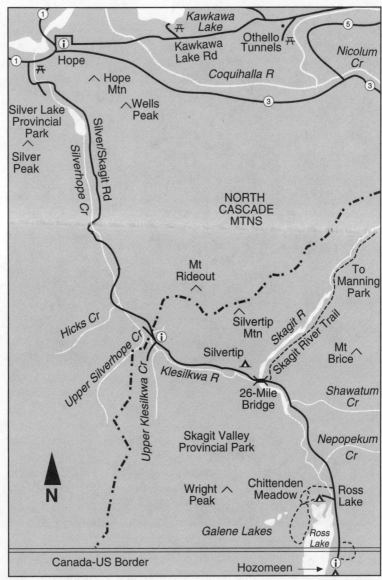

Skagit Valley and Hope area

SILVER LAKE PROVINCIAL PARK Silver/Skagit Road is paved for a short distance, then becomes well-graded gravel as it follows Silverhope Creek. Silver Lake Park lies 6 km (3.7 mi.) south. Drive 1 km

(0.6 mi.) in from the main road to reach this small lake, which is popular with locals in warm-weather months. Families come here to fish together, sometimes from old logs jutting out from the shoreline. The bottom drops off rapidly at the lake's north end, and the best swimming is at the south end of the park road. The road running along the west side of the lake leads down a narrow, treed lane to a sandy section on the bank of Silverhope Creek near where it enters the lake. This is a good picnic area, especially if you aren't planning to drive much farther south into the Skagit. Regular flooding has carved deep potholes in the fast-flowing creek. Diving into them from the thick tree trunks on the riverbank is a chilly challenge.

Windsurfers on Silver Lake enjoy the breeze that frequently gusts through the valley and that gives the Hope region such a favourable reputation for gliding. Rugged cliffs rise above the east side of the lake, with Hope Mountain and Wells Peak's jagged teeth preeminent on the skyline. The high walls catch sunlight at the beginning or end of day in a way that emphasizes the subtle colours in them, shades of iron-red above the evergreens. The trees at lakeside are aspen, water birch and cottonwood, all silver-green in summer, golden in autumn.

As Silver/Skagit Road heads south of Silver Lake, it parallels one of North America's finest river systems for fishing. Along the way, first at Silverhope Creek, then at the Klesilkwa River and finally at the Skagit River, fly-fishers pull off at designated parking spots to try for rainbow trout. Open season is summer and fall, when there are several strong runs. Watch for postings along the way. The area around the Silvertip campground (see below), where the Klesilkwa flows into the Skagit, is especially popular. Fishing is strictly catch-and-release here on the Skagit, with only barbless hooks permitted.

SKAGIT VALLEY PROVINCIAL PARK Nearly 40 km (25 mi.) south of Silver Lake along the winding gravel road, a large wooden information kiosk marks the western boundary of Skagit Valley Park. It's worth a stop to read about the natural history of the valley, which is the transition zone between the Interior and the Coast, a medley of coastal forest, open meadows populated with prairie species, subalpine and alpine areas, and marshes, all of which create a special biological mosaic.

Just south of the kiosk is the Silvertip provincial campground, one of the best-organized sites in the Skagit. From April to October there is a nightly charge of about $12 per site. Silvertip has 43 well-spaced campsites, seven of which sit on the north bank of the Skagit River.

The forest at this site is much more typical of the region than that at Silver Lake. Douglas fir and red cedar blend with western hemlock and lodgepole pine. Ponderosa pines climb the slopes of Silvertip Mountain and Mount Rideout to the north. Cool breezes come down off the slopes of Mount Rideout (2447 m/8028 ft.). It has a twin, Mount Redoubt (2730 m/8956 ft.), due south across the border, the tallest peak of six that are grouped between Chilliwack and Ross Lakes, including Nodoubt Peak.

At Silvertip, the Skagit River makes its grand entrance into the valley at 26 Mile Bridge, flowing in from its headwaters to the north in Manning Park. From here it heads to its eventual union with the Pacific near the town of Mount Vernon in Washington state's Skagit County. There's a small day-use area on the north side of the bridge with four picnic tables and plenty of parking. An information marker posted beside the river recounts the history of the Whatcom Trail, a section of which lies on the opposite bank. The 1850s Cariboo gold rush tempted Americans to build a 430-km (267-mi.) supply trail from the town of Whatcom (now Bellingham) to the Thompson River. In this way they hoped to circumvent customs and excise tax collectors stationed at the mouth of the Fraser River. The trail opened on August 17, 1858, but was abruptly abandoned two months later. Maintenance proved difficult and the route itself was just too long.

SKAGIT RIVER TRAIL To get a bit of a workout, try a section of the popular 15-km (9.3-mi.) Skagit River Trail (the old Whatcom Trail) that runs northeast from 26 Mile Bridge to Sumallo Grove in Manning Park. The first 3 km (1.9 mi.) make for an easy bicycle ride before the trail begins a short, steep climb along the edge of an extensive ancient scree slope. (If you wish to explore farther, leave your bike here.) One note of caution: in late summer, be on the lookout for bears foraging for berries along this initial part of the trail.

Red trail markers affixed to trees count down the kilometres, beginning at 14 near the bridge and decreasing as you head towards Manning Park. Treats along the way include views of nearby Silvertip Mountain and its retreating glacier, a copse of rare wild rhododendrons that bloom red in June, sandbars exposed on the Skagit and a provincial ecological reserve at km 9 protecting the stand of tall cedar and fir here. Just before the trail reaches the reserve, it crosses 28 Mile Creek. At times of high water, crossing the slim log bridge here is tricky. Tread cautiously.

CHITTENDEN MEADOW TRAIL The Skagit is a special valley because of its U-shaped profile, a rare configuration in southwestern B.C., where most valleys are steep-sided Vs dominated by high mountains. The trails through Chittenden Meadow, 16 km (10 mi.) south of the Silvertip campground, show off the valley's grandeur as the valley bottom spreads out before you. It's easy to see what attracted Washington politicians in the 1950s and 1960s, who wanted to clear trees from the American side of the valley to create the Ross Lake Reservoir. The trees were cut, and, backed up behind the Ross and Diablo Dams, the waters of the Skagit River are drawn down through hydroelectric turbines to provide power for the Seattle area.

From here on the Canadian side, it's equally evident why conservationists such as Wilfred (Curly) Chittenden, after whom the meadow is named, worked so hard to protect the valley from further flooding in the 1970s, when the governments of Washington and British Columbia seemed poised to expand the perimeter of Ross Lake north beyond the border.

Curly Chittenden was a legendary figure who died in 1995. Born in Bradner in the Fraser Valley in the early part of this century, the son of one of B.C.'s early explorers, he worked as a logger for most of his life. In 1953, he was contracted to log 200 ha (500 acres) of the Skagit Valley floor, now the Canadian end of Ross Lake. Later, when the government asked him to log even more, including the stately ponderosa pines (unique in this region because they are so far west of their usual habitat), he categorically refused and instead began lobbying for the meadowland's preservation. Thanks to his vision, the pines and surrounding meadow were saved as part of the 32,508 ha (80,326 acres) set aside by the provincial government in late 1973.

A gentle trail meanders through Chittenden Meadow, leading past a series of interpretive markers. To reach the meadow, park beside the Skagit River and cross the suspension bridge. Trail maps are usually available from the BC Parks kiosk located at the beginning of the meadow trail on the west side of the suspension bridge. The level, hard-packed Chittenden Meadow trail branches off in several directions and leads towards Ross Lake. (A trail leads north from the west side of the bridge to several good fishing spots. Depending on your technique, you can either cast from the riverbank or don waterproof gear and wade in. You'll find a cozy campsite here beneath the sheltering limbs of five magnificent red cedars, from which there is a view of Silvertip and Shawatum Mountains to the north and east.)

One of the best ways to tour the meadow is by bicycle along the old logging roads that double as pathways through the meadow. For example, from marker "4" follow a faint trail west that soon becomes much more distinct as it leads to a sign that points towards International Creek. Follow this trail as it leads through the overhanging forest, eventually emerging at the northwest corner of the lake. From here, ride through the field of stumps and tall grass back towards the meadow. A branch of the trail leads to the nearby Ross Lake campground. Allow an hour to do the trail by bike.

Cycling the trails imparts an enhanced sense of the flatness of the valley bottom that you won't otherwise experience as you pass beneath its stands of tall cottonwoods. Come fall, their leaves turn a vivid gold. At that time of year there's such a stillness in the air that the leaves make a racket as they tumble down.

ROSS LAKE PROVINCIAL CAMPGROUND Ross Lake spreads across the international border at the south end of the Skagit Valley, 65 km (40.4 mi.) from Hope. A campground and day-use area here overlook the lake. Some of the campsites are more exposed to the elements than at Silvertip, but most are sheltered in a forested area. Parents will find the nearby children's play area handy to the beach and boat launch, with a panoramic view south over the lake as well. From April to October there is a charge of about $12 per night for the use of a campsite. The park is set back a short distance from the main road. Chittenden Meadow is just 1 km (0.6 mi.) north of here. *Note:* Depending on rainfall, the time of the year and the demand for power at the Diablo generating station, Ross Lake may be full to the brim ("full pool," as it's officially designated) or there may be stumps showing above the surface. In summer, the water in the big lake is much warmer than the cold river, making this an ideal place to swim.

HOZOMEEN Just south of the Ross Lake campground lies the international border. There are no lengthy line-ups for customs inspections at the Hozomeen crossing. As the connecting road only leads several kilometres south of Skagit Valley Park into the Ross Lake National Recreation Area (itself a portion of the much larger North Cascades National Park), there's no border patrol stationed here, only a team of U.S. park rangers who greet visitors with a friendly wave. There's no need for heightened security—the rugged back-country and flooded valley floor provide a natural barrier. In a heartening display of bipartisanship, a well-stocked rack of trail maps and visitor information for both Skagit Valley and Ross Lake fronts the A-frame ranger station. Stop here for information on wilderness campsites on 37-km-long (23-mi.-long) Ross Lake.

Just past the ranger station is a boat launch, a beach and a cleared area dubbed Winnebago Flats, with a dozen campsites beside the lake. All the amenities provided at the two provincial campgrounds north of here are also present at Hozomeen. A trail runs south along the beach to a distant headland, an enjoyable stretch for your legs. Although there is plenty of driftwood for campfires strewn on the beach, signs politely suggest you try camping without one. Loons, Canada geese and dabbling and diving ducks populate the shoreline along with hundreds of tiny frogs. Aside from their various calls, cries and croaks, this is a very quiet environment most of the time. It does get busy on the major American holidays in summer, when water levels are kept high.

On the benchland above the beach are dozens of additional campsites, although with diminished views of the lake. Drinking-water pumps, picnic tables and toilets are also located here. Unlike on the Canadian side, camping in Ross Lake National Recreation Area's Hozomeen campground is free. Now *that's* an exchange rate you can afford.

As a warm-up to some of the longer hikes in the region, stretch your legs on the 1.3-km (0.8-mi.) Trail of the Obelisk that leads a short distance uphill east from the ranger station onto a ridge above the lake. Your destination is a metre-tall aluminum obelisk on the international boundary. Looking west across the valley, you can make out a thin clearing running straight up the mountain that marks the 49th parallel.

Hozomeen Mountain's distinctive peak is prominent on the southern horizon. The hike up its slope to Hozomeen Ridge is not particularly difficult and can be accomplished in 2 or 3 hours. Your reward will be a commanding view of Ross Lake, the Skagit Valley with the river's course clearly outlined and an eyeful of other North Cascade peaks.

34 HOPE & ENVIRONS

DISTANCE: 165 km (102 mi.) east of Vancouver

ACTIVITIES: Cycling, historic sites, nature observation,
            picnicking, swimming, walking

HIGHLIGHTS: The Othello-Quintette tunnels, one of B.C.'s
            most extraordinary provincial parks

ACCESS: Drive 138 km (85.6 mi.) east to Hope via the
            Trans-Canada Highway (Highway 1). Follow signs
            to the Coquihalla Highway (Highway 5). About
            15 km (9.3 mi.) east of Hope on Highway 5, take
            Exit 183. Drive west across the highway overpass
            to the Coquihalla Canyon Recreation Area and
            nearby Kawkawa Lake Park. (*Note:* In winter, all
            road signs are removed.) Alternatively, from
            Hope follow Kawkawa Lake Road, then Othello
            Road, a distance of 7 km (4.3 mi.). Kawkawa Lake
            is 2.4 km (1.5 mi.) north of Hope. The Othello-
            Quintette tunnels are 4.4 km (2.7 mi.) farther
            north. (See map page 160.)

If it weren't for the wonder derived from a visit to the Othello-Quintette tunnels, this would be almost too lengthy a day trip. Almost. This is a journey back in time to British Columbia's frontier past.

HOPE Hope's origins are in the fur trade. Fort Hope was one of the Hudson's Bay Company trading posts, built on the trail linking Fort Kamloops and Fort Langley. The British needed an overland route that would let them cross the mountains without having to tack south into American territory, and their hopes were realized when the trail opened in 1849.

Although the Ministry of Transportation seems intent on moving traffic around Hope, instead of through the pretty little river town, make a point of stopping here. A Travel Info Centre kiosk and the Hope Museum are located at the south end of Hope's main street, which fronts on the Fraser River. The Info Centre is a font of up-to-date news and directions to other sights within the Hope area. Look

Othello-Quintette tunnels near Hope

for the waterwheel, part of the restored Home Gold Mine, mounted next to the kiosk.

If you're looking for some baked goodies for your picnic, find your way to the bakery nearby. As you make your way around town, you'll notice large wooden carvings of animals mounted everywhere. A particularly colourful time to see Hope is the second full weekend in September, when the town hosts Brigade Days, a celebration of its pioneer past.

COQUIHALLA CANYON RECREATION AREA A modest trail leads from the parking lot beside picnic tables on the banks of the clear Coquihalla River. So far, so unassuming. All that changes as you walk out on the reconstructed bridges that cross the river gorge and link with four hand-chiselled tunnels. Near the entrance to the first tunnel is a replica of the scaffolding from which workers attacked the rock face. A white sign still marks the whistle stop of Othello. (As you travel the Coquihalla Highway you'll notice other Shakespearean names for former towns, such as Juliet and Iago. They were bestowed by the Kettle Valley Railway's general superintendent, who was a great fan of the Bard.)

These tunnels are not the dark, smoke-blackened, bat-infested places you might imagine. The ceilings are lofty, bleached arches, and sunlight enters from both ends. Unfortunately, the trail beyond the last tunnel is closed because of a rock fall that wiped out part of the old track. Avalanches north of the tunnels were one of the main causes of the railway's closure in 1965. (*Note:* In winter, dangerous conditions due to loose rock and ice shut down the park.)

A gold rush in the West Kootenays was the impetus behind the creation of not only these tunnels but an impressive series of other ones along the Kettle Valley Railway line, which linked Nelson with Canadian Pacific's main line at the east end of the Fraser Valley. In British Columbia, railway construction has always been the subject of controversy. The trail leads about 1.5 km (1 mi.) through tunnels that once supported track that cost $300,000 to lay in 1914. Almost all of the work was done by hand, hence the enormous expense. This is still considered the most costly mile of railway track in the world.

Most of this detail will sail right over the heads of children. What will really impress them here will be the solid presence of the rock, the rushing sound of the creek as it bores its way through the canyon, and the views from the bridges that link the tunnels. Although the tunnels are solid, ground water occasionally drips from above; darkness almost, but not quite, overtakes the daylight in the middle of the longest tunnel. The effect created here couldn't possibly be replicated elsewhere.

After the trains stopped running, Hope residents removed the wooden ties and smoothed out the railbed into a broad recreation trail, now part of the Trans Canada Trail that opened in 2000. Another option is to explore the roads around the tunnels on mountain bikes. The terrain has a pleasant, rolling aspect to it and is well worth a day trip.

KAWKAWA LAKE PARK The word *kawkawa* is a poetic term in the Halkomelem language that means "much calling of loons." See how many times you can repeat it without cracking up. Kawkawa Lake Park is a quiet, roadside municipal park with grassy picnic grounds fronted by a beach and boat launch. In summer, you'll appreciate the lake's warm water. Forest shades the approach and shelters the road between here and the Coquihalla Canyon Recreation Area.

If you are in the area during salmon spawning season, follow Kawkawa Lake Road east of Hope as it passes over the Coquihalla River. A municipal park is situated on the west bank of the river. On the other side, Union Bar Road leads off to the left past Kawkawa Creek, which flows into the Coquihalla at this point. A fish ladder for returning salmon has been constructed here, and you may be fortunate enough to see the spawning run in September. A boardwalk has been installed beside the creek to give a close-up view of the action.

FRASER RIVER ESTUARY

35 IONA & SEA ISLANDS

DISTANCE: 15 km (9 mi.) south of Vancouver, in Richmond

ACTIVITIES: Bird watching, cycling, paddling, picnicking, stargazing, viewpoints, walking

HIGHLIGHTS: Panoramic views of Vancouver, the North Shore peaks and the windswept Strait of Georgia from river, beach and jetty trails

ACCESS: Cross the Arthur Laing Bridge at the south end of Granville Street onto Grant McConachie Way. Turn right onto Templeton Street North and follow it across Sea Island to McDonald Beach and Iona Beach Parks.

SEA ISLAND During construction of the north runway at Vancouver International Airport on Sea Island in the early 1990s, a small bay at Richmond's McDonald Beach Park was enlarged to handle the off-loading of material from barges. To make up for the loss of habitat, Transport Canada converted an old sand stockpile east of the park into marsh as part of the newly created Sea Island Conservation Area. Replanted with sedges, rushes, dune barley and snowberry bushes, it has become even more attractive as Wood's roses, Pacific crabapples, willows and black cottonwoods have taken hold.

An 11-km (6.8-mi.) dike trail runs through the conservation area beside the airport and the Fraser River along Sea Island's northern perimeter. One of the best places to begin exploring is McDonald Beach Park, a municipal landmark since the 1850s. As well as being a good place to picnic, launch a boat, buy some bait or just watch the river flow, it also provides the best place for parking. From here, it's your choice: cycle or walk the trail west towards Iona Beach Regional Park (about 7 km/4.3 mi. one way), or head east towards the Arthur Laing Bridge (about 4 km/2.5 mi.). This place is also a dog magnet, and the canines seem to enjoy it as much as anyone. A grassy field on the east side of McDonald Beach Park is where many visitors with large dogs head for some ball tossing.

Views from the trail are both varied and grand. Close at hand, hefty tugboats parade along the Fraser River's North Arm like muscle cars on Kingsway. They put out a wake that you could bodysurf

McDonald Beach Park, Sea Island

on. A brow of mansions on Marine Drive dominate the ridge above Vancouver's Southlands neighbourhood. North Shore peaks rising behind them add yet another layer. Look southeast. On a clear day you get an impeccable view of Mount Baker profiled against the sky. To the south, alders and cottonwoods shield the airport from view. Late on a sunny afternoon, a lipstick sunset smears the western horizon.

IONA ISLAND Iona Island is a wild, windswept place with a slender scissor-shaped nose jutting out into Sturgeon Bank, ending at Point No Point. It sits at the mouth of the North Arm of the Fraser River, with the Musqueam Indian Reserve across the water on one hand, and Sea Island on the other. From the entrance to Iona Beach Regional

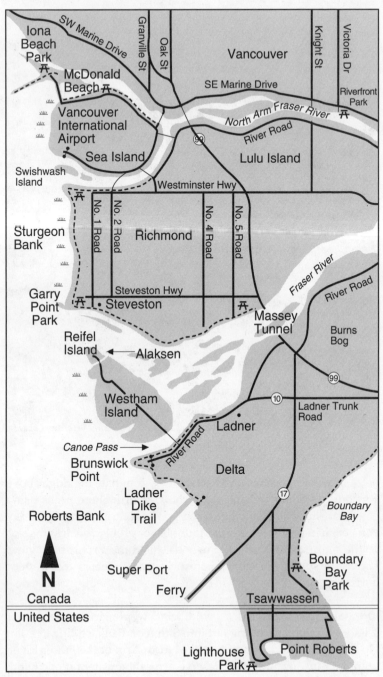

Fraser River Estuary

Sea Island Conservation Area trail

Park you can fan out to explore the sheltered or exposed sides of the island, so evidently shaped by sediment dumped at the ocean's doorstep by the Fraser River.

As you near the regional park entrance the road passes over a causeway built in the early part of this century to link Sea Island and Iona. McDonald Slough, on the east side of the road, is often lined with log booms. The road swings west past a sewage treatment plant to the park gates. Leave your car here if you plan to be in the park after sunset, as the gate is locked at dusk except on special occasions, such as stargazing evenings.

During the day birders fill their eyes with the sights of Iona's migrating flocks; stargazing visitors benefit from the increased darkness of the sky here, unhindered by the glare of city streetlights. The GVRD's Catch a Falling Star astronomy program brings high-powered telescopes from the Southam Observatory to Iona on a regular basis. There are also slide shows at the interpretive centre and hot refreshments available to ward off the crisp night air. On all your trips to Iona, be sure to dress warmly, including a hat to protect your ears against the wind blowing off the Strait of Georgia.

Iona Island is a stopover for thousands of migrating birds. More rare birds are seen here than anywhere else in the province. Mallards and teals dabble in the ocean over the tidal flats. Loons, grebes and herons fill their long curved gullets with abundant marine life found in the sheltered lagoons. Pairs of round-faced great horned, short-eared and screech owls glide by on silent wings; rare burrowing owls occasionally nest in the sand dunes that cover much of the island. Binoculars will help you see right into the thick of the flocks of dunlin that gather by the thousands on the shoreline. Depending on the height of the tide, they can be as close as the parking lot when you arrive, or you may have to head out along the long southern jetty to see them feed while the ocean ebbs. When startled, they lift off in a dizzying pattern of alternating black and white as they swoop and swirl. A predator would be hard-pressed to tell where the flock is from one moment to the next.

But you don't need binoculars to see birdlife at close range. Stalk the gently rolling reaches of the island. Find a sheltered spot beside a lagoon and watch as it comes to life, revealing itself as you wait in patient stillness. A quiet season like autumn lends itself to such unobtrusive observation.

Iona's air quality is no longer heavily influenced by the nearby sewage-treatment plant, thanks to an outfall pipe, and the 4-km (2.5-mi.) jetty over which the pipeline runs is a hard-packed gravel walkway. The service road that parallels the pipeline doubles as a cycle path. There are two Plexiglas shelters, located at the middle and end of the jetty, that allow visitors to escape the winds off the Strait of Georgia and at the same time provide an unobstructed bird's-eye view of Sturgeon Bank. Across the strait, Vancouver Island is outlined against the western sky. Closer, the mountains on the North Shore stand out, with no office towers blocking the view. For photographers who enjoy capturing a sunrise or sunset, these shelters are ideal places to position a camera. For information on Iona Beach, call the GVRD at 604-432-6359 or 604-224-5739, or visit their Web site: www.gvrd.bc.ca/services/parks/.

36 RICHMOND DIKE TRAILS & HISTORIC STEVESTON

DISTANCE:	15 km (9.3 mi.) south and west of the Oak Street Bridge
ACTIVITIES:	Bird watching, cycling, historic sites, kite-flying, paddling, picnicking, sightseeing, viewpoints, walking
HIGHLIGHTS:	Steveston's historic Cannery Row, a cycling trail that just won't quit and a park where kite-flyers hold on with both hands
ACCESS:	From Highway 99 South, take the Steveston Highway West exit (#32) just before the George Massey Tunnel and follow it to downtown Steveston. (See map page 172.) For information about getting to Richmond (including Steveston) by bus, call TransLink at 604-953-3333 or visit their Web site: www.translink.bc.ca.

Sea Island and most of Lulu Island, as well as a number of smaller islands in the Fraser River, comprise the municipality of Richmond. There's a special spot on Lulu Island that has drawn settlers since the turn of the century—former citizens of Finland, Japan and the sovereign nation of Newfoundland, for instance. The first arrivals gathered on the southwestern corner of the island at Steveston, named for a member of the Steves family, who settled here in 1877 upon their arrival from New Brunswick.

Construction of protective dikes along the western shore of Lulu Island was one of the first priorities for the newcomers. These have been improved over time and now provide a level surface that stretches for 77 km (48 mi.). Many of the old farm homes have disappeared, but enough of the original flavour of early settlement remains to make this westerly stretch of dike and historic Steveston a must-see for local adventurers. It's also a jumping-off point for exploring the whole of Richmond's western shore. Take an hour or plan an entire day to enjoy the surroundings.

Steveston and Mount Baker

GARRY POINT PARK AND WEST DYKE TRAIL If you drive to the western end of Steveston Highway, where it meets the dike at Seventh Avenue, you'll find parking for six vehicles. In another 2 minutes you can be at Garry Point Park, with parking for 60. Simply drive several blocks south along Seventh to reach the park. It's located two blocks west of the federal wharf, which forms the heart of revitalized Steveston.

Early on weekend mornings, groups of kayakers assemble at Garry Point while families on bikes head north along the West Dyke Trail and sun lovers perch on the driftwood of nearby beaches. The Canadian Coast Guard hydrofoil might skim noisily past, throwing up sea spray around its rubber skirts as it patrols the mouth of the Fraser River and around into Cannery Channel. Long-necked Steveston Island lies directly offshore, shielding from view parts of the river and the town of Ladner on the far shore. A small Japanese rock garden, opened in 1988, draws the attention of grandparents and toddlers alike; it is dedicated to the memory of the first immigrants from Japan's Wakayama Prefecture, who arrived in 1888.

For those with rubber boots and a desire to get out onto nearby Sturgeon Bank, a hillocky trail heads west off the main trail at Garry Point and out into the marsh just north of a weathered marina's dock and boathouse. The brackish marsh renews its vegetation of cattails, bulrushes, eelgrass and sedges every spring, and the air here is filled with bird calls. You can often count a half-dozen or more different territorial melodies at once, punctuated by the incongruous crowing of a rooster from a nearby farm. Although there are picnic tables at several spots along the dike trail, out on Sturgeon Bank you'll have to make do with a piece of driftwood. You can see here what much of Lulu Island must have looked like before dikes were built to begin to reclaim the land in the first half of this century.

The West Dyke Trail runs in an almost straight north-south line along the western perimeter of Lulu Island, a distance of 5.5 km (3.4 mi.). It's well used, especially on weekends. You can ride along at an easy pace, covering the entire distance one way in approximately 40 minutes.

MIDDLE ARM TRAIL As the West Dyke Trail rounds the northwestern tip of Lulu Island, it passes the parking area at the west end of River Road in the Terra Nova neighbourhood. There are picnic tables and toilets located here. The Middle Arm of the Fraser River meets the Strait of Georgia at this point. Low-lying Swishwash Island nestles offshore, with Sea Island and the airport beyond to the north. The pier at Dover Beach is an excellent spot to watch activity on the river, as across the channel jets muscle their way skyward and propeller-driven planes feather in for a landing at the seaplane dock on Moray Channel.

The Middle Arm Trail covers an east-west route beside the Middle Arm of the Fraser from Terra Nova to the Moray Bridge, a distance of 5.5 km (3.4 mi.). Distance markers beside the trail help you monitor your progress. In spring months the pungent green smell of willow buds and broom fills the air here. Nearby, in the shallows of the Fraser, dabbling ducks, Canada geese, herons and gulls feast on vegetation and small marine creatures.

The dike trail continues east along the Middle Arm, past the No. 2 Road and Dinsmore Bridges. The No. 2 Road Bridge, with its circular pedestrian ramp, is the best connection to take you across to Sea Island. A dike trail continues along the banks of the Fraser in both directions. If you head west, you pass Vancouver airport's South Terminal and several floatplane wharves and finally arrive at the gates of the coast guard station, a comfortable 15-minute ride from the bridge. Nearby is a clearing beside a stand of cottonwoods where you can picnic.

STEVESTON VILLAGE With more than a thousand boats moored in the harbour year round, Steveston has the distinction of being the largest maritime fishing community in Canada. If there's an old folks' home for tired ships, this must be it, for collected around the harbour are all manner and size of boats that would appear to have sailed their last. How much longer many of the other, livelier-looking ones will be in service depends on the continuing strength of the commercial fishery. Down Steveston way, the fishery is definitely on the wane, but it wasn't always so.

To gain an appreciation for Steveston's fishing history, visit the restored Gulf of Georgia Cannery, which originally opened in 1894. Reopened a century later as a national historic site, it presents visitors with one of the most realistic re-creations imaginable. Although the display makes the operation of the canning line easy to understand, be sure to take in the video presentation in the Boiler House Theatre just inside the remodelled entranceway. This 20-minute introduction to the entire canning process includes archival footage from the industry's heyday.

The Gulf of Georgia Cannery National Historic Site, located at 12138 Fourth Avenue, is open daily from 10 A.M. to 5 P.M. during the summer. Admission is $4 for adults and $2 for children between the ages of 6 and 16. The exhibits at the cannery have been designed with flair and on a scale that will appeal to both young and old.

Several blocks east of the cannery at the south foot of Railway Avenue is Britannia Heritage Shipyard. A brochure outlining a self-guided tour is available at the shipyard and details much of the history of the site, as fascinating in its own right as the historic cannery.

The focal point of Steveston's redevelopment is the government wharf. Fishing boats with poetic names are tied up along rows of docks. You can buy seafood directly from many of the boats: shrimp, squid, snapper, tuna, sole, cod and salmon are all available—in season—at good prices. For those with an immediate hunger, Pajo's floating café nearby serves up fish and chips along with a local favourite, steaming mushy peas.

Many new buildings constructed in the village retain the architectural flavour of old Steveston. One of the best ways to be introduced to Steveston is to join the block-by-block public tour offered by the Steveston Historical Society every Thursday during the summer at 1 P.M. For more information, contact the Steveston Museum, 604-271-6868.

If you wish to explore Steveston and the nearby dike trails by bike, rentals can be arranged at Steveston Bikes, at Second Avenue and Chatham (604-271-5544).They also rent trailers to tow kids behind.

SOUTH DYKE TRAIL The South Dyke Trail begins at the south end of No. 2 Road, Richmond's original thoroughfare. Not only are aged riverboats moored here, but the history of habitation in the south-

Steveston waterfront

western corner of Lulu Island—with the exception of the First Nations—is also detailed in words, drawings and archival photographs at several places along the dike. (Interpretive signs highlight places of local interest throughout the Richmond dike trail system.) On weekends many local residents get out their bikes for rides with family and friends. Lightly travelled Dyke Road parallels the trail.

A large wharf at the foot of No. 2 Road juts out into Cannery Channel. A gangplank leads down to a small floating dock at the far end. You could launch a hand-carried boat from it and quickly paddle across to nearby Steveston Island. Tall black cottonwoods and poplars cover the slender island. Large nests can be seen in their upper branches, home to herons and eagles. Reifel Island's migratory bird sanctuary lies just across the wide South Arm of the Fraser River.

Interpretive signs on the wharf acquaint visitors with the history of London's Landing, named for the first family to settle here, in 1885. They were the first ones to dike and farm on Lulu Island. Given the growth of Richmond since then, it's fascinating to stand where the first government wharf, school and post office were located. Just east of the wharf on Dyke Road is the entrance to London Heritage Farm, which was acquired by Richmond in 1974. The farm is open to visitors daily. A parking lot and a boat launch are located directly across Dyke Road.

Picnic tables and benches appear regularly along the South Dyke Trail. Watch for Mount Baker's ghostly profile to appear floating in the southern sky at the intersection of Dyke and Gilbert Roads. At this point you are several kilometres east of the Steveston docks.

The dike trail leads east beside the South Arm of the Fraser River all the way to the George Massey Tunnel. You can cycle this comfortably in half an hour, ending at a small municipal park at the south end of No. 5 Road in an area called Woodwards Landing. Along the way the trail passes a sleepy backwater known informally as Finn Slough. Ancient boathouses, riverbank shanties and float homes shelter in the lee of Gilmour Island, protected from storms and the wakes of large ocean freighters making their way to or from loading docks farther upriver. Much like Peggy's Cove in Nova Scotia, Finn Slough has been the subject of many paintings and photographs. Development pressures that have recently been felt along Steveston's waterfront now threaten to overtake this small enclave as well. While its fate hangs in the balance, get out and see for yourself. You can drive directly to Finn Slough; turn south from Steveston Highway on No. 4 Road and continue until in several minutes the road reaches the South Dyke Trail.

37 BURNS BOG

DISTANCE: About 30 km (18 mi.) southeast of Vancouver, in Delta

ACTIVITIES: Cycling, nature observation, walking

HIGHLIGHTS: Sheltered rain forest trails and mossy pathways lead through the largest piece of remaining wilderness in any urban centre in Canada

ACCESS: To reach Delta Watershed Park, follow Highway 91 south to 64th Avenue (Kittson Parkway), then travel east towards 120th Street. The park and a variety of entry points appear on your right.

There are several approaches to the Delta Nature Reserve. Take the 72nd Avenue exit east from Highway 91, then turn north (left) on 112th Street. Turn west (left) onto Monroe Drive beside Sungod Arena and drive several blocks to 108th Street. A trail leads downhill into the nature reserve from the main entrance here. An alternative route begins next to the Side Track Neighbourhood Pub on River Road under the south end of the Alex Fraser Bridge. Follow a gravel road behind the pub that parallels the Burlington Northern railway track and diminutive Cougar Creek until it passes under the Nordel Way on-ramp. The reserve begins here. Watch for the Machine Eating Bog Trail on the west side of the gravel road, followed a few minutes farther south by the Interpretive Loop Trail. (See map page 124.)

B urns Bog is one of the last—and by far the largest—remaining peatlands in the GVRD. Classified as an estrine or estuarine bog, it slowly formed over thousands of years in the delta where the Fraser River enters the Pacific Ocean. The best elevated view of the bog occurs as you head south across the Alex Fraser Bridge, from where it stretches out before you to the south and west. At 2715 ha (6700 acres), it's roughly half the size of nearby Richmond.

Burns Bog is a damp tangle of peat, also known as sphagnum moss. The bog supports an old-growth forest of cedar, hemlock, yew and fir, some of whose perimeter trees—such as in Delta Watershed Park—are as tall as a two-storey building. At the heart of the bog, where it's most damp, these same species have a bonsai appearance, achieving heights of less than a metre. In fact, the sign of a healthy bog is very small trees. Although the forest surrounding Burns Bog as seen from the highway has a scruffy appearance, deeper inside there are stands of remarkably healthy growth.

The image of a bog doesn't resonate with the same seductiveness as that of an ancient rain forest, even if its stunted conifer and sphagnum moss landscape is thousands of years old. (The word "bog" entered the English language from Irish or Gaelic, *bogach*, for wet, spongy ground. The British hold the term in such low esteem that it doubles as slang for lavatory.) In a sudden about-face in the 1990s, bogs went from ugly-duckling status to swanhood as the multifaceted role they play in world ecology took centre stage. Bogs capture and store carbon and nitrogen emissions, they provide habitat for unique flora and fauna, and they bestow a variety of hydrological benefits that include contributing to the health of fish stocks in adjacent river systems. The production of phytoplankton, a primary source of nutrients for fish, depends on organic iron from the lands through which rivers flow, particularly peatlands. Water in the Fraser River is not only cooled by nearby Burns Bog, but fish stocks that feed on phytoplankton are nourished by it as well.

For the moment most of Burns Bog remains off-limits to visitors. Only a small portion is currently designated as parkland. The municipality of Delta has set aside a section of its watershed and created a nature preserve on another 60.8 ha (150 acres). Hopefully this will change once negotiations are concluded between the present owners of the bog and several levels of government, and more of the bog will be preserved.

DELTA WATERSHED PARK If the technically challenging trails on the North Shore are out of your league, perhaps a walk or a bike ride along the much easier trails in Delta Watershed Park might be more your speed. Local horseback riders and joggers also appreciate the smooth trails that wind through the sheltering rain forest. These paths are a joy to discover, especially on a day when you just feel like moving at your own comfortable pace.

Growth here in the densely wooded southeast corner of the bog

Burns Bog

is noticeably different than the sphagnum moss and stunted spruce trees elsewhere. A ridge rises above the bog to the east of Highway 91. Beneath an overstorey of conifers you'll find numerous single-track mountain bike trails connected with several smooth, dirt-surfaced municipal service roads that double as recreational routes.

None of the bike trails are signed. Simply choose one of the numerous pullouts along 64th Avenue as it runs east of Highway 91 towards 120th Street. Begin riding any of the park trails that present themselves, all of which eventually connect with several gated service roads. One of the best single-track trails runs through the forest near a recently built Boy Scout shelter with smooth granite benches and a massive stone fireplace. The trail snakes its way between drooping hemlocks that in many places are spaced just slightly wider than most handlebars. Constructed so that you hardly need to apply your brakes or pedal to maintain your speed, this trail is such a treat that you'll involuntarily whoop with pleasure. As soon as you finish, you'll want to double back and try it again, just for the joy of the ride.

If you're just here for a walk and to view the bog (which looks pretty solid here compared to what you see at the Delta Nature Reserve), follow the main service road to its eastern terminus near the junction of Highways 91 and 99. In 30 minutes you'll arrive at a clearing from where agricultural land spreads out below the park's ridge and runs south to the shore of Mud Bay. Suddenly you are aware of what a welcome buffer the forest here provides from the intrusion of nearby highway sounds.

DELTA NATURE RESERVE Have you seen the bumper sticker that reads "Support Wildlife—Throw a Party"? On National Wildlife Day in April 1994, the municipality of Delta did just that, celebrating the opening of the trails in the new Nature Reserve. The reserve had actually been in place since the early 1970s. However, it took encouragement from the Burns Bog Conservation Society to get Delta to commit to maintaining a trail network in the reserve's eastern portions.

As soon as you begin to explore here, you realize this is the real thing. Hummocks of sphagnum, which are thrust upwards as the moss absorbs and stores water, are crowned with thickets of bog laurel, Labrador tea and salmonberries. In spring their blossoms carpet the bog in pink and white.

As you walk through the bog the expression "Don't get bogged down" springs to mind. The rule of thumb here is if you feel yourself sinking, just walk faster. This sinking feeling defines the mystery that surrounds bogs. A prime example is the sight of a bulldozer all but swallowed now by peat. It lies at the end of a rough track dubbed the Machine Eating Bog Trail that was blazed into the bog a decade ago by a fellow who made off with the piece of heavy equipment from a nearby construction site. For reasons unknown, he rode the behemoth into the bog, then tried to turn around when, too late, he realized he was beginning to sink in the morass. All that's left today is a small portion of the blade.

Although Burns Bog may be a somewhat forbidding place to view from the outside, once you begin to walk the cedar bark–covered trail (whose damper sections are straddled by boardwalks), it becomes a much more inviting environment. Children will find the dwarf forest here just their size. And, although city dwellers are only visitors, they'll be interested to learn that a host of wildlife call the bog home, including lynx, greater sandhill cranes and a resident population of Mariposa copper butterfly.

Plan on taking several hours to enjoy your visit to Burns Bog. If you have time, follow the well-marked pedestrian walkway on Nordel Way that leads onto the Alex Fraser Bridge. From the top of the bridge you can look south across the whole bog.

For more information on Delta Watershed Park and the Nature Reserve, call Delta Parks, Recreation and Culture, 604-946-3300.

38 DEAS ISLAND REGIONAL PARK

DISTANCE: 30 km (18.6 mi.) south of Vancouver, in Delta

ACTIVITIES: Bird watching, cycling, fishing, historic sites, nature observation, paddling, picnicking, swimming, viewpoints, walking

HIGHLIGHTS: Quiet sanctuary beside the Fraser's South Arm

ACCESS: Take Highway 99 south from Vancouver to the first major exit south of the George Massey Tunnel (#28), onto Highway 17 North to River Road. The park entrance is 2 km (1.2 mi.) east from this point on the north side of River Road.

One of the best times to visit Deas Island is early in the morning on a weekend, before traffic has begun to flow on Highway 99. Although cycling (and horseback riding, too) is permitted on Deas Island, you'll find that it's tough going in sandy sections, so be prepared to push your bike or stroller in places. Most visitors find Deas Island a good place to simply walk or paddle, not to mention exercise the dog.

Deas Island was named after its first settler, John Deas, a tinsmith who built a cannery here in 1873. It thrived through good and bad times under a series of owners until World War I. Before the George Massey Tunnel linked Delta with Richmond in 1959, a ferry operated from the mouth of Deas Slough where the Captain's Cove Marina is now located. In 1982, the Greater Vancouver Regional District took over the development of Deas Island Park and held the official opening on Rivers Day in September. (Rivers Day is an annual celebration begun in 1981 to honour B.C.'s many fine waterways.) Over succeeding years several historic Delta buildings have been relocated to the park to remind visitors of former times.

As you enter the park, the boat launch and a beach on the slough are to your left. The boathouse and dock are managed by the Delta Deas Rowing Club. Racing shells are built and stored here along with a variety of other vessels. A rowing course is laid out on the surface of Deas Slough, and you may see rowers practising as you stroll along Slough View Trail. There is a small parking lot next to the rowing facility.

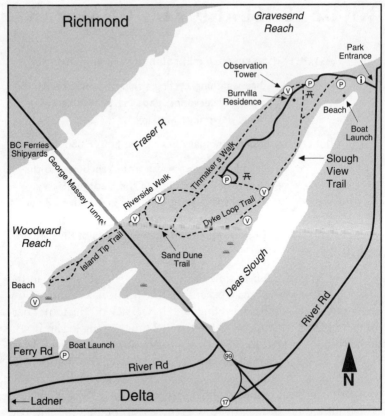

Deas Island Regional Park

You can launch a hand-carried boat from the beach and explore the slough as well as the Fraser River itself, but be careful on the river when the tide is running. One of the best times to be here is at slack tide, when the big river's South Arm is often flat calm, with the setting sun reflecting on its surface. *Note:* The park gates close at 9 P.M.; you might want to park just outside them if you're planning to be out on the slough or in the park in summer, when daylight lingers past 10 P.M.

Along the banks of the slough, wild yellow irises provide an occasional colour break from the thick green reeds and eelgrass. In early summer, the air is thick with downy white fluff, drifting from the tall cottonwood trees like snowflakes. Allow 30 minutes to paddle the slough one way. You'll pass beneath the bridge carrying motorists to and from the tunnel.

Dyke Loop Trail

Just past the rowing centre is the Inverholme Schoolhouse, which opened in 1909 and was moved to Deas Island in the early 1980s. It now houses the visitors' centre in an old-fashioned schoolhouse setting. The Burr family homestead, known as Burrvilla, was built in 1905 and also relocated to the park. Once typical of many residences in Delta, it is now one of the few reminders of those early Queen Anne–style houses. It is fronted by an observation tower that offers a broad, interpretive view of both wildlife and navigational activity on the river. Next to the Burr house is the Delta Agricultural Hall, built in 1894 and moved to the park almost a century later, in 1989. Today it's used as a park maintenance building with room for meetings and displays. The buildings stand beside wide-open Fisher's Field, with expansive views of the western sky and a covered barbecue area.

Birdsongs float through your car window as soon as you reach the western parking area. It's always a good idea to bring binoculars. Deas Island is not far from the George C. Reifel Migratory Bird Sanctuary, and there is usually an overflow crowd nesting here. Waterfowl, songbirds, shore birds, gulls and pheasants can all be seen on the island.

Riverside Walk, one of a half-dozen interconnected trails on the island, leads farther west from the western parking area. Even though the sign at the trailhead indicates the round trip takes 45 minutes, allow 2 hours if you can. You'll want to take time to sit under the shade of the cottonwood trees and watch the river traffic or clamber overtop the mouth of the tunnel and watch traffic as it disappears into the round maw. (For safety, there's a fence to separate the trail from the traffic.) A plaque mounted here commemorates the tunnel's opening by Queen Elizabeth II.

In early summer sweet flower scents perfume the air. The park is lush with purple lupines, which take over from the yellow and red broom bushes lining the river. Thickets of blackberries cover parts of the island. Their white flowers put forth a rose scent in June and are transformed into lush fruit by late August.

As you near the western end of the island, look for the BC Ferries shipyards on the river's northern shore. Follow the Island Tip Trail to a cozy bay with a grey sand beach. Slightly farther west of the beach is a rocky point to which you can walk if the tide is low enough. Slip across the eelgrass and past a rotting wooden boat hull to reach the most remote part of the island, just the place to leave the present behind for a moment.

Deas Slough is full of marshes with reed beds and stands of driftwood. Although there is a rough trail along the marshy south side of the park, in some places it might be hard to push a stroller along. The Dyke Loop Trail, which leads from Tinmaker's Walk to the Slough View Trail, is in much better condition.

Throughout July and August the park sponsors nature programs for footloose kids. For information on Deas Island Park and for event dates, call the GVRD at 604-432-6350 or visit their Web site: www.gvrd.bc.ca/services/parks/.

39 WESTHAM & REIFEL ISLANDS

DISTANCE: 38 km (23.6 mi.) south and west of Vancouver

ACTIVITIES: Bird watching, cycling, paddling, picnicking, walking

HIGHLIGHTS: Roadside produce stands and birds waiting to feed out of your hand

ACCESS: Take Highway 99 south to Highway 17 South, just past the George Massey Tunnel, and follow the signs into Ladner, an easy 20-minute drive (see map page 172). On Highway 17 there is a roadside marker announcing the turnoff to the George C. Reifel Migratory Bird Sanctuary on Ladner Trunk Road (48th Avenue). The sanctuary is located 9.6 km (6 mi.) west of Ladner on Reifel Island. To get there, once you reach the heart of Ladner, make a jog left on 47A Avenue, which leads to River Road West. Several kilometres along this diked road on the right side, past float houses and marinas, is a one-lane wooden bridge leading onto the conjoined Westham and Reifel Islands.

WESTHAM ISLAND Westham Island farmers grow delicious strawberries as well as various other kinds of fruit, and several U-pick locations are advertised at roadside. June is normally the best month for picking berries, while fall is pumpkin season.

As soon as you cross the bridge onto Westham Island, you pass the local gun club's firing range on the right side of the road. You could leave your car here and cycle the level 3.2 km (2 mi.) across Westham to the George C. Reifel Migratory Bird Sanctuary entrance on Reifel Island; however, bikes are not allowed on Reifel's trails. Otherwise, drive across Westham to the gateway.

ALAKSEN NATIONAL WILDLIFE AREA By car or bike, as you reach the causeway that links Westham with Reifel Island, the road passes beside the Alaksen National Wildlife Area, operated by the Canadian Wildlife Service. Their offices are located in the former Reifel family home. Hours are from 8 A.M. to 4 P.M., Monday to Friday except holidays, when the wildlife area is closed. Although much of Alaksen is hidden from view by trees lining the road, the property is quite extensive, over 290 ha (more than 700 acres).

Drive through the gates, down a treed lane to a small parking area with room for several cars. A modest-sized boat launch is situated here on Ewen Slough. Paddle or walk out to the Fraser River and then north as the river parallels a high dike trail that runs for about 6 km (4 mi.) around Reifel Island. If you're walking you will most likely have the trail to yourself, as this site draws far fewer visitors than the nearby bird sanctuary.

By boat you enter a backwater area where towering Lombardy poplars line the riverbank. Diminutive Albion and Harlock Islands, covered with bulrushes and pernicious purple loosestrife, provide a breakwater from the wakes of passing motorboats. This is a quiet, sheltered environment in which to enjoy a peaceful paddle. As you head northwest along the shoreline you'll find that a series of sloughs make indentations into both Westham and Reifel. These are often good places in which to drift silently with your binoculars at the ready. Spectacular displays of aerial activity often occur, seemingly just for your benefit, such as when a rare golden eagle goes ballistic riding a thermal current. As you near the northeast corner of Reifel Island you are on the opposite shore from the village of Steveston, itself sheltered by the long neck of Steveston Island. This is an attractive place to be near sunset, especially at slack tide, with the lights of Steveston flickering in the distance.

GEORGE C. REIFEL MIGRATORY BIRD SANCTUARY Located on the western fringe of the Fraser River estuary in Delta, the George C. Reifel Migratory Bird Sanctuary is the winter home for more than 230 species. Many of these are nesting year-round residents. Others head north to their summer nesting grounds. Many migratory birds stay at Reifel through the end of March; this is the best season to visit the sanctuary, before the numbers begin to thin out.

There are several picnic tables near the entrance to the bird sanctuary, both on the banks of a pond, where large numbers of mallards, coots and teals quack riotously while preening and paddling about, and inside the gate where the action is more subdued.

Wide trails wind for 3.5 km (2.2 mi.) through wooded and diked areas of the sanctuary, leading out to views of Roberts Bank on the western shore. Out on the marshes you're often treated to rare sights,

Snow geese, Westham Island

such as a northern harrier sitting on a distant fence with Mount Baker towering behind. There are a number of observation towers throughout the sanctuary as well as two blinds from which to stealthily observe the action in the marshes. If you're fortunate, you may even catch a glimpse of the resident sandhill cranes, by far the most majestic of Reifel's denizens.

A cool wind blows off the waters, so come prepared with warm clothing, a good pair of binoculars and a bird book. In case you forgot anything, there is a gift shop at the entrance to the sanctuary with a wide variety of bird-related items for sale. You can buy bags of approved bird feed for 50 cents at the entrance. *Note:* Please don't bring bread, because it provides little food value to birds. The entrance fee is $4 for adults and $2 for seniors and children under 15. A few steps past the entrance is a cozy warming hut overlooking a backwater. On cool days, a cheery fire helps take the edge off. The Reifel Migratory Bird Sanctuary was developed through the efforts of the B.C. Waterfowl Society, and it supports Canada's largest wintering population of waterfowl. Visiting hours are from 9 A.M. to 4 P.M. daily. For more information, call 604-946-6980.

40 LADNER DIKE TRAIL

DISTANCE: 30 km (18.6 mi.) south and west of Vancouver

ACTIVITIES: Bird watching, boating, cycling, paddling, picnicking, viewpoints, walking

HIGHLIGHTS: Sweeping views west across the Strait of Georgia to Vancouver Island and north to the Coast Mountains

ACCESS: To reach Ladner, drive Highway 99 to the south end of the George Massey Tunnel and take the first exit right onto River Road (see map page 172). If you miss it, take the next exit (#28) right onto Highway 17 South, then turn right again onto Ladner Trunk Road (48th Avenue) for the short drive into town. By taking the River Road exit you approach Ladner on a back road rather than through the community's newer neighbourhoods on Ladner Trunk. One home in particular along River Road has been lovingly restored. Watch for it on the south side soon after you make your exit from Highway 99.

Whether you explore the Fraser estuary by car, foot or bicycle, the views are tremendous: the broad expanse of the Strait of Georgia opens to the west; to the north the peaks of the Coast Mountains march along from the Sunshine Coast to the Fraser Valley. It's often sunnier out here, too, though cool winds do blow in off the open water. In exposed areas there's little shelter from the wind except behind an accommodating piece of driftwood on the beach. Wherever you wander the ground is level, but what's lacking in vertical challenge can be made up for in distance.

A particularly enjoyable stretch of dike trail begins in Ladner, a farming community first settled in 1868. Along with agriculture, salmon canneries were major employers. By 1899, there were 16 canneries in operation in Delta. Together with nearby Tsawwassen, Ladner grew into the commercial heart of rural Delta. Until the completion of the Massey Tunnel in 1959, residents lived in splendid isolation from Vancouver, a ferry ride to Richmond or the long drive

Ladner Dike Trail

through New Westminster the only links. Even today, in the far western reaches of Delta, the ocean breeze sings a haunting song over this secluded area.

RIVER ROAD There are two intersections of note as you travel west on River Road from Highway 99. Turning right on Ferry Road takes you out to the marina on the south side of Deas Slough (see chapter 38), glimpsed as you cross the slough on Highway 99. There is a public boat launch here, an ideal place to put in a canoe or kayak for a paddle journey through Ladner Marsh and a handful of small islands. A right turn at the next road west of Ferry puts you on McNeely Way, a paved road that becomes a dirt track, leading around the east end of Ladner Harbour and then west out towards Ladner Harbour Park, a sandy point overlooking Ladner Reach.

As River Road enters downtown Ladner it blends left onto Elliott Street. Turn right onto 47A Avenue at the town's major intersection. There are lovely examples of Delta heritage homes to admire as you drive west on 47A, which soon becomes River Road West. (If you're in no hurry, take some time to see Ladner's waterfront by turning right off River Road at Elliott onto Chisholm Street as you enter town. It's only a block long and you can then zigzag your way west through three blocks of back streets, with more heritage homes, to the intersection of 47A Avenue and 47A Street.)

LADNER DIKE TRAIL Just west of downtown Ladner the South Arm of the Fraser River meets the Strait of Georgia at Roberts Bank, the end of its 1370-km (850-mi.) journey. A large dike protects the town from periodic inundation by ocean tides and river runoff. As the Fraser sweeps past Ladner it curves around Gunn, Barber and Westham Islands on the town's north side. Westham is the only one of the three that has been settled. The best place to view these islands is from the top of the dike beside River Road.

Canoe Passage separates Ladner from Westham Island, providing moorage for the float houses rocking in the marinas beside the dike. Owing to the height of the dike, little of the waterway is visible from River Road as it winds westwards from downtown Ladner. In 3 km (1.8 mi.) it passes the bridge over Canoe Passage that links Ladner with Westham Island and the George C. Reifel Migratory Bird Sanctuary (see previous chapter); 2.5 km (1.5 mi.) farther the road ends in a gated cul-de-sac. There is roadside parking here near Brunswick Point.

As you climb up onto the gravel-surfaced dike trail the mouth of Canoe Passage presents itself all at once. The channel is several hundred metres across at this point. The flat farmland of Westham Island lies demurely on the opposite shore.

The dike trail is wide enough so that walkers, cyclists and those on horseback can share it with ease. Aside from thick hedges of blackberry brambles and a tall stand of Lombardy poplars planted long ago the land is wide open, with only an occasional willow for relief.

Old pilings march out into the Fraser from the river's edge like stalwart centurions, the last of a legion that once supported the Brunswick Cannery wharf, one of the Fraser River's earliest salmon canneries. The marshy ground at the point is usually wet, so if you want to explore out here, bring some rubber boots. One of the best times for this is midsummer, when much of the marsh is in bloom. Driftwood stranded above the high-tide line by winter storms provides natural bridges to clamber over. Some trunks are weathered smooth and curved just right for sitting back on while listening for bird calls. Don't forget your binoculars, or your paint box if you're so inclined. It's calm out here on a good day and usually there aren't more than a handful of others with whom to share the trail.

From this starting point the trail swings south for 7 km (4.4 mi.) in a gentle curve around Roberts Bank towards the superport causeway, an easy hour's walk one way and half that on a bicycle. Viewpoints occur at regular intervals, with a bench or two set off beside the trail.

At any time of year the view west over the Strait of Georgia is compelling, an enormous seascape of ever-changing light and dark. This is the panorama you dream of longingly when cooped up in the city. Offshore in the shallow waters of the strait, flocks of ducks and geese bob along. Depending on the direction of the wind, they take shelter on either side of the long causeway that runs out to the loading dock where ocean freighters take on coal. A hundred black railway cars sit motionless in a line while the quiet drumming of a half-dozen diesel engines harnessed in tandem carries across the water towards the dike.

There is a trail running along the causeway that juts out into Roberts Bank. This little diversion can easily add another half-hour of exploration time to the journey. When you look shoreward from out here, Ladner is eerily remote. Mount Baker and other peaks in the Cascade Mountains rise up to the east. Southwards, a large BC Ferries vessel heads off towards Vancouver Island. A freighter is silhouetted against the shores of the Gulf Islands, with the peaks of Vancouver Island's mountains rising above Nanaimo to the west.

Returning to Ladner after time spent out on top of the dike is like returning from a sailing trip. The water has been expansive and ever-present. Soon you are back on sheltered land with the horizon closing in on all sides, but you come away with a feeling of inner tranquillity and give silent thanks to the dike builders for allowing you to get away for a few hours.

If you'd care to find out more about the building of the dike, visit the Delta Museum and Archives back in town at 4858 Delta Street, one block west of Elliott. The museum is in the restored 1912 Tudor-style building that once housed the Delta municipal offices (now located in more modern quarters on Highway 17).

41 BOUNDARY BAY REGIONAL PARK

DISTANCE: 40 km (25 mi.) south of Vancouver in Tsawwassen, part of the municipality of Delta

ACTIVITIES: Beachcombing, bird watching, boating, cycling, nature observation, paddling, picnicking, playground, swimming, walking, windsurfing

HIGHLIGHTS: A broad salt marsh with a magnificent natural sand beach at its southwestern edge

ACCESS: Boundary Bay Regional Park is an easy 45-minute drive south of Vancouver. (See map page 172.) Take the Highway 17 South exit from Highway 99 towards the Tsawwassen ferry terminal, then turn south on 56th Street (Point Roberts Road), which leads into Tsawwassen. Turn left onto 12th Avenue and follow it around to Boundary Bay Road and Third Avenue, which lead south to the park entrance at Centennial Beach.

From our vantage point here in B.C.'s southwestern corner, it often appears that the farther from the city we explore, the greater are the natural rewards of the landscape. After all, B.C. has some really enormous expanses of protected land, particularly in the more remote corners of the province. Back here in the city, all that parkland looks pretty exotic.

The sheer distance between Vancouver and these remote locales contributes to their allure. If you have three days' driving time at your disposal, you might just make it as far as the jumping-off place into one of them. On the other hand, if you have 30 minutes to spare here at home, you could be exploring the sandy shore and broad waterway of one of B.C.'s more wondrous locales, Boundary Bay. This fascinating area has few equals along the coast for size and setting, yet because of its proximity to the city, much of the bay's natural grandeur is curtained behind farmland, recent housing development and commuter roads.

These days not only does the bay's shoreline enjoy protection as parkland, but so too does much of the offshore area, as part of the

Boundary Bay and Mount Baker

Lower Mainland Nature Legacy Plan. And what an offshore area! As much as you might enjoy exploring the sand dunes and dike trails that characterize Boundary Bay's shoreline, you'll delight in paddling the bay in calm weather, especially at high tide. Gliding across the clear waters of the shallow bay in a kayak or canoe imparts a feeling of flying above the undulating, shadowy ocean floor below.

When agitated, Boundary Bay affords both a challenge and a thrill to sailors and windsurfers. As waves surge in, young swimmers strive to ride slippery driftwood logs that bob in the sun-warmed water. (You can plan on enjoying a swim here well into September.) Mired high above the tide line, logs tossed up by past storms shelter picnickers when strong breezes arise. On the northern and eastern skyline, the Coast and Cascade mountain ranges converge in the far distance of the Fraser Valley. To the south, Mount Baker and its companion peaks to the west, the Sisters, shore up the sky. This is a fine spot to catch a sunset, when shafts of sunlight tint the clouds above with a palette of pastel hues. No two evenings are the same here, which is why I'm drawn back time and again.

There are a small number of parking spaces at the intersection of 12th Avenue and Boundary Bay Road. If you plan to explore the dike by bike, this is a good place to begin. A 16-km (10-mi.) dike trail runs

Boundary Bay

clockwise from the park around the north end of the bay. This is a popular trail with walkers and cyclists. In fact, there is such an extensive length of level trail that the challenge will be to decide at what point you've had enough and wish to turn back. If you persist, the dike stretches to the eastern end of Mud Bay in distant Surrey. (See chapter 42 for a comprehensive description.)

For those wanting to launch a boat or windsurfer, a ramp is located at the east end of 1A Avenue, several blocks south of Centennial Beach via 67th Street. If you plan on boating, it's always a good idea to consult a tide table in advance. When the tide goes out at Boundary Bay it goes *way* out, revealing an expanse of firm, clean, inviting sand—great for exploring on foot but an obstacle to launching a boat.

CENTENNIAL BEACH Watch for Cammidge House at the Centennial Beach entrance to the park off Boundary Bay Road. This stately farmhouse, ringed with porches, has been a fixture here since 1907. It has been restored by the GVRD at the south end of the park road, where it is now used as a community meeting place. The GVRD is also undertaking habitat-enhancement work on the Spetifore Lands, a buffer zone between Tsawwassen and Boundary Bay, planting a variety of native and indigenous plants to benefit wildlife.

The main parking area at Centennial Beach has picnic tables

beside a treed area, drinking water, changing facilities and wash-rooms, and a playground. A concession stand is open during the busiest times in summer. From here, a network of short walking trails fans out to the north, perfect for wildlife viewing. Even on a crowded weekend, Centennial Beach always has room to spare, especially if you avoid the immediate area of the parking lot. The beach runs north for more than 2 km (1.2 mi.), so stretch out.

Be careful of incoming tides when walking out into the bay. If you're here for a picnic, try putting up a marker, such as an umbrella or piece of driftwood, to act as a beacon by which to fix your position on the beach. Otherwise, from a distance out in the bay you may find that you have only a vague idea of where you left your picnic basket.

The ocean drains out of the bay past Point Roberts to the south-west, with Crescent Beach and White Rock to the east. From a vantage point on the dunes it's possible to get one of the best views of Mount Baker in the entire Lower Mainland. On a hot day, when the ocean rises over the sand floor heated by the sun's rays, Boundary Bay is as warm as bath water; in very cold weather, the shallow bay can freeze solid.

Two elevated viewing platforms are located along the 1-km (0.6-mi.) 12th Avenue Dyke Trail, which connects Centennial Beach and the 12th Avenue entrance to the park. During seasonal migrations thousands of waterfowl stop at Boundary Bay. Black brant are especially noted for their spring stopovers—20,000 to 30,000 visit during April. The best viewing is at high tide, when the incoming water forces the ducks who have been out feeding on the sand flats to move closer to shore. Here they mingle with gulls, terns and herons.

The intertidal plants and animals of the salt marsh attract other birds as well. Several species of hawks and owls are found here. Boundary Bay, especially at the foot of 64th and 72nd Streets, is a well-known place to spot snowy owls. To be silently overflown by a white-faced pair is a mind-altering experience.

For more information on wildlife viewing programs and other nature activities offered by the GVRD at Boundary Bay Regional Park, call 604-432-6359. For general information on the park, call 604-224-5739 or visit their Web site: www.gvrd.bc.ca/services/parks/.

42 MUD BAY

DISTANCE:	22 km (13.6 mi.) southeast of Vancouver, on the Delta-Surrey border
ACTIVITIES:	Bird watching, cycling, historic site, nature observation, picnicking, viewpoints, walking
HIGHLIGHTS:	A lengthy stretch of dike trail curving around a shallow bay where flocks of shorebirds fly evasion formations at the tide line
ACCESS:	If you take the Highway 10 exit (#20) off Highway 99, you'll be within a mile of Mud Bay (see map page 124). The only alternative is to take the Highway 17 South exit (#28) and then turn east onto the Ladner Trunk Road (Highway 10 under another name). From Highway 10, cross south onto Hornby Drive at the first set of stoplights. There is an RCMP detachment at this intersection. Take the first right turn off Hornby onto 96th Street and drive to the south end. There is parking on the dike and beside the road. At this point you're no longer on Mud Bay, having come out onto much larger Boundary Bay. As if to make the distinction clear, beyond is the Boundary Bay Airport, much grander in turn than the nearer Delta Heritage Air Park. Another approach is to stay on Hornby to 104th Street. If you are travelling with small children this might be the better approach, for it's closer to the features they'll likely find most intriguing at Mud Bay, such as the antiquated airplane fuselage that graces the entrance to the air park.

The junior member of a triad of bays, Mud Bay is a broad, shallow expanse of gumbo on the border where Delta and South Surrey meet. Boundary and Semiahmoo Bays are its senior partners. You pass beside Mud Bay when you drive along Highway 99 between Ladner and Crescent Beach. Only the Burlington

Mud Bay

Northern railway line gets to cross the bay's shallow waters; we road travellers have to circle around it.

Much of the time Mud Bay looks as if someone has pulled the plug and forgotten to clean the tub. Two rivers, the Serpentine and the Nicomekl, empty into the bay's eastern end. They bring silt from runoff and from headwaters many miles inland. This is the dumping ground for all that mud, deposited year after year. The Boundary Bay Regional Trail, which includes the East Delta Dike Trail, winds around both Mud and Boundary Bays, skirting the mud flats that once extended much farther inland. You can put in a full day of cycling making the 33-km (24-mi.) round trip between the Surrey-Delta border and Boundary Bay Regional Park in Tsawwassen (see previous chapter).

Beginning earlier in this century, crude dikes were built around the shorelines of Mud and Boundary Bays to hold back the ocean. They have been improved considerably in the years since then. Greenhouse gardeners and turf farmers are the main occupants of the land behind the dikes. A few cows, sheep and horses are pastured around the old Delta homesteads scattered along the roads leading down to the bays. Urban sprawl is eating up many of the fields closer to Tsawwassen, but down around Mud Bay, agricultural reserve land still holds sway.

When hard-packed, dike trails are wonderfully level surfaces to roll along on a bicycle, and the East Delta Dike Trail on the north side of Mud Bay is no exception. The surface of the dike is wide enough for walkers, cyclists and horseback riders to share. Hawks, eagles and owls patrol the fields on one side, while on the other, shorebirds in the thousands flock back and forth. The sandpipers are particularly active. Their ability to instantly change direction in midflight is a survival technique against raptors. To onlookers they present an ever-changing pattern in white and black: one moment they are a white cloud, the next they blend invisibly with the dark background of the ocean.

As you progress along the dike eastwards from 96th Street, you pass the historic Delta Heritage Air Park, out of which the Boundary Bay Flying Club operates. Several dozen light planes of various vintages are parked here. If the wind is blowing cool off the bay, you might wish to visit the small clubhouse next to the runway for a quick warm-up. Unfortunately, it's only open on weekends.

Mud Bay comes into its own east of the air park as the dike leads towards the foot of 112th Street. The dike's surface becomes increasingly rough east of here as it curves inland past a point of marshland that juts out into the bay, then parallels the bay once more. Here and there are the shells of old boats, mired in the mud. Highway 99 edges closer to the trail until only a small fence separates the two. The surface of the dike is loose gravel or sand, and the going is tough if you're wheeling a bike or a stroller. The trail swings away from the highway after 10 minutes of this. Your reward will be some isolated viewpoints on the bay's shoreline—perfect picnic spots.

Find a seat on the driftwood "furniture" here and take time to admire the light show over the bay. The mud is speckled with small ponds of water that reflect the colour of the sky; sunlight striking the surface of the ponds turns them a silvery-blue colour. One of the best times of the day for making this journey is late afternoon, when, even on overcast days, the bay lights up with a brilliance all its own.

43 POINT ROBERTS

DISTANCE: 50 km (30 mi.) south of Vancouver

ACTIVITIES: Boating, camping, cycling, historic site, nature observation, paddling, picnicking, swimming, viewpoints, walking

HIGHLIGHTS: Sweeping ocean views from a beach at land's end where killer whales feed offshore

ACCESS: Take Highway 99 south through the George Massey Tunnel to the Highway 17 South exit (#28). (See map page 172.) Turn south off Highway 17 South to Tsawwassen on Point Roberts Road (56th Street) and follow it to the Canada-U.S. border. You can leave your car on Wallace Avenue on the Canadian side and cycle or walk from here. By car, head south on Tyee Drive, then west on Marine Drive to reach Lighthouse Marine Park.

The famous borderline that demarcates this tiny American enclave from adjoining Tsawwassen is celebrated by a stone marker laid in 1861 under the terms of the Treaty of Washington. To search out the monument, turn right onto Roosevelt Way immediately after crossing the border. Make your way the short distance to the western end of the road before it veers sharply south onto Marine Drive. Far below, the waters of the Strait of Georgia lap the beach, and the jetties of the Tsawwassen ferry causeway and the Roberts Bank coal facility jut into view.

Don't bother trying to make your way down the slippery slope here. Instead, continue farther south along Marine to much more hospitable approaches to the sea at Lighthouse Marine Park.

LIGHTHOUSE MARINE PARK Land's end. There's a special allure in those words. They hook the imagination and draw the curious to the shoreline. By implication, this is where one slips off the mooring lines that ground us. Even if we don't physically ship out to sea, in our minds at least, we sail off across the earth's watery surface.

Such is the mood at Lighthouse Marine Park. Stand on the pebble-strewn beach at the southwestern tip of the Lower Mainland. Spread out before you are three broad straits: Haro, Georgia and Juan de Fuca. This is a dramatic point of convergence. An ever-shifting line formed by a rip tide dances off towards the horizon. Shipping lanes merge in the distance. Perspective plays tricks on your eyes. Freighters appear, then are seemingly swallowed whole behind distant islands in the San Juan and Gulf Islands chains. A mist renders them dull-coloured, mere outlines in the haze. So vast and complex is this panorama that, at best, one can only form a sketchy notion of the power of nature's forces at play here.

Lighthouse is a treasured part of the Whatcom County parks system. Marooned from the rest of Washington state by a political twist of fate, it and the rest of Point Roberts are frequented almost entirely by Canadians. Since its inception in 1973, Lighthouse Park has grown beyond being a simple beach destination. A network of boardwalks and trails now runs through the windswept dunes. Constant breezes gust in off the straits. Stunted pines with a bonsai appearance and wild rose bushes thick with fragrant pink and white blossoms help anchor the dunes. Slope-roofed shelters supported by sturdy log posts provide picnickers with welcome relief. The wind only loses its edge in summer. A dip in the ocean demonstrates how chilly these waters are year round.

Set back off the beach on the west side of the park is a tusk-shaped slab of polished black granite. Known as the *Sunsweep* sculpture, this small installation is one of three such markers placed along the Canada-U.S. border in the 1980s as part of an international art project. The other two are at Roosevelt-Campobello Park in New Brunswick and on American Point Island in Ontario's Lake of the Woods Park. Inscribed on the base of the Boundary Bluff marker are these words:

> Aligned to the north star, solstices and equinoxes, portrays the path of the sun from east to west. Designed by David Barr in 1985 and given to the people of this community as a symbol of international friendship.

Unfortunately, vandals seem to have missed the point of Barr's gesture. The tusk has been broken in two, but willing hands have glued it back together and it stands solidly in place once more, less vaunted but undaunted, facing Vancouver Island in the western distance and Mount Baker rising above the waters of Semiahmoo Bay in the east. Two enormous anchors have been moved into position

Point Roberts cyclists, Lighthouse Marine Park

around the sculpture. They lend an air of rusty grandeur to the site.

Here at land's end, winds and countervailing currents swirl against each other, encouraging the water into playful surf. Between swells, kayakers nimbly launch out into the strait. For their efforts they are rewarded with views of the North Shore mountains that are otherwise, on the beach, concealed from sight by the dunes. Occasionally, an unwary paddler will be unceremoniously upended by the choppy motion of the waves. A modest breakwater of wooden pilings valiantly but vainly tries to hold back the surf rolling towards the lighthouse (which, in this case, is less of a house and more of a metal scaffolding).

Perched inland a short distance from the beach, a three-storey observation tower rises above a small orca interpretive centre. Profiles of three pods of killer whales—denoted as J, K and L pods—that frequent the waters off the point are presented on murals. The distinctive dorsal fin markings of some of the older pod members are displayed in a photographic exhibit inside the centre. Using these as clues, visitors fortunate enough to sight the whales can positively identify individual animals. The matriarch of J pod is estimated to be 88 years old.

June to October is the best time to come whale watching here, when all three pods pass near the park, usually on a daily basis. It often takes them as long as an hour to journey past. Attractions for them include coho, chinook and pink salmon (also called humpy by the Americans) and rock fish that school up in the nutrient-rich waters off the point. It's worth overnighting in the adjacent campground to increase your chances of seeing the whales. The orcas forage for food, slap their flukes and occasionally surface for some spy hopping, leaping skywards for a look-see of their own. A Vancouver-based organization, Lifeforce Foundation, is often present during these times. Members not only provide helpful insight on the behaviour and personality of individual killer whales, they also update information in the interpretive centre.

In summer, a fee of US$3 is charged park users who arrive by car, with extra charges if you use the boat launch or wish to stay overnight. For information, call Whatcom County Parks and Recreation, (360) 733-2900. For information on the Lifeforce Foundation, call 604-669-4673.

SEA TO SKY CORRIDOR

44 PORTEAU COVE PROVINCIAL PARK

DISTANCE:	43 km (26.7 mi.) north of Vancouver
ACTIVITIES:	Boating, camping, paddling, picnicking, scuba diving, swimming
HIGHLIGHTS:	Beach play or overnight stay on the shores of a dramatic fiord
ACCESS:	Off Highway 99 North, 22 km (13.7 mi.) north of Horseshoe Bay.

For all of its beauty, Howe Sound provides few points of public access along its rugged shoreline. In most places the mountains plunge sharply into the waters of the deep fiord (Canada's most southerly), forcing the railroad and the highway close together, with scant room left over for visitors to spread a picnic blanket, let alone set up a tent. One of the few places where these things are possible is the provincial park at Porteau Cove.

There was once a small settlement in this sheltered bay. Little remains except the formal stone wall around the cove's hidden west side. In fact, from the road it is almost impossible to see the cove that is one of this park's most attractive features. Instead, as you travel Highway 99, the beach and jetty are what catch the eye. Only in winter, once the leaves are down, is it possible to see through the surrounding forest into the little cove itself.

As you turn into the park, you pass information signs, directed at divers, that detail the location of several marine vessels scuttled offshore specifically for underwater exploration. The first of these boats was sunk in 1981 when the park was opened. Marine life is attracted to such wrecks, making a dive even more exciting. Watching divers hardly qualifies as a spectator sport. That said, there is something rather entertaining in seeing a group of rubber-clad people entering or emerging from the cold waters of the sound while you enjoy your picnic at one of the numerous tables spread around the broad, driftwood-littered beaches on both sides of the jetty. Small floats positioned offshore help divers orient themselves. Divers affix a flag to the top of these if they are diving below, warn-

Porteau Cove

ing boaters to stay well away. Porteau Cove is also a designated provincial marine park with sheltered moorage.

If you are visiting Porteau for the day, you can use the large parking area beside the jetty. This is a wonderful place to take a break from highway traffic and enjoy the spectacular views of Howe Sound, with Anvil Island's obvious profile to the southwest and the peaks of the Tantalus Range rising in the northwest. The gravel beach slopes gently into the sound. On days when the tide is low and the sun high, the gravel heats up and warms the incoming waters, making swimming here a pleasure.

As this is the only provincial park on the sound accessible by car, the 59 campsites are in constant use (15 are walk-in sites). Even if you are visiting just for the day, have a look at Porteau's camping facilities with an eye to making plans for a future visit. If you head here with the intention of staying overnight in summer, arrive early and have a contingency plan in case all the spaces have been taken. You can also reserve a campsite here by calling Reservations BC, 604-689-9025.

The drive-in sites go quickly throughout the summer and on Friday and Saturday nights from May to October, but there is usually a good chance of getting one of the walk-in sites even if you arrive late, except in the months of June to August. A user fee is collected from April to October: about $18.50 for drive-in sites and $9 for walk-ins.

As soon as you enter the campground, bear right to check out the oceanfront sites. In the middle of the campground is a washroom facility complete with showers. The walk-in sites are located at the far end of the campground road. From the walk-in parking lot to the sites is only a short distance, easily covered in several minutes. An amphitheatre is located between the drive-in and walk-in campsites. Interpretive displays are presented here at one of the most scenic locations in the park on summer evenings. Because there is so little level land, most sites are relatively closely spaced compared to other provincial parks. Campsite 44, at the westernmost end of the road next to the walk-in parking, is one of the few that have some breathing room. It sits in the shelter of the Sitka spruce forest and commands an attractive view of the sound. The only drawback is its proximity to the railroad tracks. Visitors can count on several trains passing by at all hours of the day and night.

Discreetly tucked in behind the walk-in sites is the cove itself. There is an open lawn beside the cove, and a small bridge spans the narrow backwater. Take a walk to the viewpoint on the trail that leads west from the walk-in sites and up onto the forested bluff. Stunted shore pines (a coastal variety of lodgepole pine) and stately Sitka spruce provide shelter on the point, from where you can look down on the cove or out across the waters of the sound. This is a quiet place in which to enjoy the surroundings, especially in the early or late hours of the day, or to stop for an off-season breather from the highway.

The boat launch at Porteau Cove is the only public one accessible from Highway 99 between Horseshoe Bay and Squamish. There are often times when Howe Sound is flat calm, a perfect invitation to enjoy a paddle; however, always be aware that strong winds can rise quickly. Sticking close to shore you can safely enjoy views of the Howe Sound Crest and Britannia ranges that are not otherwise revealed from land. If you paddle north to Furry Creek, look for pictographs painted on the rock face on the north side of the small bay just past the creek's entrance into Howe Sound.

45 SQUAMISH

DISTANCE: 60 km (37.2 mi.) north of Vancouver

ACTIVITIES: Bird watching, camping, fishing, group functions, hiking, mountain biking, mountaineering, nature observation, paddling, picnicking, viewpoints, walking, windsurfing

HIGHLIGHTS: A place to scale a granite monolith, explore an estuary trail with eagles or just hold onto your hat at the spit's tip

ACCESS: The well-marked entrance to Shannon Falls Provincial Park is located on the east side of Highway 99. You can drive to the base of Stawamus Chief via the designated turnoff at the viewing area on Highway 99 just north of Shannon Falls. Follow the road that leads up the embankment in the middle of the viewpoint and south to the provincial campsites.

To reach the Squamish estuary, turn west from Highway 99 into Squamish at the second traffic lights, where an Esso station is the anchor tenant, and drive south along Cleveland Avenue, the town's main drag, to Vancouver Street; then head three blocks west, to the trailhead to the Squamish estuary.

To reach Squamish Spit, turn west from Highway 99 at the third set of traffic lights onto Industrial Way, then turn north on Queensway, which feeds into Government Road. The gravel road to the spit starts off Government Road's west side. It is 4.3 km (2.7 mi.) from the turnoff to the end of the spit. Just before the road climbs up on the dike, turn left onto a service road and follow it south to the very end.

Alice Lake Provincial Park is located 12 km (7.4 mi.) north of downtown Squamish just east of Highway 99 (see map page 220).

Squamish Smoke Bluffs

S quamish is a year-round destination for a variety of outdoor pursuits. And owing to its proximity to the ocean,
low-elevation trails remain snow-free for most of the year. Just getting here is a thrill. Enjoy the drive between Horseshoe Bay and
Squamish. There are plenty of viewpoint pullouts that will help
tame the intensity of the journey.

SHANNON FALLS AND STAWAMUS CHIEF PROVINCIAL PARKS Out-of-
province licence plates adorn the cars parked at the base of the
Stawamus Chief, attesting to Squamish's decades-old drawing power
among the international climbing community. Even a casual passer-
by would find it hard to ignore the mountain's lumpy magnificence.

At the same time as the granite features of the Stawamus Chief

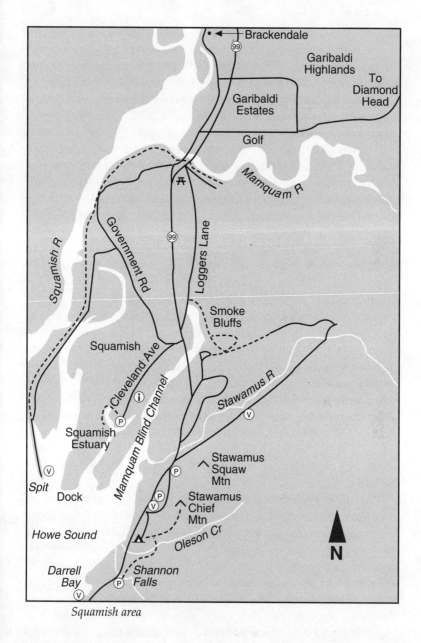

Squamish area

catch your eye, Shannon Falls, B.C.'s third-highest waterfall, presents itself for admiration. Linked by a 1.6-km-long (1-mi.-long) trail, these two natural wonders constitute a double whammy for those in search of adventure. Shannon Falls' white veil of water drops 335 m (1100 ft.) from a ridge above Highway 99 to a creekbed below, then empties into nearby Howe Sound. Almost a century ago, the falls drove a wooden waterwheel to provide energy to a nearby sawmill. A replica of the large wheel is mounted beside the creek.

It takes only a minute to walk up to the falls from the parking lot. A well-built system of wooden staircases and bridges leads to a viewing platform near the base of the falls. There are some impressive firs and cedars here. Starting at the platform is a rough trail that leads higher, for those who like to taste the spray created by the tumbling water.

The first half of the well-maintained trail that links Shannon Falls and Stawamus Chief Parks is over level ground through an alder forest. Plan on 15 minutes to cover the route that begins north of the loggers' sports area. Orange and red markers affixed to a large cedar indicate the way. At the base of the mountain, the trail begins to climb beside the smooth rock face, which is covered in places by green lichen. You might have to clamber over the occasional blow-down blocking the trail just before the small bridge over Olesen Creek, which gurgles down through a cleft in the mountainside. The Stawamus Chief Mountain Trail begins across the creek, slightly above its trailhead in the Stawamus Chief provincial campground.

When you stand next to the Chief, you look up and up at a wall of smooth granite. It's awe-inspiring. Hiking from here to the top will take you an hour or longer. Altogether there is a 600-m (1970-ft.) elevation gain on this hike; you will be climbing almost constantly until the top. Although this particular trail is the most popular with hikers, it is only one of the hundreds of possible routes on the Chief. There is little shade on the trail, so pack plenty of liquid for the higher parts of the climb.

The trail is smooth and wide in most places. The higher you get, the more exhilarating it becomes until finally, near the top and above the tree line, you reach a very broad and open, windswept spot. The steepest part is now behind you; if you've brought lunch, keep you eyes open for an appropriate place to picnic on this final section.

From here you can see Shannon Falls in profile to the south, with the ribbon of Highway 99 curving beyond it. To the north, the Squamish River cuts through the valley that widens between Brackendale and Howe Sound. Across the water to the west are the glaciated peaks of the Tantalus Range.

Rock climbing's popularity around Squamish is not limited to the Chief. Close by to the north are the Smoke Bluffs, a small ridge easily reached by road. Because of the ridge's southern exposure, the granite walls dry quickly in the morning sun. Climbers groom the rock face with wire brushes to obtain an ideal smoothness. Rough trails lead up to the base of the ridge from a parking lot on Loggers Lane just east of Highway 99. Small groups of climbers practise here. Although this isn't a spectator sport, they won't mind you watching if you are quiet; safe climbing requires great concentration.

SQUAMISH ESTUARY When your aim is to get outdoors, especially in the Sea to Sky corridor, downtown Squamish might seem like an odd starting point. However, the town's estuary trails make it a good place to begin your adventure.

At the trailhead, a wooden sign bears a detailed map of the estuary and the dike trail that rambles west from here. The grass-covered trail leads past the channelled waterways of the estuary, home to a large population of migratory waterfowl during spring and fall as well as an overwintering population of geese and raptors. Out here the uncluttered views really open up. Stawamus Chief, the town's centrepiece, looms large. Equally arresting, if the skies are clear, is the dagger point of Atwell Peak and its broad-shouldered companion, the Dalton Dome. Together they dominate the skyline of Garibaldi Park to the north.

A cool breeze often blows across the marshy sloughs of Howe Sound's shoreline, so dress accordingly for maximum enjoyment. Bring binoculars so you can follow the flight of hawks or eagles over the marshland as they search for a meal. The path is bordered by brick-red rosehips, and drifts of sedges pattern the surface of the slough. The white stalks of pearly everlasting rival Shannon Falls' snowy tress, which can be seen cascading down the slopes to the south of the Chief. Spires of solitary, stunted Sitka spruce anchor the estuary's perimeter.

This portion of the estuary trail ends at a log-sorting yard. If you are exploring on foot, this is a good place to turn around. Several side trails passed along the way offer opportunities to extend your visit. By bicycle, you can continue on the gravel back road from the sorting yard. It leads around a long finger of the estuary whose east side is diked by the Squamish Spit. If you have enough time, you can easily tack on another 10 km (6.2 mi.) or more riding out to the windsurfing centre at the spit's tip.

SQUAMISH SPIT The Squamish Spit is a long finger of dike at the mouth of the Squamish River where it flows into Howe Sound. The spit helps keep the harbour free of silt so that large freighters can tie up nearby to take on loads of lumber. On busy summer weekends there can be more than a hundred cars parked here. At the very end of the spit is the windsurfer launch area. The views from the spit are spectacular, the best in the area: Shannon Falls, the Stawamus Chief, Sky Pilot Mountain and Goat Ridge, Mamquam Mountain, Atwell Peak and Mount Garibaldi all stand out in one great panorama.

Year round, a strong wind known as a "squamish" blows each afternoon across Howe Sound with such force that unwary wind-surfers in the waters off the Squamish Spit often can't right themselves if they get dunked. Fortunately, there is an emergency rescue service on standby.

The spit is administered by the Squamish Windsurfing Society. Launch fees are currently $10 per day or $75 for a season's pass. For information on daily wind conditions from May to October, dial 604-926-9463 in Vancouver or the society's Wind Talker phone line in Squamish, (604) 892-2235.

ALICE LAKE PROVINCIAL PARK Alice Lake is the largest of four tightly knit lakes nestled in the woods below Alice Ridge. Camping with all the amenities of home—at least hot showers and indoor plumbing—is a big attraction here. An overnight fee is charged from May to October: $18.50 for one of the 96 vehicle campsites, $15 for one of 12 new walk-in sites. Reservations may be made by calling 604-689-9025. A group campsite is available; call (604) 898-9680 to reserve.

Of the four lakes in the park, Alice is the one most suitable for paddling. (Motorized boats are not permitted on any of the lakes.) There are launch sites at each end of the lake beside the picnic areas. Rows of tables ring the shore, each with its own barbecue. The setting, with its manicured tranquillity, is quite pleasant. There is a pier to fish from at the south end. Lakeshore Walk links the two picnic areas, shaded by cedar groves that thrive on the moisture provided by the lake. The view from Alice Lake's north end is one of the best in the park, short of climbing nearby DeBeck's Hill.

The most popular trail in the park links Alice with its three smaller companion lakes. Budget 2 to 4 hours to complete the loop. All of the trails are well marked, with both directions and distances indicated to Stump, Fawn, Edith and Alice Lakes. This is a good trail for cycling as well as walking, though it is restricted to pedestrians in summer.

Stump Lake's name conjures up images of decrepitude, so it's a pleasant surprise to discover that the only stumps in sight stand beside the trail, not in the lake itself. The smooth trail divides as it rounds the small lake. On one side it's quite level; on the other it climbs the hillside. Looking down you may see anglers casting for rainbow, cutthroat and brook trout. Unlike at Alice, there are no lawns or beaches here or at either of the other two lakes.

From Stump Lake's north end the trail winds close beside the Cheekye River for a time, then begins to climb gently towards Fawn Lake. The forest floor is thick with ferns; beside the trail delicate wildflowers such as white trilliums and dusty-rose bleeding hearts appear in clusters. Beneath several large old-growth cedars is an especially pretty viewpoint overlooking the river. (If you are walking with young children, this may be as far as you care to go on the Four Lakes Loop Trail. Instead of retracing your steps, you can take a short connector to an old logging road that leads back to Alice Lake.)

Fawn Lake is smaller and shallower, and its shoreline is not as accessible as those of Stump and Alice. It's possible to swim from the banks of a small clearing. This is exactly what many cyclists do after the long ride uphill on the old road.

A former logging road and the Four Lakes Loop Trail merge for the short 10- to 15-minute walk between Fawn and Edith, most of whose waterfront is not within the park boundary. (The old logging road doubles as a mountain bike trail called Tracks from Hell, leading south from Edith Lake to the Garibaldi Highlands neighbourhood. The shorter Mike's Loop Trail begins here as well.) There are some steep stretches as the Four Lakes Loop Trail from Edith to Alice keeps company with a small creek. Simple wooden bridges span the creek in several places.

If you like views, try tackling DeBeck's Hill, an option that presents itself at Alice Lake's south end. During some seasons you may find yourself fending off the persistent bugs, but the cool breeze that usually blows across the top of DeBeck's Hill will dissipate the insects as quickly as the panoramic views appear. You'll get the complete picture of local geography from up here. If you're exploring by bike and consider DeBeck's Hill too challenging, head south to Garibaldi Highlands along Jack's Trail, which begins at the bottom of the hill.

The Squamish Chamber of Commerce and Visitor Info Centre at 37950 Cleveland Avenue in Squamish is a good place to find out about events and services in the area. Alternatively, call them at (604) 892-9244 or visit their Web site: www.squamishchamber.bc.ca.

46 DIAMOND HEAD

DISTANCE: 84 km (52 mi.) north of Vancouver

ACTIVITIES: Camping, cross-country skiing, hiking, mountain biking, picnicking, snowshoeing, viewpoints

HIGHLIGHTS: A mountain road leads gently upwards to an alpine landmark where colours blaze in fall

ACCESS: From Highway 99 in Squamish's Garibaldi Highlands neighbourhood take the Diamond Head (Garibaldi Provincial Park) turnoff east and follow Mamquam Road 16 km (10 mi.) to the trailhead parking lot. *Note:* Dogs are not allowed in Garibaldi Park.

Diamond Head is a fortresslike ridge that rises above the Squamish Valley in Garibaldi Provincial Park. Accompanied by craggy Atwell Peak, Diamond Head makes a bold statement about the elevation of the Coast Mountain peaks here, which tower from 1980 m (6500 ft.) to well over 2440 m (8000 ft.) You'll be surprised at how quickly you can get a close look at these peaks.

There is a large map of the Diamond Head region at the trailhead. From the parking lot to the subalpine zone is an 11-km (6.8-mi.) hike along an old road. Because the grade is gentle for most of the road, you should be able to reach the Elfin Lakes in 2 1/2 hours if you are reasonably fit. The map at the trailhead gives a longer estimate of 4 hours. You can also journey into this region of Garibaldi Park by mountain bike.

Profound silence envelops Diamond Head. Few birds sing, no dogs bark. Visitors cross into this realm of tranquillity almost as soon as they embark on the old road, along which supplies and lodge guests were once transported. Allow 75 minutes to reach Red Heather Meadows. BC Parks maintains a day shelter and small campground here, with six wooden tent pads and a clutch of food ropes from which to suspend food bags beyond the grasp of bears. An elevated pit toilet, fronted by a steep, nine-step staircase, hints at the depth of snow in winter. It also adds new starch to the term "throne room."

Sky Pilot Mountain from Paul Ridge

The Elfin Lakes are 90 minutes up the road from here on Paul Ridge. All sense of time redefines itself en route. Much like the altered state induced by stargazing, one's mind is drawn into another world where the rhythms of change occur on a vastly amplified scale. Crevasse-laced glaciers that took millennia to form speak of a time frame that eclipses mortal comparisons.

The scale of the mountains in the Pacific ranges that transect Garibaldi Park is truly astonishing. It's easy to see what drew a trio of entrepreneurs to hew a log chalet here. Diamond Head Lodge welcomed guests from the mid-1940s to the early 1970s. Although reduced in size and sagging at the corners, the lodge is still standing. Given the volumes of snow recorded locally in past winters, it's a wonder the building hasn't fallen in on itself. Sheets of plywood cover the windows. Saggy soffits outline the roof like lipstick applied by a dipsomaniac. Nestled in a meadow beside the twin Elfin Lakes, with peaks surrounding it on all sides, the old lodge still enjoys one of the best prospects in Garibaldi Park.

A loyal following of day trippers and campers trek year round to Diamond Head. With the demise of the lodge, BC Parks opened a

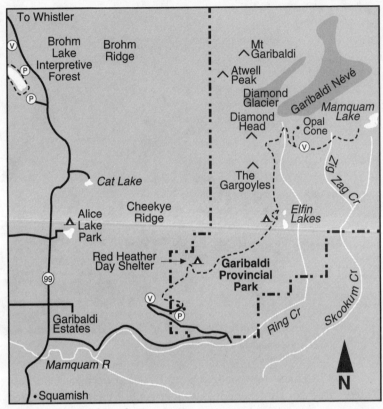

Diamond Head

campground nearby. A stone's throw from the former lodge stands the alpine-gothic Elfin Lodge, a two-storey, 34-bunk shelter, complete with kitchen facilities at a cost of $10 each per night, $25 per family. It's quite cozy inside, a favourite nest for Nordic skiers on cold winter nights. From this vantage point, lava beds on the south flank of a stubby feature called the Opal Cone are visible through binoculars, at least on a clear day. Clouds frequently cluster around the tips of the dominant peaks, Mount Garibaldi to the north and Mamquam Mountain to the east. It's usually much cooler at this elevation than in the Squamish Valley, visible far below.

A narrow trail leads beyond Elfin Lakes to the Opal Cone, an intriguingly shaped granite plug formed when the spew of molten lava hardened. The cone is neither conical nor opalescent in appearance. It squats like a green-grey molar at the foot of Mount Garibaldi's south tower, dagger-nosed Atwell Peak, surrounded by a battleship-grey moonscape scoured clean by the retreating Garibaldi and Lava Glaciers. As topsoil will be scarce for a while, vegetation has yet to become established here. The few traces of flora that do cling to the sides of the cone flourish somewhat mysteriously. At this elevation, above 1400 m (4593 ft.), growth is very slow. Core samples taken from stunted groves of cypress on nearby Paul Ridge indicate the trees are many hundreds of years old. This qualifies them for membership in the vaunted "ancient" category of forest appellations.

If the lava is rather bland in appearance, it only serves to heighten the intensity of hues in the broader panorama. Frost triggers dramatic displays of fall colour in these alpine meadows. Pumpkin-yellow and orange leaves blaze on black huckleberry and oval-leafed blueberry bushes, augmented by an understorey of white partridge-foot, green Alaska clubmoss and pink-tipped Pacific mountain-heather. Even if you're not up for going much farther than Diamond Head, at least explore the first stretch of the Opal Cone Trail as it leads to the rough bridge across Ring Creek. The aptly named Gargoyles, then the Dalton Dome, Atwell Peak and Mount Garibaldi's snow-capped summit present themselves as a reward for your effort. Some of the richest fall colours carpet the gulleys that plunge beside the trail.

Spend a night here. The view from the campground is superb. Immersed in the silence of the surroundings, revel in the view of the Tantalus Range to the west when first lit by the early morning light. At that magic hour, you'd think that the sun was pouring forth lava like primordial plasma, the cosmic soup from which matter evolved.

47 GARIBALDI LAKE & BLACK TUSK

DISTANCE: 99 km (61 mi.) north of Vancouver

ACTIVITIES: Camping, cross-country skiing, fishing, hiking, paddling, picnicking, snowshoeing, swimming, viewpoints

HIGHLIGHTS: Views of the most stunning setting in Garibaldi Provincial Park are the reward for a lengthy, though not demanding, hike

ACCESS: The turnoff to Black Tusk and Garibaldi Lake is just south of Daisy Lake, 19 km (11.8 mi.) south of Whistler. Watch for the BC Parks signs on Highway 99. This paved road runs 2.5 km (1.6 mi.) east to a large parking lot beside Rubble Creek. A 9-km (5.6-mi.) trail to Garibaldi Lake begins here. There are campgrounds beside the lake and in nearby Taylor Meadows, 7.5 km (4.7 mi.) from the parking area. Along the way the elevation gain is 810 m (2660 ft.) to the lake, slightly more to the meadows.

The trail to Garibaldi Lake and Black Tusk offers so many choices for adventure that you could easily revisit the area for years before exhausting the possibilities. Visitors are attracted to Black Tusk and Garibaldi Lake in astonishing numbers. If you can arrange to go on a weekday you will have the area more to yourself. On weekends, the trail back to the parking lot at the end of the day can be as congested as the highway—just be patient and revel in your new memories.

Even if you don't intend to walk the trail, you should at least drive the short distance in from Highway 99 to the parking lot to enjoy the wide-open view of the Barrier. The broad wall of red volcanic rock is especially appealing when lit by the setting summer sun. It's a unique formation in this region, the result of a flow of molten lava coming face to face with a glacier that once occupied what is now Rubble Creek. The ice cooled and hardened the lava, forming the

Black Tusk from Whistler Mountain

thick rock face that holds back the waters of Garibaldi Lake, a basin that filled as the surrounding glaciers melted and retreated.

The popularity of the Garibaldi Lake and Black Tusk trails makes for a full parking lot on weekends between May and October. Vandalism here is an unfortunate problem, so leave nothing of value in your car if you're planning to be away for long. Consult the information kiosk at the trailhead for a detailed map of Garibaldi Park.

THE APPROACH You can walk from the parking lot to the "4 km" sign in an hour along an easy trail that starts straight and then changes to switchbacks farther up the mountain. The Douglas firs and western red cedars lining the beginning of the trail are smaller

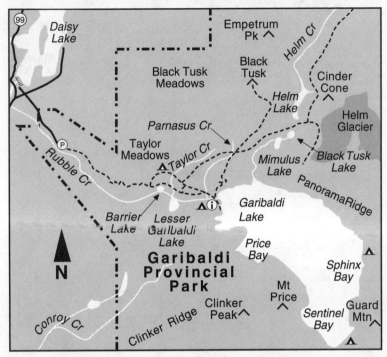

Garibaldi Lake and Black Tusk

in girth than those higher up, a result of a great landslide in 1855 that wiped out much of the forest at lower levels.

You will be relieved to reach the "6 km" marker because by now you might be suffering from visual deprivation. There are no views from the trail until just past this important divide. At the small shelter is a map of the area to help you decide which way to head from this point. The trail to the left leads up to Taylor and Black Tusk meadows and beyond there to the Tusk itself, as well as a host of other destinations. The trail to the right leads almost immediately to the viewpoint for which you've been waiting. Take a few minutes to enjoy the view even if you do not intend to follow the trail beyond to Garibaldi Lake, 3 km (1.9 mi.) farther along. Next to you is the Barrier. Its face is shaded in the morning light, a subdued texture compared to its visage later in the day. To the southwest you have sweeping views, from the broad white swath of the Tantalus Range rising above the Squamish Valley around to Powder Mountain above the Callaghan Valley.

GARIBALDI LAKE Depending on what time of year you visit, water may or may not be flowing out of nearby Barrier Lake. The outflow occurs only in late summer when water levels are at their highest. Year round the waters from Barrier, Garibaldi and Lesser Garibaldi Lakes percolate down through a layer of scoria (porous volcanic rock), venting into Rubble Creek through a series of springs at the base of the Barrier.

The best time to enjoy the visual delight of the three lakes is in August and September; not only are water levels at their highest, but this is also when they are the most intense blue. Just around the corner from the viewpoint the scene is even more astonishingly beautiful. Barrier Lake lies spread like a table before you. Fish jump in full profile. Without turning your head you can see white water entering and leaving the small lake at each end. If you look back along the trail you'll see Cloudburst Mountain framed by the notch at the lake's west end. You'll have a bounce in your step as you walk around Barrier Lake to Lesser Garibaldi Lake because it feels so good to be here. Near the bridge over Taylor Creek, whose waters feed into Lesser Garibaldi, there is an approach to lakeside that anglers will find helpful. The trail rings the lake on the hillside above but offers little other access.

Past the lake the trail enters the forest once more, dividing again just before the "8 km" sign. The trail to the left is one of several that lead to the Taylor Meadows campground. You are now cloistered among the evergreens, 15 minutes from Garibaldi Lake. This is to prepare you for the screamingly grand views that await at the big lake. From the bridge over Parnasus Creek you may see other hikers taking in the view from a bridge over the outflow creek from Garibaldi Lake, framed in a cleft of red volcanic rock and evergreens with the white of the glaciers behind them. By this time you may be wondering whether your nervous system can handle the volume of visual stimuli being fed to your brain.

Cross the bridge and walk (or wade) around to the Garibaldi Lake campground. There are three dozen campsites scattered on the hillside above the lake. Some of them have wooden platforms on which to pitch a tent, helpful when the ground is wet. You are allowed a stay of up to 14 days. At present the fee per night is $10. There are four covered shelters for day use, with picnic tables situated both inside and in front of them. Nearby, the rangers that patrol the park and put on interpretive programs for visitors have a cabin of their own.

Just offshore are the Battleship Islands, a string of small, rocky outcroppings. There are several benches along the lakeside trail and on the largest island. A sign on the lakeside trail lets you know that you've reached the "9 km, Elev. 1470 m" mark. When lake levels are at their highest, sections of the boardwalk leading out to the islands double as rafts from which you can swim, fish or just stretch out and relax.

BLACK TUSK Black Tusk is the magnet that has been attracting attention since the first mountaineers arrived to explore it in 1912. No other rock formation in the surrounding fortress of Coast Mountain peaks is as noticeable or so readily identifiable.

A trail from Garibaldi Lake climbs through the forest above the lake, meeting up with the trail from Taylor Meadows after a 30-minute walk. Along the way it passes a series of small ponds dotting the mountainside. The views from the open meadows around these ponds change constantly as you gain altitude. Below you Garibaldi Lake unfolds, revealing the full extent of its long, broad contour.

At this point you have a choice of several trails: you may climb to Black Tusk, 3 km (1.9 mi.) above, or head to Helm Lake and Panorama Ridge, closer by. The Helm Lake Trail leads north to Cheakamus Lake, 14 km (8.7 mi.) distant, through a distinctly volcanic zone. Even if you are not prepared to go the distance, you can still visit the area a little over a mile away around the lake and glacier. Panorama Ridge lies 3 km (1.9 mi.) farther along. From here you get unlimited views around Garibaldi Lake, with features that were hidden at lower altitudes now revealed in detail. To the south, the peaks of Mount Garibaldi rise higher than all others.

The trail to the Tusk begins to climb steadily towards a nearby ridge. Little streams constantly parallel or cross the trail. Even if you find the hike strenuous, it's worth going at least a short distance up the trail to get a view of Garibaldi Lake. In midsummer, the meadows on all sides bloom with blue lupine, red heather, Indian paintbrush and yellow cinquefoil.

If you persist, in an hour you will reach the ridge. Now nothing stands in the way of views of the Black Tusk's south face. The last of the alpine firs fade away and a barren expanse of degenerating granite takes over. A dusty trail leads across the flats and up to the Tusk, whose peak is still another hour away. The going isn't easy, and it's not for novices. It's prudent to wear a helmet when making the final ascent, as the terrain is unstable. On top your reward is being able to see every place from which you've ever viewed the Tusk, and then some.

48 CHEAKAMUS LAKE

DISTANCE: 123 km (76 mi.) north of Vancouver, in Whistler

ACTIVITIES: Camping, cross-country skiing, fishing, hiking, mountain biking, paddling, picnicking, snowshoeing, viewpoints, walking

HIGHLIGHTS: A gentle trail through a towering forest leads to a turquoise lake at the foot of Whistler Mountain; bright alpine wildflowers

ACCESS: To make your way to the Cheakamus Lake trailhead parking lot, follow Cheakamus Lake Road, which begins across from Whistler's Function Junction industrial neighbourhood, 45 km (27.9 mi.) north of Squamish. The trailhead lies some 8 km (5 mi.) east of Highway 99 along this well-marked road.

Glacier-fed Cheakamus Lake lies within the shadow of Whistler Mountain to the north. In winter, the big lake freezes solid, and getting to the trailhead in Garibaldi Provincial Park, let alone the lake, is a challenge. In summer, this is one of the most rewarding destinations in Whistler.

The gentle trail to Cheakamus Lake does not rank as a true hike; most of its 3.5-km (2.2-mi.) distance is over level terrain. Its length, however, qualifies it as an energetic walk or jog. It takes slightly more than 1 hour to travel one way to the lake. From there it's another hour along the shore to the trail's terminus at the mouth of Singing Creek. Simple campsites are located at the near end of the lake (the outflow point for the Cheakamus River) and at the end of the trail. Park rangers patrol the trail during the busy season, answering questions and giving directions. In a friendly way they also check to make sure there are no dogs, which are not permitted in Garibaldi Park.

A rich, resinous smell of balsam hangs in the air at this entrance to Garibaldi Park. It's always there, although the fragrance only lasts a moment before it is gone. Visitors must bend down to clear the low-hanging boughs of a sturdy western red cedar as they enter the dimly lit grove. During one especially snowy winter in the late 1990s, one of the mature amabilis fir near the park boundary snapped, and it now

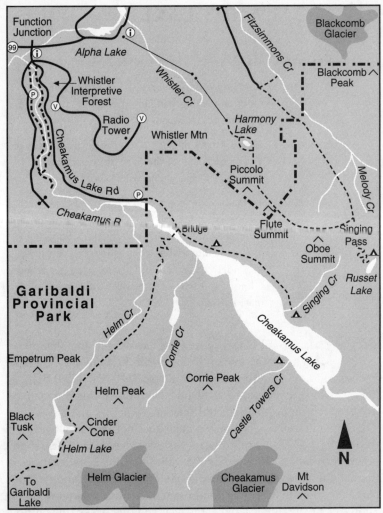

Cheakamus Lake and Whistler Interpretive Forest

bars the route as effectively as a wall. It's a bit of a scramble to get around it.

The first part of the trail is hilly and hugs a steep embankment above noisy Cheakamus River below. The trail is well established and slightly spongy underfoot. Walkers can set their own pace. Kids can run on ahead and still be seen and heard among the tall trees. A cool wind often blows down off the glaciated peaks, and the sunlight is diffused as it filters through the large overhead branches. Dress

Cheakamus Lake Trail

accordingly. Moss grows in a dozen shades of green on all sides of the tree trunks.

A bridge spans the Cheakamus River near its outflow from the lake. The wood-and-steel structure provides hikers access to the Helm Creek Trail, which begins on the opposite bank and eventually leads to Garibaldi Lake. The Helm Creek Trail, an all-day, 12-km (7.5-mi.) excursion to a small lake on the slope high above Cheakamus Lake, is suitable for summer and early fall hiking. The bridge also permits intrepid mountain bikers to loop back from the Cheakamus Lake Trail to Whistler via a rough riverside trail that links with the Westside Main logging road. (*Note:* Watch for an aluminum marker the size of a business card affixed near the base of a sturdy amabilis fir past the bridge. It has been placed about knee-high and engraved with these words: "Cody Lormair, born under this tree December 20, 1985, 11 A.M. Happy parents Erica and John." Look for the plaque on the north side of the trail past the bridge, just west of a prominent creek crossing.)

As the trail nears Cheakamus Lake it brings you closer to the emerald-coloured Cheakamus River, which broadens and becomes even noisier where it leaves the lake. Soon after you sight the lake, several rough campsites appear. Just beyond the first campsites is a cathedral-like grove of trees that for many visitors will crown the journey. The scale of the rain forest at Cheakamus is imposing. There is a hush here found only at exalted elevations.

SINGING CREEK Trees shelter two-thirds of the trail to Singing Creek's 3.5-km (2-mi.) distance, but the woods occasionally open up into thickets of blackberry and alder where small creeks flow down from the ridge of Whistler Mountain. Small meadows are evident above natural clearings around each creek. In places the trail rises above the lake. Here semi-arid banks of sand and stone sprout clumps of alpine flowers, small but brilliantly coloured patches of orange paintbrush, wild tiger lily, white valerian and blue lupine that climb up the hillside in summer.

In late spring the earth is still damp in many places and the ground cover is just beginning to show itself. Lush ferns thickly carpet the slopes above the lake, vividly green in the forest twilight. At several places along the way to Singing Creek, rockslides have cut paths down from the southern ridge of Whistler Mountain. In places the trail is so overgrown with nettles that you will want to be wearing long pants for protection. The nettles also hold the dew or raindrops; brushing past them can quickly soak a pair of jeans.

The farther along the trail you go, the more the views to the east and west open up. Brandywine Mountain is northwest in the distance, the Overlord group (hidden by forest for the most part) behind you to the east, the McBride Range to the southeast. Whistler Mountain is to the north and west, very evident as a long ridge above the trail. The Cheakamus Glacier covers the near side of the mountains at the southwestern end of the lake. A cool wind is always blowing down off the slopes.

Sounds of rushing water in Singing Creek and wind in the tree boughs harmonize with the deep bass notes emanating from Castle Towers Creek on the far shore. There is one particularly good campsite here, perched above a small beach and equipped with a hammock woven from an old fire hose. There are few access points to the lake, so the one at Singing Creek is a welcome opening. Families of mergansers summer here and share the lakeside with visitors. Because Cheakamus Lake is fed by numerous creeks that originate in the surrounding glaciers and snow fields, the water is chilly year round. Don't expect to do more than give your feet a refreshing soak to revitalize them for the return trip.

49 BROHM LAKE, WHISTLER & SHADOW LAKE INTERPRETIVE FORESTS

DISTANCE: 78 to 140 km (48 to 87 mi.) north of Vancouver

ACTIVITIES: Mountain biking, nature observation, picnicking, swimming, viewpoints, walking

HIGHLIGHTS: Well-built mountain biking and walking trails lead across swing and trestle bridges to dramatic viewpoints

ACCESS: The Brohm Lake Interpretive Forest is located 14 km (8.7 mi.) north of downtown Squamish on the west side of Highway 99 (see map page 220).

The Whistler Interpretive Forest lies beside Cheakamus Lake Road east of Highway 99 at Whistler's Function Junction intersection, 44 km (27.3 mi.) north of Squamish (see map page 228). The road is initially paved, then turns to gravel. Detailed maps are available at the blue information kiosk on the north side of Cheakamus Lake Road near the intersection with Highway 99.

Shadow Lake Interpretive Forest lies 10 km (6.2 mi.) north of Whistler beside the BC Rail Green River Crossing. To reach the lookout, turn west off Highway 99 onto the Soo River Forest Road just south of the BC Rail crossing. Alternatively, trails to the lake and lookout lead off from the crossing, where there is ample parking.

Over the past decade, B.C. Forest Service recreation sites in the Sea to Sky corridor have gained new respectability. Coupled with this is the emergence of its interpretive forests, which highlight remedial forest practices such as replanting and thinning. At first, these model forests seemed like little more than cosmetic fixes applied to recent clear-cuts. Then new trail construction, funded in large part by Forest Renewal BC, made three such interpretive forests between Squamish and Pemberton increasingly welcoming to those on mountain bikes as well as on foot.

BROHM LAKE INTERPRETIVE FOREST Many travellers have stopped at Brohm Lake to swim and on occasion walked the rough trail that encircles it. They may be surprised to discover an extensive network of trails running through the forest to the south and west of the lake as well. One reason these trails often escape notice is that their best approach is from a gated entrance 1 km (0.6 mi.) south of the lake rather than from the main paved parking area. There's plenty of room to pull off Highway 99 here, and the trailhead is marked by a large brown Forest Service sign beside which is a covered box with trail maps.

You'll enjoy a walk through the woods even if you haven't brought a mountain bike. There's probably more ground to cover on foot than you can explore in one visit, which makes the Brohm Lake Interpretive Forest an ideal destination for repeat visits. Although the lake itself is the main magnet, particularly for families in summer, the more remote forest trails have a quiet charm of their own. The sounds of the highway quickly fade away as you begin walking. At several places the trail divides, offering visitors a choice of directions. For example, the High Trail leads north to Brohm Lake, while the Cheakamus Loop Trail leads west onto a ridge.

Within an hour's walk from the southern parking lot, starting on Alder Trail and then branching onto the Cheakamus Loop trails, you reach two viewpoints that look across Paradise Valley to the glacier-clad Tantalus Range. Staircases assist visitors up the steepest stretches. Here, next to a covered lookout shelter, is one of the best picnic spots. The Cheakamus River flows past far below, and the Squamish waterfront is visible in the distance. All of the peaks in the Tantalus Range—including Mount Tantalus itself as well as Alpha, Omega, Zenith, Pelion and Serratus Mountains—stand revealed in their glory.

WHISTLER INTERPRETIVE FOREST Whistler forester Don MacLaurin spearheaded the Whistler Interpretive Forest's development. It's a joint project of the B.C. Ministry of Forests and the Resort Municipality of Whistler as well as other players from both government and industry. Various aspects of a managed second-growth forest are explained at pullouts along the logging roads that run through the forest on both the east and west sides of the Cheakamus River.

The Whistler Interpretive Forest's major recreational feature is

Shadow Lake Interpretive Forest

the extensive network of narrow trails, especially suited to mountain biking, that crisscross both the Eastside Main and Westside Main roads. The trails have quickly garnered a reputation as some of the best-built and, therefore, most enjoyable rides in Whistler. In addition, there are signs that indicate time, distance and elevation gain for biking.

A suspension bridge links the trails on both sides of the Cheakamus. Named MacLaurin's Crossing, it lies several kilometres upstream from the entrance to the forest. Paired with a BC Parks bridge farther upstream in Garibaldi Park near Cheakamus Lake (see previous chapter), the new addition has enhanced the long-term potential for adventuring along both sides of the river.

A good place to begin is the Riverside Trail that runs along the east side of the Cheakamus. It's easy to find and, aside from several short, steep stretches, suited to all ability levels, whether you're exploring on foot or by bike. If there's one drawback here it's the limited access to the fast-flowing river, which frequently channels through steep-sided granite walls, best appreciated from midspan on MacLaurin's Crossing.

SHADOW LAKE INTERPRETIVE FOREST An easier approach to water can be found at Shadow Lake. As Highway 99 leads north of Whistler towards Pemberton, it passes through the Shadow Lake Interpretive Forest. Signs point to a sheltered wooden lookout above the lake. Diminutive Shadow Lake lies nestled below beside the Soo River. A series of loop trails runs through the forest and to the viewpoint. Parts of these trails go back a century or more. Trappers and traders, both Native and non-Native, passed through here on their way to and from Pemberton and the Coast. Little remains of a logging operation that flourished at Shadow Lake in the early 1900s.

Unlike the hard-packed trails beside the Cheakamus River, these ones are softened by a thick covering of leaves and evergreen needles. Although they don't run for nearly the distance of those in the Brohm Lake or Whistler Interpretive Forests, the route around Shadow Lake offers other rewards. For one thing, the views of surrounding peaks, including Wedge Mountain and the sunbaked bluffs above the Soo River, are superior. Lush displays of wildflowers, such as Pacific bleeding heart and trailing yellow violet, carpet the forest floor in a wetland zone between the lake and the river. Follow the section of trail that leads through a stand of old-growth fir and cedar out onto a sandbank where tall black cottonwood trees tower above the Soo. This is a sunny spot to enjoy a picnic.

For more information on interpretive forests, contact the Squamish Forest District office in Squamish, (604) 898-2100.

50 WHISTLER PARKS

DISTANCE: 115 km (71.4 mi.) north of Vancouver

ACTIVITIES: Cross-country skiing, cycling, in-line skating, nature observation, paddling, picnicking, playgrounds, sailing, skateboarding, snowshoeing, swimming, viewpoints, walking, windsurfing

HIGHLIGHTS: A paved recreation trail loops through Whistler Valley, linking a series of lakeside parks

ACCESS: Follow Highway 99 north to Whistler, a 2-hour drive.

VALLEY TRAIL If there's one facet of Whistler that garners as much praise from visitors as do the mountains, it's the Valley Trail. Whistler's neighbourhoods are knit together by an extensive network of pathways that together comprise this 20-km (12.4-mi.) trail system. For recreationalists and commuters alike, when it comes to getting around Whistler, the Valley Trail functions as an alternative to busy Highway 99.

Almost entirely paved, the Valley Trail passes beside seven parks, five lakes, a river and several creeks. In summer, it's a cycling and in-line skate path as well as a walkway; in winter, it's primarily a cross-country ski trail, though with a good pair of snow boots you can tramp along quite comfortably. Whistler Village sits at its hub. The beauty of the Valley Trail is that you can get onto it easily from almost anywhere in Whistler. Each year it gets longer, keeping pace with the resort's growth. It's difficult to say where the trail begins and ends; most of it forms a loop.

Before you start out on the Valley Trail, decide whether you are going to do the entire loop or make one of the parks or lakes your destination. On foot, it takes 3 hours to complete the loop; by bike, half that or less. You don't have to go the whole distance to enjoy the trail.

WHISTLER'S MUNICIPAL PARKS As befits a town that annually welcomes millions of visitors, a necklace of parks adorns the Whistler Valley. Many of these are located beside lakes where you'll find picnic tables, beaches, boat rentals and splendid viewpoints. Several of the parks, such as Alpha Lake and Meadow, feature play areas specifically

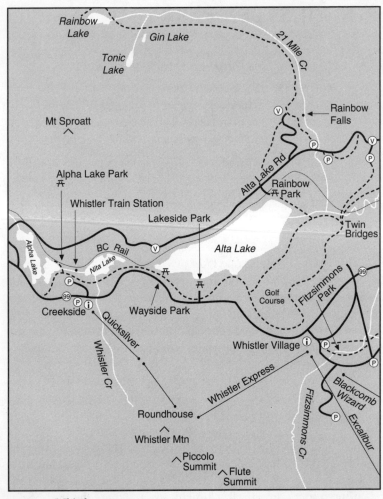

Whistler area

designed for younger children. One of the parks, Fitzsimmons, is dedicated to skateboarding.

As Highway 99 winds between the Creekside and Village neighbourhoods south of Whistler Village, a distance of about 4 km (2.5 mi.), it passes Wayside and Lakeside Parks. Both are situated on the west side of the highway and their entrances are well marked. Lakeside Park is an open area on the southeast side of Alta Lake. A lawn runs down to the beach, where there are two L-shaped docks. There are six well-spaced picnic tables, most with their own barbe-

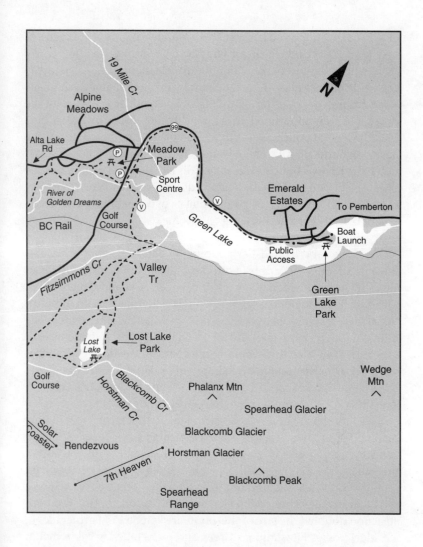

cues. There is no lifeguard, and dogs are not allowed on the beach. In summer you may rent boats and windsurfers here; guided tours of the lake and the colourfully named River of Golden Dreams nearby (see below) can also be arranged.

Wayside Park is smaller than Lakeside. Four picnic tables, each with its own barbecue, sit on a sloped hillside overlooking the south end of Alta Lake. There is a modest beach with an open lawn above for sunbathing. A dock is moored just far enough offshore to make swimmers appreciate reaching it after a plunge into the cold waters of Alta Lake. Canoe and Laser sailboat rentals (slightly less expensive here than at Lakeside Park) are handled from a small boathouse.

Two of the largest parks, Rainbow and Meadow, are located on the west side of the valley. To reach them by car, travel along Alta Lake Road from its intersection with Highway 99 either across from the Bayshores neighbourhood in south Whistler or from the Alpine Meadows neighbourhood north of the village. Rainbow Park, at the northwest end of Alta Lake, stands on the site of Whistler's first lodge, which was built here in 1914. This location still commands the finest viewpoint in the valley, hands down. A sandy beach, a grassy playing field, an array of picnic tables, two floating docks and a quaint collection of heritage log cabins make this a spot where you can easily spend an entire summer's day enjoying Whistler.

Meadow Park, in Whistler's Alpine Meadows neighbourhood, is linked to Rainbow Park by both the Valley Trail and the River of Golden Dreams, which flows north between Alta and Green Lakes. Meadow has many of the same amenities as Rainbow, with the additional treat of a children's water park, but is often far less crowded. The municipal swimming pool and enclosed ice rink are situated nearby. The only drawback to swimming outdoors at Meadow Park is that there is no beach. Bathers here simply dive into the River of Golden Dreams and haul out onto the riverbank. Because the water is cold and deep, this is not a suitable place for young children to swim.

Lost Lake hasn't gone missing in years. Still, it is the most remote of Whistler's parks. Tucked on the benchland beside the Chateau Whistler golf course, it is most easily approached via the section of the Valley Trail that begins at the well-marked Lost Lake parking lot on Blackcomb Way, across from the municipal offices. Near its outset, the trail passes beside the Fitzsimmons Skatepark. (In 1999, construction doubled the size of this popular skatebowl.) Farther along, a bridge crosses Fitzsimmons Creek and passes the log cabin that in winter houses the cross-country ticket office and concession stand.

A network of gravel and paved trails traces the slopes around Lost Lake. Take your pick, depending on your fitness and skill level. This applies equally to those exploring in summer on foot or by bicycle and those adventuring in winter on cross-country skis or snowshoes. A sandy beach and grassy picnic area are located at the lake's south end. From here, a trail circles the lake. A floating dock juts out from the shoreline at the lake's midpoint; an access trail branches off the main loop to reach it. This more remote location offers bathers a quieter environment from which to enjoy splendid views of Blackcomb.

Rainbow Park, Whistler

Discreet clothing-optional sunbathing has been a hallmark of this part of the lake since Whistler's hippie days.

RIVER OF GOLDEN DREAMS Whistler is located at the summit of a pass. Balanced here on the fulcrum between north and south is Alta Lake, which, until the 1960s, was the name by which the town of Whistler was known. (Whistler Mountain was still called London Mountain.) Alta Lake drains into Nita Lake from its south end and into Green Lake from its north. The storybook-titled River of Golden Dreams (more properly named Alta Creek) links Alta with Green Lake and provides paddlers with a perspective on the valley that can only be appreciated from a canoe or kayak. All signs of habitation vanish behind riverbanks thick with low-lying willows. The river's channel is hidden by tall stands of reeds but is not difficult to locate. If you have your own canoe or kayak, the beach at nearby Rainbow Park is the most convenient place to put in. If you're renting, launch at Lakeside or Wayside Park (see above).

Just east of the Valley Trail bridge across the river that provides access to and from Rainbow Park, paddlers will encounter a small concrete weir. This is the only man-made obstacle paddlers will face on the River of Golden Dreams. A portage is required, albeit only a few steps. River shoes come in handy. Beyond here the river's course is squeezed between railway tracks on the west and high banks on the east. At low-water times it may be necessary to help your canoe or kayak across short sections of the creekbed along this stretch.

Once the river begins to oxbow its way towards Green Lake, the best views of the trip begin to open up before you. Wild canaries swoop past and muskrats swim in and out of their riverbank burrows. Allow an easy hour to make the journey from Alta Lake to the well-marked pullout beside a bridge that carries Highway 99 traffic.

If the river current permits (remembering that you must paddle against it to return to the pullout), complete the journey to Green Lake. Stately Sitka spruce and black cottonwood trees line the riverbank along this final stage of the journey. A telephone is mounted at the parking lot next to the pullout. Call a taxi (numbers are posted by the phone) to arrange transport back to Rainbow Park or make other plans, such as leaving bikes at the pullout so that you can ride back to Rainbow Park on the Valley Trail to retrieve your vehicle (and then your boat). (Although this might seem complicated, it's actually quite straightforward. Return transportation for those who rent canoes or kayaks on Alta Lake is prearranged.)

INDEX